INTERMEDIATE LANGUAGE LESSONS
Teacher's Guide

Catherine Andrews

B.A. English Education, National Board Certified, Teacher of English, Hayesville Middle School, Hayesville, North Carolina

Mary Jane Newcomer

B.A. English Education, Teacher of English, Frostproof Middle-Senior High School, Frostproof, Florida

Lost Classics
Book Company

Lake Wales, Florida

PUBLISHER'S NOTE

Recognizing the need to return to more traditional principles in education, Lost Classics Book Company is republishing forgotten late 19th and early 20th century literature and textbooks to aid parents and teachers in the education of their children.

This guide is designed to accompany *Intermediate Language Lessons,* which was reprinted from the 1914 copyright edition. The guide contains all the original questions and exercises from the reader along with suggested answers. It also includes new "Extended Activities" that reinforce and enhance the original study sections. In most cases, items that appear in the textbook for dictation lessons are not repeated in the guide for the sake of brevity, in an effort to produce a more affordable guide for the teacher and parent. Some exercises have responses that are impossible to predict. At times examples of possible responses are given and at other times the parent or teacher must evaluate each response from cues in the exercise's description.

There have been multiple printings of this grammar text, and while we strive for perfection, there will be rare errors or ommisions in different printings. These errors are corrected in subsequent printings as they are found. The contents of this guide, therefore, reflect the contents of the textbooks as they were intended to be printed, which may differ very slightly from what appears in a particular printing of the textbook.

Intermediate Language Lessons by Emma Serl, which this volume is meant to accompany, has been assigned a reading level of 760L. More information concerning this reading level assessment may be obtained by visiting www.lexile.com.

Lost Classics Book Company

ISBN 978-1-890623-34-0

Designed to Accompany
Intermediate Language Lessons by Emma Serl
ISBN 978-0-9652735-7-2

Contents

Objectives

The activities in this edition will meet the following objectives:

1. The student will identify words and construct meaning from text and illustrations, phonics, and context clues.
2. The student will determine the main idea through illustrations.
3. The student will recognize basic patterns and functions of language.
4. The student will understand that word choice can shape ideas, feelings, and actions.
5. The student will use and identify repetition, rhyme, and rhythm in oral and written text.
6. The student will use text and previous readings to make predictions.
7. The student will use a simple outline.
8. The student will use knowledge of developmental-level vocabulary in reading.
9. The student will increase comprehension by summary and discussion.
10. The student will recognize the beginning, middle, and end in passages.
11. The student will write questions and observations about familiar topics, stories, or new experiences.
12. The student will analyze an author's perspective, noting the differences between fact and opinion.
13. The student will use reference materials to obtain information.
14. The student will justify an argument with logical, relevant reasons, clear examples, and supporting details.
15. The student will retell details of information, including sequencing of information.
16. The student will produce final documents that have been edited for correct spelling, punctuation, capitalization, and sentence structure.
17. The student will use knowledge and experience to tell about experiences or to write for familiar occasions, audiences, and purposes
18. The student will follow simple sets of instructions for simple tasks using logical sequencing of steps
19. The student will use different forms of words, including contractions, possessive nouns, and present, past, and future tenses.
20. The student will determine how to draw conclusions from texts.
21. The student will understand sentence varieties, paragraph writing, and punctuation.

Lesson 1

Selection for Study— "The Finding of Moses"

1. Read the story and tell it.
2. Describe the picture.

Teacher Note

"The Finding of Moses" was painted by Paul Delaroche, a popular French painter in the early 19th century. Born in 1797 in Paris as Hippolyte Delaroche (later known as Paul), he began exhibiting his works in 1822. He specialized in paintings that depicted historical and religious subjects such as this painting of *The Finding of Moses*. His works were characterized by their attention to detail. Delaroche died in 1856.

Extended Activity

A. The king's daughter named the baby Moses because she "drew him out of the water," as seen in this work of art. Using the Internet or baby name books, have the students research the meanings of their names and write a brief report detailing the events surrounding their births. In the report answer the following questions: What is your name? What does it mean? How was your birth unique? Who was there? How did your family celebrate your arrival?

B. The story of Moses is most often depicted through art work showing his cradle floating in the Nile from which he got his name. Have the students create a piece of art that depicts the meaning of their names.

Lesson 2

Names of Persons and Places

1. From the story, "The Finding of Moses," copy:
   A. The name of the baby
   The baby's name was Moses.
   B. The name of the baby's sister
   The sister's name was Miriam.
   C. The name of the king
   The king was named Pharaoh.
2. With what kind of letter does the name of a person or place begin?

The name of a person or place begins with a capital letter.

3. **Make a rule for this use of the capital letter.**

A proper noun is the name of a particular person or place. All names of particular people and places must begin with a capital letter.

4. **Write the names of—**
   A. two countries
   B. five boys
   C. two celebrated men
   D. four cities
   E. two states
   F. five girls
   Answers may vary.

Lesson 3
Selection for Study—"The Stone in the Road"

1. **Tell the story from the following outline:**
   A. **The king**
   The king loved his people and tried to help them but they were selfish, so the king decided to teach them a lesson by placing a stone in the middle of the road, then hiding to see what would happen.
   B. **The people**
   The people were selfish and did not try to help each other.
   C. **The stone in the road**
   The king placed the stone in the road that passed his palace. He wanted to see what the people would do with the stone.
   D. **The people who passed**
   First a woman came along with some goats and scolded about it, but she went around the stone and continued on her way. Next came a man riding a donkey and also complained about the stone but rode around it and moved on. Others also passed by and commented on the stone but made no attempt to remove it from the road.
   E. **The miller's boy**
   The miller's boy came by carrying a bundle, stopped and decided to move the stone so no one would fall over it. He put down his bundle and with great effort pushed the stone to one side.
   F. **The bag of gold.**
   When the stone was moved, the miller's boy found a bag where the stone had been with these words written on the bag, "This bag of gold belongs to the one who helps others by removing the stone from the road." So he carried his treasure home with a happy heart.

2. **Read in the last part of the story what the king said.**
   The king returned to his palace saying, "I'm glad that I found someone who is unselfish enough to think of the comfort of others."

3. **With what kind of letter is the word *I* always written?**

The word I is always written with a capital letter.

4. **Make a rule for this use of the capital letter.**

   I is always capitalized when used as a word.

Lesson 4
Selection to be Memorized

Teacher Note

Refer to the memorization rubric, page 218, for evaluation.

1. Copy the quotation and memorize it.

Extended Activity

In Lessons 2 and 3, the students created rules for capital letters. Have the students list the words of this poem that begin with capital letters and create a rule for the manner in which they are used in this poem. The capitalized words are the first words of each new line of poetry: True, In, Some, Of, For, And, There's, And. The first word in each new line of a poem begins with a capital letter. Have the students read other poems in the book to see if their rule is true for other poems as well. See Lesson 6, Lesson 13, and Lesson 30 as examples.

Lesson 5
Composition—A Prince Story

1. Read the story, "The Stone in the Road," then make a similar story about a prince and a beautiful jewel. The prince places the jewel in a bucket far down in a deep well, then he dresses himself up as a poor old man and asks all who pass to draw water for him to drink.
2. Make an outline of your story.
3. Tell the story from the outline.
4. Begin your story in this way: Once upon a time, a prince...

Lesson 6
Selection for Study—"The Wise Fairy"

1. Explain the third stanza.

As the fairy watched the poor, lonely women spinning clothes day after day, she hid a lump of gold in the flax for them.

2. **What is a distaff?**

   A distaff is a a staff that holds the flax or wool the spinner is spinning.

3. **Explain the seventh stanza.**

   The fairy gave a gift of gold to any who spent their money for the essentials of life such as shoes for their feet, bread to eat, or a coat to keep warm.

4. **Explain the eighth stanza.**

   If the poor spent their money on expensive jewels, wine, silk, or foolish pleasures, they found only a lump of clay from the fairy.

5. **Tell the story of the wise fairy.**

   The wise fairy lived in a tree so she could see far and wide. She kept an eye on the poor women, ditchers, children, and fishermen so she could reward them for work well done.

6. **Who wrote this poem?**

   Alice Cary wrote this poem.

7. **What lesson did the author wish to teach?**

   The author wished to teach the lesson that when we use our time and money wisely, there will always be enough to sustain us. When we spend our money on expensive things, not necessary for sustaining life, we will not find happiness.

8. **What part of the poem do you like best?**

   Answers may vary.

Extended Activity:

Alice Cary draws pictures with her words so the reader can visualize the scene she describes. Choose one stanza and create a piece of art that best shows the image in that stanza.

Lesson 7
Oral Composition

Frank and Mary Rogers each received two dollars for a Christmas present. Tell a story showing how one of the children spent the money foolishly and one wisely.

Lesson 8
The Sentence

   A. A fairy lived on the other side of the sea.
   B. Where did she hide the lumps of gold?
   C. Do not spend gold foolishly.

1. Which of the groups of words tells something? Note: A group of words that tells something is a statement.

   A. The group of words that tells something is "A fairy lived on the other side of the sea."

2. What mark of punctuation is placed after a statement?

   A period is placed after a statement.

3. Which of the groups of words asks something? Note: A group of words that asks something is a question.

   B. The group of words that asks something is "Where did she hide lumps of gold?"

4. What mark of punctuation is placed after a question?

   A question mark is placed after a question.

5. Which of the groups of words makes a command? Note: A group of words that orders something is a command. Note: A group of words that tells, asks, or commands is a sentence.

   C. The group of words that makes a command is "Do not spend gold foolishly."

6. With what kind of letter does the first word of every sentence begin?

   The first word of every sentence begins with a capital letter.

7. Write five statements about "The Wise Fairy."

   Statements may vary.

8. Write five questions about "The Wise Fairy."

   Questions may vary.

9. Write five commands that the fairy might have given to the people, or that they may have given to each other.

   Commands may vary.

Lesson 9
Picture Study—
The Flower Girl

1. What story does the picture tell?
2. How old do you think the little girl is?
3. From what kind of home do you imagine she may have come?
4. Why do you think she is selling flowers?
5. What do you think the boys are saying?
6. Do you imagine that they will buy any flowers?
7. How do you think these boys make money?
8. Can you suggest another name for the picture?

Answers will vary.

Teacher Note

This particular picture is also named *Tough Customers* or *Street Arabs* as the homeless children in New York were called. It was painted in oil on canvas in 1881 by John George Brown, who began his successful painting career about 1860. He specialized in humorous paintings of children at play that became popular after the Civil War, since they represented the future hope of the country. For additional information regarding this piece of art as insightfully written by Kenneth W. Maddox see:

http://www.museothyssen.org/thyssen_ing/coleccion/obras_ficha_texto_print120.html

Lesson 10

Composition

1. Write the story that one of the boys in the picture, *The Flower Girl,* might tell his sister. Begin it in this way: As I was going down the street I...

Lesson 11

Use of the Dictionary

1. **How are the words in the dictionary arranged?**
   Words in the dictionary are arranged alphabetically.
2. **How is the pronunciation of the word indicated?**
   The pronunciation of a word is indicated by pronunciation symbols.
3. **Write words containing the following sounds:**
   Answers will vary but may reflect the following sounds:

   a—c<u>a</u>t, m<u>a</u>t, s<u>a</u>t, b<u>a</u>t
   ā—n<u>a</u>me, s<u>a</u>me, c<u>a</u>me, t<u>a</u>me
   ä—f<u>a</u>ther, <u>a</u>rm, c<u>a</u>rt, c<u>o</u>tton, b<u>o</u>ttle
   e—f<u>ea</u>ther, <u>e</u>lephant, b<u>e</u>d
   ē—h<u>ea</u>t, s<u>ea</u>t, m<u>ea</u>t
   i—<u>i</u>gloo, t<u>i</u>p, ch<u>i</u>p
   ī—<u>i</u>ce, m<u>i</u>ce, t<u>i</u>me
   ȯ—<u>a</u>ll, s<u>aw</u>, c<u>au</u>ght
   ō—<u>o</u>ld, c<u>o</u>ld, b<u>o</u>ld
   u̇—b<u>oo</u>k, h<u>oo</u>k, p<u>u</u>ll
   ü—<u>you</u>, <u>u</u>nicorn, <u>u</u>se
   ǝ—b<u>a</u>nan<u>a</u>, <u>a</u>bout
   ȯi—c<u>oi</u>n, j<u>oi</u>n, t<u>oy</u>

aú—out, now, ouch

ŋ—sing, ring, thing

4. Study in your dictionary the following: hedge, mirror, meadow, compassion, flax, refer, dictation, paragraph, shelter, stanza, powerful, description, brim, initial, orchard.

5. Copy the words, dividing them into syllables and placing marks of pronunciation as given in the dictionary. Pronounce the words.

hedge, hej; mirror, ˈmir-ɛr; meadow, ˈme-dō; compassion, kɛm-ˈpa-shɛn

flax, ˈflaks; refer, ri-ˈfɛr; dictation, dik-ˈtā-shɛn; paragraph, ˈpar-ɛ-graf

shelter, ˈshel-tɛr; stanza, ˈstan-zɛ; powerful, ˈpȧu(ɛ)r-fɛl; description, di-ˈskrip-shɛn

brim, ˈbrim; initial, i-ˈni-shɛl; orchard, ˈȯr-chɛrd

Lesson 12

Correct Use of Words

A. Did you call him?

B. Did you call me?

C. Did you call him and me?

D. Mother bought some candy for you.

E. Mother bought some candy for me.

F. Mother bought some candy for you and me.

1. Study the sentences.

2. Write a sentence containing the word me.

3. Write the sentence again, using him and me instead of me.

4. Write another sentence using the word me.

5. Write the sentence again, using you and me in place of me.

6. Write another sentence containing me.

7. Write the sentence again, using her and me in place of me.

8. Write a sentence containing the word us.

9. Write the sentence again, using them and us in place of us.

Answers to above will vary.

Lesson 13

Selection to be Memorized—"The Robin"

1. Find in the dictionary words that might be used for *caroled, piping, blissful, rapturously, jubilant.*

A thesaurus (a book of synonyms) should be used for this activity. Possible answers might be:

caroled —warbled, twittered, chirped, trilled

piping—whistling, tuning up, lilting,
blissful—happy, joyful, enchanting, rapturous
rapturously— joyfully, enchantingly, delightfully
jubilant—exulting, triumphant, rejoicing

2. **Which do you like better, the words you found in the dictionary or the ones the author uses? Note: A single line of poetry is called a verse. Note: The parts into which a poem is divided are called stanzas. This poem contains three stanzas.**
    Answers will vary.

3. **With what kind of letter does the first word of each line of a poem begin?**
    The first word of each line of poetry begins with a capital letter. (See Lesson 4 in this guide for a reference to first words of poems.)

Lesson 14
Correct Use of Words

1. **Copy the following sentences, filling in the blanks with *is* or *are*:**
    A. There *is* a tall elm tree in the meadow.
    B. There *is* a robin in the tree.
    C. There *are* green fields nearby.
    D. There *are* rain clouds in the sky.
    E. There *is* a warm wind blowing from the south.
2. **Copy the sentences again, filling the blanks with was or were.**
    A. There *was* a tall elm tree in the meadow.
    B. There *was* a robin in the tree.
    C. There *were* green fields nearby.
    D. There *were* rain clouds in the sky.
    E. There *was* a warm wind blowing from the south.
3. **Use in sentences: is, are, was, were**
    Answers will vary.
4. **Begin each sentence with *There*.**
    Each sentence should begin with There.

Extended Activity for Lessons 15-21

A. **Before completing the next seven lessons related to birds, take the students on a nature walk to identify types of local birds. Have the students create a "bird wall" listing pictures and names of the birds they've seen, their habitats, their eating habits and their migratory patterns, if any. See Lesson 16, number 2 for a descriptive writing outline to help students organize and jot down their findings.**
B. **Research and build simple bird houses. (The Internet provides simple plans.)**
C. **Create a haven for birds that includes food and water.**

Lesson 15

Conversation—Birds

A. quail B. bluebird C. goldfinch D. heron E. stork F. meadowlark G. oriole H. flicker
I. hawk J. crane K. owl L. swan M. duck N. woodpecker O. sparrow

1. **Which of these birds are swimmers?**

   The birds which are swimmers are the swan and the duck.

2. **What kind of feet have they?**

   They have webbed feet which they use as paddles.

3. **Which of these birds have long legs and wade in the water?**

   The birds with long legs and wade in the water are the heron, the stork, and the crane.

4. **Which are birds of prey? What kind of bills have they?**

   Birds of prey are the hawk and the owl. They have hooked, razorlike bills for tearing flesh.

5. **Which are seed eaters?**

   Seed-eating birds include the quail, the bluebird, the goldfinch, the meadowlark, the oriole, the flicker, the woodpecker, and the sparrow. While these birds prefer seeds, they also eat insects and fruits.

6. **Which are sweet singers?**

   The birds known for their singing are the bluebird, the goldfinch, the meadowlark, and the oriole.

7. **Tell what you can of the habits of these birds.**

   Habits of birds vary depending on their species. The birds of prey are largely meat-eaters while other species eat only insects, fruits and seeds. Some birds find their food on dry ground while others climb trees to hunt for insects and still others hunt their food in wetlands and ponds. Nearly all birds communicate through songs or calls. Most birds search for food during the day and sleep at night. They protect themselves from their predators by staying still and blending into their habitat, made possible by their markings. Others fly or hide. While some birds lay their eggs on the ground, many build nests made of leaves, twigs, and grass. Many species of baby birds are born blind, featherless, and unable to stand on their spindly legs. The parents provide all their food. Other species of babies can hunt their food within hours of hatching. All birds can fly without being taught. Many types of birds migrate from northern countries when winter comes because their source of food may be covered in snow. Other species that live in the tropics may migrate during the dry season to find food and water. Most small birds live only a year or two while larger birds may live longer.

Lesson 16

Composition—Description of a Bird

I am thinking of a bird that is not as large as the robin. Its colors are orange and black. It eats bugs and worms. It weaves its nest, hanging the nest in a tree. It swings sweetly.

1. Of what bird am I thinking?
   I am thinking of the oriole.
2. Write a similar description of one of the birds mentioned in Lesson 15, or of some other bird that you have seen. Follow this outline:
   A. Size
   B. Color
   C. Food
   D. Nest
   E. Song
   F. Other habits
   Answers will vary.
3. Read your description aloud, and let the rest of the class guess the answer.
   Answers will vary.

Lesson 17
Correct Use of Words

1. Write three sentences telling about what you have taught a dog or other pet to do.
   Answers will vary.
2. Write three sentences telling what you have learned at school.
   Answers will vary.
3. Write two sentences telling something you have learned outside of school.
   Answers will vary.
4. Write a sentence telling what birds teach their young.
   Answers will vary.
5. When is it correct to use the word *learn*?
   Learn *means to take in or get information. I learn from another person or experience.*
6. When is it correct to use the word *teach*?
   Teach *means to give information. I teach another person information.*
7. Use in sentences the following: *this bird, that bird, these birds, those birds.*
   Answers will vary.
8. Which of the sentences refer to birds *near* you?
   This bird and these birds refer to birds near you.
9. Which sentences refer to birds far *away from* you?
   That bird and those birds refer to birds far from you.
10. Which of the sentences refer to *one* bird?
    The sentence referring to one bird uses this or that.
11. Which refer to *more than one* bird?
    The sentence referring to more than one bird uses these or those.

12. **Make a rule for the use of *this, that, these, those*.**

This and that refer to one person, place, thing, or idea. These and those refer to a group of persons, places, things, or ideas.

Lesson 18
Selection for Study— "The Red-Headed Woodpecker"

1. **Tell something of the red-headed woodpecker.**

Woodpeckers get their name from pecking on wood in search of insects for their food. They use their sharp beaks to drill holes in tree trunks for their nests. They also tap dead or hollow branches to announce their presence and protect their territory. Woodpeckers have strong feet with sharp claws for climbing up and down tree trunks. They have strong neck muscles which help them to move their heads rapidly while drilling. They have long, sticky tongues with barbed tips that help them draw the insects from under the bark. They can also snare insects in mid-flight and on the ground. Woodpeckers are losing their habitat to housing developments and logging. As a result, woodpeckers may damage telephone poles in their search for food and survival.

2. **What other birds build nests in holes which they make in the sides of trees?**

Other birds that make their nests in holes in the sides of trees are sapsuckers, yellowhammers, and flickers.

3. **How does a woodpecker cling to the side of a tree?**

Woodpeckers have strong feet and sharp claws that allow them to climb up and down tree trunks and cling to the bark. With two front toes and two hind toes they can climb without falling backwards. Their stiff tail feathers help brace them against the trunk of the tree.

4. **This story is divided into five parts. The first part tells about the home of the woodpeckers.**
   A. What does the second part tell about?

   The second part describes why they chose the oak—near people who had thrown them food.

   B. The third part?

   The third part describes how they dug out their home, taking turns of about twenty minutes each to complete the nest.

   C. The fourth?

   The fourth part describes the home, a snug, clean pocket in the side of the tree.

D. The fifth?

The fifth part describes how they cared for their babies with insects they caught in the air or under bark using their sharp sawlike tongues.

Teacher Note

Each of these parts is called a *paragraph*. Paragraphs are composed of one or more sentences referring to the same central thought. Notice that the first word of each paragraph is usually set a little to the right of the margin. The first word of each paragraph is said to be *indented*. (In printed text the first word may also be set to the left of the margin and is called a *hanging indent*. See "Recommended answers" on the next page, Lesson 21.)

Lesson 19
An Imaginary Dialogue

1. Write in dialogue form an imaginary conversation between the two. Use this form:
   Robin: _____
   Mrs. Robin: _____
   Robin: _____

Lesson 20
Words of a Series

A. The canary and the meadowlark and the oriole and the bluebird can sing.
B. The canary, the meadowlark, the oriole, and the bluebird can sing.

Note: The names of birds in sentences A and B are said to be in a series.
1. What word connects the names in A?
   The word and *connects the names in sentence A.*
2. Where are commas used in B?
   Commas are used after canary, meadowlark, *and* oriole *in sentence B.*
3. What punctuation mark separates words of a series, when not all the connecting words are expressed?
   A comma separates words of a series when not all the connecting words are expressed.
4. Write a sentence stating four things a robin can do.
   Answers may vary.
5. Write a sentence containing the names of five kinds of animals.
   Answers may vary.
6. Write a sentence containing the names of five kinds of fruit trees.
   Answers may vary.
7. Write a sentence mentioning any six objects.

Answers may vary.

8. **Write a sentence containing the names of the colors of the rainbow.**

   The seven colors of the rainbow are: violet, indigo, blue, green, yellow, orange, and red.

9. **Write a sentence containing the names of three of the states. Note: Do not use *and* more than once in any sentence.**

   Answers may vary.

Lesson 21
Paragraphs

Arrange the following sentences into four paragraphs; be sure that each paragraph contains sentences referring to one central thought.

Recommended answers:

A priest went forth in the early dawn. The sky was clear. The grass and flowers waved in the breeze that rose as the sun threw its beams over the earth. Birds of all kinds vied with each other as they sang their joy on that glorious morning.

The priest stood listening. Suddenly, off to one side he heard a trill that rose higher and clearer than all the rest. He moved toward the place whence the song came that he might see what manner of bird it was that could send farther than all the others its happy notes.

As he came near, he beheld a tiny brown bird with open bill, the feathers on its throat rippling with the fervor of its song. It was the wren, the smallest, the least powerful of birds, that seemed to be most glad, and to pour out in melody to the rising sun its delight in life.

As the priest looked, he thought, "Here is a teaching for my people. 'Everyone can be happy; even the weakest can have his songs of thanks.'" So he told to his people the story of the wren, and it has been handed down from that day—a day so long ago that no man can remember the time.

Lesson 22
Conversation—Indians

1. **Tell what you can of the following:**
   A. **Indian homes**
   B. **Occupations of the men**
   C. **Occupations of the women**
   D. **Education of the boys**
   E. **Wigwams**
   F. **Canoes**

G. Weapons

H. Food—how prepared

Student responses to number one, A-H, will vary.

Allow the students to research using the Internet and encyclopedias to get detailed information. A general overview might include the following information.

A. Indian homes—Because Indians lived in many different climates and terrain they had many types of homes. While some Indians traveled and built simple shelters they could carry with them, other tribes stayed in one location and built more permanent structures. Some of the more common types of structures were the wigwam: it consisted of a pole framework covered with leaves and bark; long house: a long rectangular structure that could house multiple families, with a low door to keep in the heat and a high ceiling to keep the smoke from the hearths away from the people; wickiups: huts made of brush and matting; earth lodges: homes built in pits and covered with sod roofs; hogans: built with poles or logs and covered with earth; teepees: pole homes in the shape of a cone covered with animal skins or tree bark; adobe: made of sun-dried bricks and resembled apartment houses

B. Occupations of the men—Men were occupied with hunting and fishing; they also did simple farming such as planting corn, beans, and squash.

C. Occupations of the women—women helped with the farming, cooked the food, and created the materials for their home including pottery, basketry, beading, and weaving their fabrics

D. Education of the boys—boys were taught survival skills and in many tribes participated in initiation ceremonies that tested their bravery and strength. If they met the challenge they became adults and were ready to get married and become full-fledged members of the tribe.

E. Wigwams—see note above

F. Canoes—probably the most popular Indian canoe was the birch bark canoe, built by designing a framework of lightweight and decay-resistant wood and covered with birch bark

G. Weapons—Indians hunted with bows and arrows, clubs, and spears. They fished with hooks and lines, harpoons, traps, spears, and nets. Some Indians also used certain types of plants that attracted the fish and drugged them, paralyzing their gills momentarily so that when the fish came up for air, the fishermen could catch them.

H. Food—how prepared: meat was usually roasted, boiled or broiled. Indians often preserved their food by smoking or drying it. They often cooked in a pit oven using hot stones from the fire to line a pit and produce the heat required for cooking their food.

2. **Bring to school Indian relics or pictures of Indian life.**

Lesson 23
Composition—Indians

1. **Write a short composition about Indians. Follow the outline given in Lesson 22. Begin the composition in**

this way: Long before the white people came to America, Indians roamed here and there over this broad country.

Extended Activities

After researching the lifestyles of the Indians, have the students choose a name for an Indian boy or girl and write a creative story about a day in the life of that child. Be sure to include why the Indian child got that name and how he or she lived out its meaning.

Lesson 24
Titles and Abbreviations

    A. President Adams
    B. Doctor Johnson
    C. Uncle George
    D. Admiral Evans
    E. Judge Fuller
    F. Cousin Ada

1. With what kind of letter does a title begin when it is written with the name of a person?
   A title that is written with the name of a person must begin with a capital letter.
2. Make a rule for the use of the capital letter. Note: Words are sometimes written in a shorter way; they are then said to be abbreviated.
   Capitalize titles and/or their abbreviations when used with names of persons.
3. Write the names of the months and their abbreviations.
   Names of the months and their abbreviations:
   January, Jan.; February, Feb.; March, Mar.; April, Apr.; May, June, and July are not abbreviated because they contain four or fewer letters; August, Aug.; September, Sept.; October, Oct.; November, Nov.; December, Dec.
4. Write the names of the days of the week and their abbreviations.
   Names of the days of the week and their abbreviations. Sunday, Sun.; Monday, Mon.; Tuesday, Tues.; Wednesday, Wed.; Thursday, Thurs.; Friday, Fri.; Saturday, Sat.
5. Write the name of the state in which you live and its abbreviation.
   Answers will vary.
6. With what kind of letter does the name of each day of the week and month begin?
   A capital letter begins the name of each day of the week and month.

What punctuation mark follows an abbreviation?
A period follows an abbreviation.

Write the names for which the following abbreviations stand:
    A. Rev.
    Reverend
    B. Dr.

Doctor
C. Ave.
Avenue
D. St.
Street
E. Jr.
Junior
F. Sr.
Senior
G. Mr.
Mister
H. Mrs.
Mistress

Lesson 25
"Helen Keller"

1. **Why is Helen Keller's teacher called wonderful?**
Helen Keller's teacher is called wonderful because she opened the world to Helen by helping her to know that words stand for things and are a way to express one's feelings.
2. **Tell the story of Helen Keller.**
Answers will vary.
3. **Find out anything else you can about her.**
Answers will vary.
4. **What is the central thought in each paragraph of the selection?**
Paragraph 1 tells about Helen's birth and an illness that left her blind and deaf.
Paragraph 2 tells how Helen learned to associate words with things and began to communicate with people by using her fingers.
Paragraph 3 tells how Helen learned to speak and went on to complete both high school and college. She was an inspiration to the world.
5. **Use the following words in sentences: A. communicate B. imitate C. graduate**
Sentences should include: A. communicate B. imitate C. graduate.
6. **Can you find in this lesson a word which is divided at the end of the line? What mark shows that the word is continued on the next line?**
Note: When the word is divided at the end of a line the division should be made between syllables. A hyphen (-) is used at the end of a line to connect the syllables of a divided word.
In paragraph 3, progress is divided at the end of the line. A hyphen shows that the word is continued on the next line.
7. **Tell how the following words might be divided at the end of a line: *dreadful, imitated, excited.***
The following words might be divided at the end of a line: dreadful, dread-ful; imitated, im-i-tat-ed; excited, ex-cit-ed.

Extended Activities

A. Helen grew up both blind and deaf. Close your eyes for several minutes. Can you describe what is going on around you by the sounds you hear? Now cover your ears and tell what you think is going on in the space around you. Write a paragraph describing what it might be like to live without sight and hearing.

B. If you had to give up a sense, sight, hearing, touch, taste, smell, which one would it be and why? Make a collage of the sense that you would find the easiest to give up. What images would you put on it to show the things you would miss without that sense?

C. Memorize the sign language alphabet and learn to sign your name.

Lesson 26

Letter Writing—"Helen Keller to Oliver Wendell Holmes"

Teacher Note

This letter is taken from *A Story of My Life*, by Helen Keller.

1. **How old was she when she wrote this letter?**
   Helen Keller was nine years old when she wrote this letter.

2. **Compare the date with the date of her birth.**
   Helen was born in May 1880, and the letter was written March 1, 1890.

3. **To what does she compare butterflies? How do you suppose she could gain any knowledge of such insects?**
   Helen compares butterflies to "boys and girls when they forget books and studies, and run away to the woods and fields to gather wild flowers or to wade in the ponds for fragrant lilies, happy in the bright sunshine.

4. **Mention the central thought of each paragraph of this letter.**
   The central thought of each paragraph is as follows:
   Paragraph 1 is the introduction and tells the poet of Helen's love and concern for him.
   Paragraph 2 describes how visitors came to see the blind children, and Helen entertained them.
   Paragraph 3 describes a sad story Helen has been reading, and she has learned that sadness teaches us to be brave and patient.
   Paragraph 4 tells how Helen is studying insects and what she has learned about butterflies.
   In paragraph 5 Helen tells the reader about her little sister.
   In paragraph 6 Helen tells her reader good-bye and ends with the closing "From your loving little friend."

5. **Arrange the topics in the form of an outline.**
   A. Thinking of you
   B. Entertaining visitors
   C. What I am reading/what I have learned
   D. What I am studying
   E. Upcoming visit
   F. Saying good-bye

Extended Activity

Helen Keller wrote this letter to Oliver Wendell Holmes, a famous American poet. This was just one of several letters she wrote her good friend Holmes. After reading his poems entitled "Spring" and "Spring Has Come," Helen wrote him another letter thanking him for writing such good poems. She wrote that they helped her to enjoy spring even though she was blind and deaf and could not hear and see the beauty of springtime that he wrote about. Using the Internet, research Holmes to find his poems "Spring" and/or "Spring Has Come." Then find the letter she wrote in April, 1891, thanking him for the poems. How does she enjoy spring without her sense of sight and sound?

Lesson 27
Letter Writing

1. Read again the letter in Lesson 26.
2. Where was the letter written? What punctuation mark is placed between the name of the city and that of the state? Note: The part of the letter that tells where it was written and when it was written is the heading. The letter begins, "Dear kind Poet." This part of the letter is called the salutation. The body of the letter follows the salutation. The letter closes with "From your loving little friend." This is called the complimentary close. The signature of the person writing the letter follows the complimentary close.
   The letter was written in South Boston, MA.
3. What mark of punctuation follows the salutation? The complimentary close? The signature?
   A comma is placed between the name of the city and that of the state. 3. A comma follows the salutation and the complimentary close. The signature is not followed by any mark of punctuation.
4. Write these headings from dictation:
   A. Boston, MA, Jan. 6, 1914
   B. Jacksonville, FL, June 16, 1914
   C. Colombia University New York, NY, Mar 13, 1914
   D. 1104 South Wabash Ave. Chicago, IL, May 1, 1914

Lesson 28
Letter Writing

1. Write one of the following letters:
   A. Your friend, Charles White, who lives in the country, has sent you a puppy by express. Write a letter telling how you received the box, what the puppy did when you opened the box, what you named him, and how you expect to train the dog. Thank your friend for

sending you such a fine present, and invite him to visit you.

B. Your Uncle Frank has sent you a fine box of fruit. Write a letter telling when it arrived and how pleased you were to receive it. Tell with whom you shared part of your gift. Say that your parents have agreed to let you visit your uncle next summer and that you are looking forward to your summer vacation with much pleasure. Tell any items of interest concerning your family that your uncle might like to know.

Note: your letter should have heading, salutation, body, complimentary close, and signature.

Teacher Note

An outline of the friendly letter shows five basic parts: The heading includes two lines for the writer's address and the date in the upper right-hand corner of the letter. The salutation or greeting appears at the left-hand margin two lines below the heading and begins with Dear followed by the name of the person being addressed and a comma. The body is the main part of the letter and includes the ideas or information you wish to tell your friend. Skip a line after the salutation and between each paragraph. The complimentary closing follows the body and begins two lines below the body and just to the right of the middle of the letter. The first word is capitalized and the closing ends with a comma. The signature is written beneath the closing and is usually just your first name.

> 1620 St. Charles Avenue
> New Orleans, LA 70112
>
> Dear Fred,
>
> It was so nice to hear from you yesterday and to know that all is well with you and your family.
>
> We are well, also, and hope to visit you during the summer when school is over for the children.
>
> Johnny is growing quickly and now is almost four. It is hard to believe that he was just a baby at your last visit. Julie and Andrea are doing well at school, and Andrea has even been named valedictorian for her class.
>
> I will write more later and let you know when we might be able to arrange a visit.
>
> Yours affectionately,
>
> George

Lesson 29
Addressing an Envelope

Note: The envelope should contain the name of the person to whom the letter is to be sent, the street and number if the person lives in the city, the name of the city or town, and the name of the state.

1. Address the envelopes to the following:
   A. Mrs. A. D. Clark, 1234 Avalon St., Milwaukee, WI, 53202
   B. Mr. Franklin D. Blackburn, 2313 Tara Drive, Birmingham, AL, 35216
   C. Miss Helen Brady, 2014 Third Avenue, Minneapolis, MN, 55416.
   See the blank envelope outlines in the Teacher Aides section, page 226, at the back of this book.
2. Where should the postage stamp be placed?
   The postage stamp should be placed in the upper right hand corner of the envelope on the side without the flap.

Lesson 30
Selection to be Memorized

1. Memorize the selection.

Extended Activity A

Bryant's poem begins with a question: "What plant we in this apple tree?" He never mentions the apples that result from the planting.

What does he say is planted in the tree?
Bryant says buds, boughs, shadows, and shelter are planted in an apple tree.

How does each one help us?
Each helps us in the following ways: Buds "lengthen into leafy sprays," boughs grow for the thrush to "haunt and sing and hide her nest," shadows cool us in "the noontide hour," and the shelter protects us "from the summer shower."

Extended Activity B

This poem was written by William Cullen Bryant, known as the first great American poet. Research Bryant using the Internet and/or an encyclopedia to answer the following questions.

1. When was Bryant born?
   William Cullen Bryant was born November 3, 1794.
2. Where was he born?
   He was born in Cummington, Massachusetts.

3. **What did his father do for a living?**

   He was the second son of Peter Bryant, a prominent doctor.

4. **How old was he when he published his first poem?**

   He was 13 when he published his first poem.

5. **What was the title of his first poem and what was it about?**

   His first published poem was entitled "The Embargo" and it ridiculed the policies of President Thomas Jefferson.

6. **In what important political action was Bryant engaged?**

   Bryant was active in the antislavery movement.

7. **In what other careers did Bryant excel besides writing poetry?**

   Bryant was also a lawyer and a journalist.

8. **Bryant later became an editor of a newspaper. What newspaper was it?**

   He was editor of the Evening Post until his death.

9. **When did Bryant die?**

   William Cullen Bryant died June 12, 1878.

10. **Bryant wrote many other poems about nature. Find and list five of his other nature poems. Choose one of his poems and copy it.**

    Answers may vary but may include some of the following: "To a Waterfowl," "Inscription for the Entrance to a Wood," "The Yellow Violet," "Green River," "A Winter Piece," "A Forest Hymn," "The Death of Flowers," "The Prairies," "Lines To a Waterfowl," "The Rivulet," "The West Wind," "The Forest Hymn," To the Fringed Gentian," "June," "The Skies," "October," "November," "The Gladness of Nature."

Lesson 31
Dictation

   If you live in a large city, you may not know the apple tree. In winter it is a short, grayish tree with a flat or rounded top. Its stout, thick branches are irregular and rigid.

   In the spring it is a white tree. Its large clusters of white and pink flowers look like short-stemmed bouquets with a margin of leaves below.

   In autumn it is a green tree filled with fruit of red and gold.

1. **What is the central thought of each of these paragraphs?**

   Paragraph 1 describes the apple tree in winter as a short grayish tree with flat or rounded top and thick irregular and rigid branches.

   Paragraph 2 describes the apple tree in spring as a white tree with large clusters of pink and white flowers.

   Paragraph 3 describes the apple tree in autumn as a green tree full of red and golden apples.

2. **Write the paragraphs about the apple tree from dictation.**

Lesson 32
Conversation—Fruits

1. **Tell what you can about the following fruits:**

   A. grapes

   Grapes grow in clusters on woody vines. They are grown throughout the world and come in a variety of colors. Besides fresh fruit, they are used in wines, juices, and jellies and are dried to produce raisins.

   B. peaches

   Peaches grow on trees in temperate climates around the world. They have a hard pitted stone in the center of the fruit. Peaches are tasty fresh or in pastries, pies, and jellies.

   C. currants

   Currants grow on low, bushy shrubs in cool, moist climates. They have a tart flavor and are used in wines, jams, jellies, and pies.

   D. blackberries

   Blackberries are small black fruits that grow wild throughout much of the world. They may grow on vines or bushes which may have thorns. Blackberries can be used in jams, jellies, wines, pies, or as a fresh fruit snack.

   E. oranges

   Oranges are a citrus fruit grown on trees in sub-tropical climates. They are rich in vitamins C, A, and B. They are popular as fresh fruit or can be used in juices, candy, jellies, soft drinks, and baked goods.

   F. apples

   Apples are among the most famous fruits that grow on trees. They grow anywhere except in extremely cold or hot climates and come in all sorts of colors and flavors from tart to sweet. Apples contain vitamins, pectin, and potassium and are used for baking cakes, pies, and other desserts as well as apple butter, cider, jellies, applesauce, wines, and vinegar.

   G. strawberries

   Strawberries grow close to the ground and grow best in cooler climates. They are rich in vitamin C. Strawberries are often eaten fresh as well as in desserts such as pies and are used to make jams and jellies.

   H. pears

   Pears also grow on trees in temperate climates and may have a gritty, sandy texture. They have a core similar to an apple with tiny seeds in the center. They contain carbohydrates, vitamins, calcium, phosphorus, and iron among other nutrients and are used in desserts or eaten fresh.

   I. lemons

   Lemons are a type of citrus that grow on trees and are rich in vitamins C and B. Because they are very tart, they are seldom eaten raw but are used in a wide variety of dishes such as puddings, pies, drinks, and seasonings.

   J. bananas

   Bananas are grown in the tropics around the world. They are a nourishing fruit that contain carbohydrates, phosphorus, vitamins, and potassium. They grow on stalks that may look like trees but don't have woody trunks or boughs. Their blossoms develop into tiny green bananas known as fingers. Each cluster of fingers is called a hand. Bananas are used in pies, cakes, snacks, and drinks.

K. plums

Plums grow on trees around the world. Like peaches they have a hard pit in the center of the fruit. Plums are dried to produce prunes and are eaten fresh or used to make jams and jellies.

L. cranberries

Cranberries grow on vines in specially prepared bogs and have pink or white flowers that produce red sour berries. They are rich in vitamin C and are used in sauces, jellies, and juices.

2. **Write sentences answering the following questions, each sentence to contain a series of words:**

   A. Which of these fruits grow on trees?

   Peaches, oranges, apples, pears, plums, and lemons grow on trees.

   B. Which grow on vines?

   Grapes, blackberries, and strawberries grow on vines.

   C. Which grow on bushes?

   Currants, cranberries, and some blackberries grow on bushes.

   D. Which grow only where it is always warm?

   Bananas, oranges and lemons grow only where it is always warm.

   E. Which have you seen growing?

   Answers may vary.

   F. Which fruits can be shipped long distances?

   With modern packaging and ease of travel, all fruits can now be shipped long distances.

Lesson 33
Description—A Fruit Store

1. **Write a description of a fruit store using the following outline:**
   A. Location of store
   B. Owner
   C. Kinds of fruit in the store
   D. Parts of the world from which the fruit came
   E. Losses in the fruit business
   Answers may vary.
2. **Parts A and B of the outline may be combined in one sentence.**
3. **Part C should contain words in a series.**
4. **Into how many paragraphs should your description be divided?**
   The description should be divided into four or five paragraphs.

Lesson 34
Correct Use of Words

    A. Set the fern on the table.
    B. You may sit in this chair.
    C. Sit in a good position when you write.
    D. We set the flowers in the window.
    E. I sat under the big tree.

1. In which of the above sentences is an object referred to as placed in a certain position. Note: The word *sit* means to take a seat. Note: When an object is placed in any position the word *set* may be used.

   Sentences A and D refer to an object as placed in a certain position.

2. Write six sentences telling
   A. Where you set the dishes
   B. Where you set the geraniums
   C. Who set the dishes on the table

   Sentences A to C should use set or sets.

   D. Where you like to sit
   E. Who sits near you at school
   F. Who sits nearest the teacher's desk

   Sentences D to F should use sit or sits.

3. Copy the following sentences, filling the blanks with set, sit, or sat:
   A. Mary, <u>set</u> the basket on the porch.
   B. Bring your chair and <u>sit</u> near me.
   C. <u>Set</u> your doll in the doll carriage.
   D. The dog likes to <u>sit</u> near the fire.
   E. I <u>sat</u> near the window yesterday.
   F. Do not be afraid; I will <u>sit</u> near you.
   G. <u>Set</u> that bottle of ink on the desk.

Lesson 35
Selection for Study— "The Barefoot Boy"

1. Consult the dictionary for meanings of the following words; divide the words into syllables and mark the accented syllables: jaunty, habitude, architectural, artisans, eschewing.

   jaunty, ˈjaun-ty, spirited or lively in manner; habitude, ˈhab-

*i-tude, habits or customs of a character; architectural, ar-chi-*ᐟ*tec-tur-al, the overall design or form of a structure; artisans, *ᐟ*ar-ti-sans, craftsman; eschewing, es-*ᐟ*chew-ing, avoiding or shunning*

2. **Describe the boy as the first stanza of the poem pictures him.**

   The boy, tanned by the sun, has red lips from which come a merry whistle.

3. **How was he dressed?**

   He is barefoot and wearing turned-up pants and a torn hat.

4. **How old do you think he was?**

   Answers may vary.

5. **If you were to draw a picture of him, what would you have him doing?**

   Answers may vary.

6. **What background would you use?**

   Answers may vary.

7. **Would the fifth and sixth lines suggest anything for your picture?**

   Lines five and six refer to red lips "kissed by strawberries on the hill" and "sunshine on thy face."

8. **How did the poet know so much about a barefoot boy?**

   The poet knew so much about the barefoot boy because he "was once a barefoot boy!"

9. **How does the barefoot boy have more than the rich man can buy?**

   The barefoot boy has more than the rich man can buy because he has "outward sunshine, inward joy."

10. **Why is the wasp called a "mason"?**

    The wasp is called a "mason" because he builds his "walls of clay" by making mud from saliva, mixing it with small pebbles and shaping his nests much like a mason builds a wall.

11. **Tell what you can of an oriole's nest.**

    An oriole builds its nest at the tip of a tree limb weaving vines, fibers, string and hair to create a purselike nest.

12. **What knowledge does the boy have that he never learned in school?**

    Lines 21-37 describe the knowledge the boy has that he never learned in school: knowledge of the wild bees' chase, the wild flowers time and place, flights of fowl and habits of the woods creatures, how the tortoise carries his shell and the mole sinks his well, how the robin feeds her young and the oriole's nest is hung, where the whitest lilies grow and the freshest berries grow, where to find the ground nuts and wood grapes, the black wasp's cunning ways and the art of the hornets.

13. **Name some of the "tenants of the wood" that the boy might know.**

    Some of the tenants of the woods might be the birds, squirrels, rabbits, moles, and insects that live in the woods.

14. **Write the names of three insects, two birds, and three animals mentioned in the poem.**

    Three insects mentioned in the poem are bees, wasps and hornets; two birds mentioned are robins and orioles; three animals mentioned in the poem are a tortoise, a woodchuck, and ground moles.

15. **Write sentences telling something of the habits of each.**

    Answers may vary.

16. **What flowers and fruits are mentioned?**

    Flowers mentioned in the poem are wild flowers and white lilies; fruits are fresh berries and wood grapes.

Extended Activity A

This poem was written by John Greenleaf Whittier, who along with William Cullen Bryant, was
     another great American poet. Research Whittier using the Internet and/or an encyclopedia
     to answer the following questions.

1. **When was Whittier born?**
     John Greenleaf Whittier was born December 17, 1807.
2. **Where was he born?**
     He was born in Haverhill, Massachusetts.
3. **What did his father do for a living?**
     His father, John Hussey Whittier, was a farmer.
4. **How old was he when he published his first poem?**
     He was 19 when his first poem was published.
5. **What was the title of his first poem?**
     The title of his first poem was "The Exile's Departure."
6. **In what important political action was Whittier engaged?**
     Whittier was active in the antislavery movement founding the antislavery Liberty party in 1840.
     In the mid-1850s he was also instrumental in starting the formation of the Republican party.
7. **What other careers did Whittier pursue besides writing poetry?**
     Besides writing poetry, Whittier edited and published a variety of magazines and newspapers.
8. **Whittier wrote several books. What was the first book he wrote?**
     Whittier's first book, published in 1831, was titled Legends of New England.
9. **When did Whittier die?**
     Whittier died September 7, 1892.
10. **Whittier wrote many other poems about nature. Find and list five of his other nature poems.**
     Choose one of his poems and copy it.
     Answers may vary and may include some of the following: "In School Days," "Snow-Bound,
     "Telling the Bees," "What the Birds Said," "The Worship of Nature."

Extended Activity B

Point of view is the position or angle from which a story is written or told. There are three points
     of view a writer or story teller can take: first person point of view in which the narrator is
     part of the story using words like I, me, my, us, and we to tell the story; second person point
     of view is used when the writer refers to a second person besides himself and uses words
     like you and your; third person point of view means that someone else outside the story is
     narrating using words like he, she, it, they, them. An omniscient third person point of view
     allows the writer to describe not just the actions, but the thoughts and feelings of all the
     characters in his story.

In what point of view does Whittier write this poem?
     Whittier writes this poem from the first person point of view.
What lines can you find to prove what point of view he uses?
     Lines nine and ten prove what point of view he uses: "From my heart I give thee joy-I was once
     a barefoot boy."

Read Lesson 26 again and identify the point of view Helen Keller uses in her letter. What words does she use to show you the point of view she is using?

Lesson 26: the point of view Helen Keller uses in her letter is first person. She uses words like "I have thought of you..." "I am going to write you a letter because I love you."

Read Lesson 21 and identify the words that show what point of view the narrator is using.

"An Indian Legend," is third person omniscient; the words that show this point of view are "As the priest looked, he thought."

What point of view is used in the poem in Lesson 54? What words does the poet use to show point of view?

Lesson 54, "Don't Give Up," is second person. The writer is talking to you. "If you've tried and have not won, Never stop for crying;" "If by easy work you beat, Who the more will prize you? Gaining victory from defeat, That's the test that tries you!"

Lesson 36
Conversation—The Farmer

1. **Tell of the work of the farmer A. in spring B. in summer C. in autumn D. in winter.**

    A. In the spring the farmer prepares the soil for planting by tilling the ground. He may use a plow to turn over the soil, followed with a disc or harrow that breaks up the clods and makes the ground smoother for planting. Major crops include alfalfa, barley, beans, corn, cotton, fruits and vegetables of all types, oats, peanuts, potatoes, rice, rye, sorghum, soybeans, sugar, tobacco, and wheat. Springtime may also bring newborn animals that need to be cared for.

    B. In summer the farmer tends his crops by cultivating the growing plants, fertilizing them, and perhaps using pesticides and herbicides to kill harmful insects and weeds. The farmer also cuts the hay and stores it for animal food.

    C. In autumn the farmer is busy harvesting the crops and storing them for the winter's food supply for the animals and/or selling it for human consumption.

    D. In winter the farmer may repair tools and implements and order seed for the coming spring to begin the planting process again.

2. **What implements does the farmer use in his work?**

    The farmer uses many implements in his work depending on the type of farming he is doing. He may have tractors, plows, discs, harrows, cultivators, sprayers, combines, harvesters, balers, wagons, elevators, rakes, and trucks to name a few.

3. **How have modern inventions lightened the work of the farmer?**

    Modern inventions have helped the farmer immeasurably. In the 1700s and early 1800s, farmers lived on small farms and everyone worked hard with only hand tools or simple machines as their implements. They could scarcely raise enough to feed their families. Scientific advances have made farming much easier and more productive. Farmers have now developed better plant varieties, stronger fertilizers, and better herbicides that have increased production and developed healthier animals that produce more meat. While early farmers could barely produce enough food to feed their own families, individual farmers today can produce enough to feed 100 people. Farmers' surplus food is exported around the world.

4. **In what ways does the success of his work depend on nature?**

   The farmer's success depends heavily on nature. Sufficient sun and rain are critical for crops since drought or lack of sun can destroy crops. In addition temperate climates are essential for production. If farmers plant too early their crops may freeze; if they plant too late their crops may not mature in time for a plentiful harvest before the winter months arrive. If summer storms bring high winds or hail, crops can be destroyed in minutes. Nature can be a farmer's best friend or his worst enemy.

5. **What kinds of crops are raised on farms in your section of the country?**

   Answers may vary.

6. **Notice that the names of the seasons do not begin with capital letters.**

Lesson 37
Possessive Form

   A. The barefoot boy knows how the oriole's nest is hung.
   B. He knows the black wasp's cunning ways.
   C. He has seen the woodchuck's cell.

1. **Whose nest is mentioned in sentence A?**

   The oriole's nest is mentioned in sentence A.

2. **To what words are the apostrophe (') and s added to show ownership or possession? Note: Words written in this way to show ownership are said to be in possessive form.**

   The apostrophe and s are added to nouns that show ownership or possession.

3. **What words in sentences B and C are in the possessive form?**

   In sentence B the word wasp *is in the possessive form; in sentence C the word* woodchuck *is in the possessive form.*

4. **Find examples of the possessive form in Lessons 1, 3, 13, and 26.**

   Examples of the possessive form in Lesson 1: king's, (3 times) baby's, Pharaoh's; Lesson 3: miller's, (2 times); Lesson 13: robin's, earth's; Lesson 26: Washington's

5. **Write sentences containing the following:**
   A. the miller's boy
   B. Pharaoh's daughter
   C. the barefoot boy's hat
   D. the rich man's house
   Answers will vary.

6. **Use in sentences the possessive form of each of the following words:**
   A. man
   B. king
   C. bluebird

   D. squirrel
   E. angel
   F. sister

Answers will vary but must include the following: A. man's, B. king's, C. bluebird's, D. squirrel's, E. angel's, F. sister's.

Lesson 38
Composition

One morning in spring, Farmer Davis said, "I see that old Speckle wants to raise some more chickens. I think I will let her raise some ducks instead. I will get some ducks' eggs when I go to town this afternoon."

1. Copy the paragraph and complete the story by telling how long Speckle had to wait for the eggs to hatch, how the ducklings differed from little chickens, how Speckle took care of them, and what happened one day at the pond. Let the sentences in each paragraph of your story be about one central thought.

Lesson 39
Names

John Greenleaf Whittier wrote beautiful poems.
Note: Whittier is the family name or surname.
Note: John is the name that was given to the poet by his parents and is called the given name.
Note: The name between the given name and the surname is the middle name.
   1. With what kind of letter does each word of the name of a person begin?
      Each word of the name of a person begins with a capital letter.
Note: The first letter of a word is called an initial. Mr. Whittier's initials are J. G. W.
   2. What punctuation mark is placed after an initial when used alone?
      A period is placed after an initial when used alone.
   3. Write these names using initials only for the given and middle names.
      A. Oliver Wendell Holmes *O. W. Holmes*
      B. James Russell Lowell *J. R. Lowell*
      C. Ralph Waldo Emerson *R. W. Emerson*
      D. William Cullen Bryant *W. C. Bryant*

Lesson 40
Selection for Study—
"Story of the Flax"

1. **Make a list of changes through which the flax passed.**
   The flax bloomed, was pulled out, soaked, dried, broken, combed, spun into linen, sewn into a dress, worn out, discarded for rags, taken to a mill, resoaked in hot water, ground into pulp, pressed under rollers, and made into fine paper upon which were written the words of a great poet.

2. **Tell the story of the flax.**
   First the flax bloomed. Secondly, the farmer pulled it up by the roots and soaked it then dried it out. Then the flax was broken and combed to extract the fibers. Finally the spinning wheel spun the fibers into linen which a mother purchased to sew a dress for her daughter. After the dress was worn out and turned into rags, it was salvaged by a rag picker and taken to a mill where it was soaked again, ground into pulp and pressed under rollers where it became fine linen paper. A bookmaker purchased the paper and used it to print the words of a poet.

3. **Into how many paragraphs is this story divided?**
   This story is divided into six paragraphs.

4. **What is the central thought in each paragraph?**
   The central thought of paragraph one, the growth of the flax plant; paragraph two, the farmer harvests the flax; paragraph three, the flax is spun into linen; paragraph four, a mother buys the linen for a dress; paragraph five, the flax is recycled into paper; paragraph six, the flax is sold and used for great poems.

5. **Tell what you can of looms and methods of weaving.**
   Have students research both the weaving process and the printing process on the Internet. See 6.

6. **Tell something about the process of printing.**
   See 5.

7. **Write the first and second paragraphs from dictation.**
   Paragraph one: The flax plant was in bloom; its little blue flowers were as delicate as the wings of a butterfly. The sun shone on it, the rain clouds gave it water, and the soft south wind blew it gently to and fro.
   Paragraph two: One day the farmer and his men came into the field. They took hold of the flax plant and pulled it up by the roots. Then they laid it in water, as if they were going to drown it, and after that they put it near a hot fire until it was almost burned up.

Lesson 41
Composition—Description

1. Write a paragraph describing this book. Tell about
   A. The cover—material, color, design
   B. The paper—thick or thin
   C. The print—large or small
   D. The margins—narrow or wide
   E. The illustrations

Lesson 42
Composition—"The Thirsty Crow"

"The Crow's Story"

   I am so thirsty! I have had no water to drink for a long time. If I do not find some water soon, I shall die. There is a pitcher, perhaps—

1. Copy these sentences, and complete the story as the crow might have told it. Write your story in paragraphs.

Lesson 43
Composition—Dialogue

   A grasshopper that loved to sing and dance met an ant that was putting away food for winter.

1. Write a conversation which may have taken place between the two when the grasshopper urged the ant to play with him. Use this form:
   Grasshopper: Good morning, _____.
   Ant: _____.
   When winter came the grasshopper went to the ant's house begging for food.
2. Write the second conversation.

Lesson 44
Conversation—
The Cat Family

1. **Talk about the house cat from the following outline:**
    A. Size
    Adult cats may average about eight to ten inches at the shoulder and weigh from five to fifteen pounds.
    B. Color
    Cats come in a variety of colors and shades including smokes, solids, calicos, Siamese, and tabbies to name a few. Students may opt to select one type and identify its varying degrees of color.
    C. Covering of body
    A cat's coat serves two purposes—to provide insulation and protect its skin. Generally cats have two layers of hair: an undercoat of soft, short hair and an outer layer of longer hair.
    D. Feet—claws and soft pads
    A cat uses its claws for climbing, hunting prey, and defense. Its claws are curved and long for better grip when the cat climbs and/or pounces on its prey and retract when not in use. The soft pads allow the cat to move quietly and sneak up on its prey.
    E. Eyes
    Cats' eyes vary in color. The iris contracts and widens to allow the cat to see well in dim and bright light. Cats have a third eyelid that lubricates and protects the eye.
    F. Use of whiskers
    Cat whiskers are keen touch organs located on the chin, above the eyes and on the sides of the face. They transmit signals to the brain when they brush objects. They help a cat find its way in dark places, protect a cat's eyes, and sense wind direction.
    G. Roughness of tongue
    The papillae covering the tongue help cats to groom themselves and lick their food.
    H. Teeth
    Adult cats have 30 teeth to grab and shred their food.
    I. Food
    Cats need a healthy diet of vitamins and minerals, fats and proteins and clean water. They enjoy beef liver, dairy products, eggs, vegetables, and fish.
    J. Method of hunting
    While untamed cats must use their hunting skills, house cats do not generally have the keen hunting ability needed to find their food and kill it for consumption. They rely on their pet owner to provide their food. Cats in the wild stalk their prey with the use of their silent paws,

long, curved claws, sharp eyes, keen hearing, and agile jumping ability. They use their claws to grab the prey's throat and strangle it or sever its spinal cord.

K. Habits

Cats love to run, climb, jump, and play.

L. Varieties of cats

Cats are generally divided into two varieties—long and short haired breeds. Within those two general categories there are many varieties.

M. Use

Household cats are used for companionship and pleasure. Farm cats are often used to keep down rodent populations that might otherwise eat feed and grain.

N. Cleanliness

Cats clean themselves using their rough, coarse tongues to groom their fur. They also use their soft paws to wash their faces.

O. Friendliness

Cats communicate their affection through purrs, meows, and playful pouncing. They may raise their tails in greeting and rub against the owner's legs.

P. Affection for young

Mother cats lick their kittens at birth and dry them to stimulate their breathing. Mother cats provide milk for their babies and keep them clean and protected until they are old enough to wean—about 6 to 8 weeks.

Q. Means of protection

Cats may flick their tail from side to side, arch their backs, and puff their fur to warn of danger. They may hiss and growl to indicate fear and use their claws for protection.

Note: Animals that are similar in general structure and habits are said to belong to the same family.

2. The following animals belong to the cat family; compare those you have seen with the house cat using the points in the outline:
   A. lion
   B. panther
   C. leopard
   D. puma
   E. tiger
   F. wild cat
   G. jaguar
   H. lynx

3. Write ten questions about an animal of the cat family. Read your questions, and call upon other pupils to answer.

4. Find and bring to class pictures of any of the animals mentioned in this lesson.

Lesson 45
Composition—Description of an Animal

1. Write a description of one of the following animals: A. tiger B. bear C. cat D. rabbit E. squirrel F. dog G. wolf H. fox I. giraffe J. elephant (Model your description after the one given in Lesson 44)

Teacher Note
   The outline in Lesson 44 follows but may need to be adapted for the chosen animal and available information. A. Size B. Color C. Covering of body D. Feet—claws and soft pads E. Eyes F. Use of whiskers G. Roughness of tongue H. Teeth I. Food J. Method of hunting K. Habits L. Varieties M. Use N. Cleanliness O. Friendliness P. Affection for young Q. Means of protection

Lesson 46
Dictation— "Description of a Lion"

1. Use in sentences: A. height B. tawny C. shaggy D. terror E. prowls F. creature G. concealed.
   Answers may vary.
2. Why is the lion called "the king of beasts"?
   The lion is called "the king of beasts" because of its great strength and royal appearance. It is a symbol of power and beauty.
3. Tell any stories of lions that you may have heard or read.
4. Make an outline of the description.
5. Write the description from dictation.

Lesson 47
Reproduction—A Fable

1. Write this fable in dialogue form. Begin it in this way:
   First Cat: This is my piece of cheese.
   Second Cat: No, it is not yours. I saw it first.
   First Cat:

Second Cat:

First Cat:

Monkey:

2. **What punctuation mark is placed after the word** *no*? **Note: The words** *yes* **and** *no*, **when used in answering questions, are generally followed by commas, except at the end of a sentence.**

   A comma is placed after the word no.

3. **Find examples of the use of yes and no in your readers.**

   Examples of the use of yes and no in the textbook: Lesson 56, Lesson 58, Lesson 63.

Lesson 48
Composition

1. Read once more the story of "The Quarrel," Lesson 47.
2. Write a similar story about two little girls, a larger boy, and a ripe peach.
3. Where did the little girls get the ripe peach?
4. Why did they quarrel about it?
5. Whom did they ask to settle the quarrel?
6. What did the larger boy say?
7. What did he do?

Lesson 49
Reproduction—A Fable

Write in your own words one of the following fables:

   A. The Fox in the Well
   B. The Hare and the Tortoise
   C. The Dog and His Shadow
   D. The Fox Who Lost His Tail
   E. The Wind and the Sun
   F. The Lion and the Mouse
   G. The Fox and the Crane.

If you do not know any of these, write some other fable.

Extended Activity

Students should become familiar with Aesop, the creator of many familiar fables told today. Aesop was a Greek slave who lived about 600 B.C. Most of his stories or fables describe animals who behave and talk like humans and illustrate their virtues and vices humorously. Each fable ends with a moral, or piece of advice about life. At www.aesopfables.com the students will find information about Aesop and hundreds of his fables along with their morals. Students should be encouraged to research Aesop, choose one of his fables to complete this lesson, then create a piece of art work depicting that fable.

Lesson 50
Imaginative Letter

1. A boy or girl has gone away for a visit, leaving a kitten at home. Write a letter from the kitten which tells how it is being treated, what the other children in the house are doing, and how it wishes for the return of its master or mistress. Include some incident that might happen in the life of a kitten.

Lesson 51
Summary—To Remember

The following test may be assigned to the students as a review of the skills covered in Lessons 1-50. Please rewrite the following sentences correcting their errors.

1. what is your favorite animal
    What is your favorite animal?
2. what is special about that animal
    What is special about that animal?
3. dr seuss wrote stories about strange animals and characters
    Dr. Seuss wrote stories about strange animals and characters.
4. no i can not create animals as well as he did
    No, I cannot create animals as well as he did.
5. the animal he created that i like best is yertle
    The animal he created that I like best is Yertle.
6. some of his other animals are thidwick mulligatawny horton iota and bustard
    Some of his other animals are Thidwick, Mulligatawny, Horton, Iota, and Bustard.
7. he also wrote about strange people like thing one and thing two
    He also wrote about strange people like Thing One and Thing Two.
8. i also remember marvin k mooney.
    I also remember Marvin K. Mooney.
9. my favorite book by dr suess is oh, the places you'll go
    My favorite book by Dr. Suess is Oh, the Places You'll Go.
10. yes dr suess had a great imagination
    Yes, Dr. Suess had a great imagination.
11-17. List the days of the week and their abbreviations.
    Days of the week: Sunday, Sun.; Monday, Mon.; Tuesday, Tues.; Wednesday, Wed.; Thursday,

Thur.; Friday, Fri.; Saturday, Sat.

18-29. List the months of the year and their abbreviations.

Months of the year: January, Jan.; February, Feb.; March, Mar.; April, Apr.; May; June; July; August, Aug.; September, Sept.; October, Oct.; November, Nov.; December, Dec.

Fill in the blanks choosing the correct answer from the word bank below:
stanzas, sentence, paragraph, capital, statement, hyphen, question

30. The first word of every line of poetry begins with a *capital*.
31. A *hyphen* is used at the end of a line to connect the syllables of a divided word.
32. A group of words that states something, or asks something, or expresses a command is called a *sentence*.
33. A *paragraph* is composed of one or more sentences about the same central thought.
34. A sentence that tells something is a *statement*.
35. A sentence that asks something is a *question*.
36. The parts into which a poem is divided are called *stanzas*.

True or False

37. A period is placed after a statement.
    True
38. Words of a series are separated by hyphens.
    False
39. A sentence that asks something is a command.
    False
40. The first word and all important words in a title begin with capital letters.
    True

Lesson 52
Dictation—Quotation Marks

1. **Read what the hen said. Note: The marks that enclose the exact words spoken by the hen are called quotation marks ("").**
   The hen's exact words are; "Who will plant this wheat?" "I will."
2. **Where do you find other quotation marks?**
   Other quotation marks can be found around the exact words of the rat, the cat, and the pig: "Not I."
3. **Write the sentences from dictation.**
   A little red hen found a grain of wheat. She said, "Who will plant this wheat?" The rat said, "Not I." The cat said, "Not I." The pig said, "Not I." "I will," said the little red hen, and she did.

Extended Activity A

Have students scan the book to find quotation marks used in other lessons.

Lesson 1: "This is one of the Hebrews' children." "Shall I go and call a nurse of the Hebrew women, that she may nurse the child for thee?" "Go." "Take the child and nurse it for me, and I will pay thee thy wages." "I drew him out of the water."

Lesson 3: "This stone should not be here," he said. "Someone might fall over it. I will move it out of the way." "This bag of gold belongs to the one who helps by removing the stone from the road." "I am glad that I have found someone who is unselfish enough to think of the comfort of others."

Lesson 21: "Here is a teaching for my people. Everyone can be happy; even the weakest can have his song of thanks."

Extended Activity B:

Hand out several comic strips to students. Explain that the balloons showing what people said in the strips are visual symbols for quotations marks. Have students rewrite the words in the strip, using quotation marks instead of balloons around exact quotations.

Lesson 53
Meaning of Words

1. Write a word opposite in meaning to each word of the following list; write the words in pairs, thus, busy-idle:

   A. **honest** *dishonest*

   B. **certain** *doubtful*

   C. **broad** *narrow*

   D. **deep** *shallow*

   E. **high** *low*

   F. **heavy** *light*

   G. **wide** *thin or narrow*

   H. **valuable** *cheap*

   I. **rare** *common*

   J. **large** *small*

   K. **bitter** *sweet*

   L. **sour** *sweet*

   M. **industrious** *lazy*

   N. **generous** *stingy*

   O. **quiet** *noisy or loud*

   P. **tame** *wild*

   Q. **slow** *fast*

   R. **difficult** *easy*

2. **Write other words that are opposite in meaning.**
   Answers may vary.
3. **Write five sentences containing words and their opposites.**
   Answers may vary.

Lesson 54

Selection for Study—"Don't Give Up"

1. **What does this poem teach?**
   This poem teaches us that persistence pays off. We should never give up.
2. **Explain "patient trying." What lessons in school require "patient trying"?**
   "Patient trying" means tackling our tasks with patience even if at first the task may be difficult and we may fail. Class work, tests, friendships, sports, art, or music may require "patient trying."
3. **How may victory be gained from defeat? What may be learned from defeat?**
   Victory may be gained from defeat by proving to ourselves that if we keep trying, we will conquer the difficulty. Defeat teaches us patience and may help us to find other ways to solve a problem that we may not have thought of before.
4. **If a football team is defeated, what may the players learn that will help when they play again?**
   Multiple answers may emerge in class discussion.
5. **If a pupil fails an examination, what may he learn from his failure?**
   Multiple answers may emerge in class discussion.
6. **Write the first and second stanzas of the poem from dictation.**
   First stanza: If you've tried and have not won, Never stop for crying; All that's great and good is done Just by patient trying.
   Stanza 2: Though young birds, in flying, fall, Still their wings grow stronger; And the next time they can keep Up a little longer.
7. **Memorize the poem.**

Lesson 55

Contractions

1. **What does *you've* mean, Lesson 54?**
   You've means you have.
2. **Write the two words for which *you've* stands.**
   You have.
3. **What letters have been omitted?**
   H *and* A *have been omitted.*

Note: The mark showing that a letter or letters have been omitted is called an apostrophe.

Note: You've is a contraction.

4. Find another contraction in Lesson 54. For what words does it stand?

    That's stands for that is.

5. Write the words for which the following contractions stand: I'm, can't, don't, I'll, they'll, we'll, you've, he's, it's, they're, couldn't, wouldn't.

    I'm, I am; can't, cannot; don't, do not; I'll, I will; they'll, they will; we'll, we will; you've, you have; he's, he is or he has; it's, it is or it has; they're, they are; couldn't, could not; wouldn't, would not.

6. Write sentences containing five of these contractions.

    Answers may vary.

Lesson 56
Quotations

    A. The teacher said, "Someone is at the door."
    B. Tom said, "It is not I."
    C. "Perhaps it is Frank," said the teacher.
    D. "I am sure it is not he," said Tom.
    E. "Is it Lucile?" asked the teacher.
    F. "It is not she," Tom replied.
    G. "Then it must be Harry and Frank," said the teacher.
    H. "Yes, it is they," said Tom.

1. Read the teacher's exact words, as used in sentence A. Note: These words are called a direct quotation.

    "Someone is at the door."

2. Read the direct quotation given in sentence B.

    "It is not I."

3. What marks enclose the direct quotation?

    Quotation marks enclose the direct quotation.

4. What punctuation mark separates the direct quotation from the rest of the sentence?

    A comma separates the direct quotation from the rest of the sentence.

5. With what kind of letter does the first word of a direct quotation begin?

    The first word of a direct quotation begins with a capital letter.

6. Notice the use of *I, he, she,* and *they* in the sentences.

Lesson 57
Dictation

1. Copy from Lesson 56 the conversation between the teacher and Tom. Pay special attention

to punctuation.

A. *The teacher said, "Someone is at the door."*

B. *Tom said, "It is not I."*

C. *"Perhaps it is Frank," said the teacher.*

D. *"I am sure it is not he," said Tom.*

E. *"Is it Lucile?" asked the teacher.*

F. *"It is not she," Tom replied.*

G. *"Then it must be Harry and Frank," said the teacher.*

H. *"Yes, it is they," said Tom.*

2. **Write the conversation from dictation.**

Lesson 58
Correct Use of Words

1. **Write questions which might be answered by the following:**

   A. It was I.

   B. It was not I; it was he.

   C. I think it was she.

   D. I am sure it is he.

   E. It was we.

   F. It might have been they.

   G. It is I.

   H. It was he and I.

   I. It was they.

   J. No, it is not he.

   K. Yes, it is she.

2. **Write the answer after each of your questions.**

   Answers will vary.

Extended Activity

Have half the students write these statements A-K on notecards, one statement per card. Have the other half of the students write simple questions asking who. Pair the students and have them match their questions and answers and make any corrections that may need to be made.

Lesson 59
Description of a Game

Select one of the following exercises:

1. A. Draw a diagram of a baseball ground.
   B. Write a description of the game, telling how many players there are on a side, where the different players stand, and what points count in winning.
   C. Write three or more rules for the game.
2. A. Draw a diagram of a tennis court.
   B. Write a description of the game.
   C. Write two or more rules for the game.
3. A. Draw a diagram of a croquet ground.
   B. Write a description of the game.
   C. Write two or more rules for the game.
4. Write a description of the game you like best to play.

Lesson 60
Letter Writing

1. Your Aunt Ellen has sent you a ball and a bat, a tennis racquet, or a croquet set for a birthday present.
   Write a letter thanking her. Say how kind you think she was to remember your birthday, tell where you play your games, and include any family news that you think might be of special interest to her.

Review

2. Why does *Aunt* begin with a capital letter?
   Aunt begins with a capital letter because it is used as part of Ellen's name
3. Name other words that begin with capital letters when used as parts of names.
   Answers will vary.

Lesson 61
Picture Study—
Gambols of Children

1. Tell what you see in the picture.
   Answers may vary.
2. What is the meaning of the word "gambols"?
   Gambol means to skip or hop about.
3. Can you suggest another name for the picture?
   Answers may vary.
4. Are these American children? Give a reason for your answer.

Answers may vary.

5. **Describe the background of the picture.**

   Answers may vary.

6. **Tell a story that the picture suggests to you.**

   Answers may vary.

7. **Which child do you think is the oldest?**

   Answers may vary.

8. **Which is the youngest?**

   Answers may vary.

9. **What do you think the man is telling the child on his lap?**

   Answers may vary.

10. **What in the picture suggests happiness?**

    Answers may vary.

Lesson 62
Correct Use of Words

A. Birds sing in the leafy trees.
B. The artist draws pictures of strange scenes.
C. The bells ring loud and clear.
D. The rain comes to the thirsty flowers.
E. We see ripe apples in the orchard.
F. The farmer boy drives the cows to pasture.
G. The author writes a beautiful poem.
H. The cows go down to the river to drink.
I. The snow falls on the frozen ground.
J. The squirrel eats the sweet acorns from the oak trees.

1. Use one of the following groups of words in each of the above sentences, and change the italicized word in each sentence to show past time.
   A. a few days ago
   B. last summer
   C. yesterday
   D. last week
   E. day before yesterday
   F. a year ago
   G. last September
   H. two weeks ago
   I. a month ago
   J. last Christmas
   K. a long time ago
   L. last fall

Answers may vary but all should reflect the past tense of the actions in A-J. Possible answers:

A. *Birds sang in the leafy trees a few days ago.*
B. *The artist drew pictures of strange scenes last summer.*
C. *The bells rang loud and clear yesterday.*
D. *The rain came to the thirsty flowers last week.*
E. *We saw ripe apples in the orchard day before yesterday.*
F. *The farmer boy drove the cows to pasture a year ago.*
G. *The author wrote a beautiful poem last September.*
H. *The cows went down to the river to drink two weeks ago.*
I. *The snow fell on the frozen ground a month ago.*
J. *The squirrel ate the sweet acorns from the oak trees last fall.*

2. **Write sentences A-J with one of the following groups of words in each; change the form of the italicized word if necessary, and use it with the word *will*; in sentence E use shall instead of *will*:**

   A. **next week**
   B. **tomorrow**
   C. **soon**
   D. **in a few days**
   E. **next summer**
   F. **next year**
   G. **in a month**
   H. **next Christmas**
   I. **next September**
   J. **next winter**

Answers may vary but all sentences should reflect future tense using will with the exception of sentence E which should use shall instead of will.

A. *Birds will sing in the leafy trees next week.*
B. *The artist will draw pictures of strange scenes tomorrow.*
C. *The bells will ring loud and clear soon.*
D. *The rain will come to the thirsty flowers in a few days.*
E. *We shall see ripe apples in the orchard next summer.*
F. *The farmer boy will drive the cows to pasture next year.*
G. *The author will write a beautiful poem in a month.*
H. *The cows will go down to the river to drink next Christmas.*
I. *The snow will fall on the frozen ground next winter.*
J. *The squirrel will eat the sweet acorns from the oak trees next September.*

3. **Which sentences refer to present time?**
   Sentences A-J refer to present time.
4. **Which sentences refer to past time?**
   Sentences under activity 1 refer to past time.
5. **Which sentences refer to future time?**
   Sentences under activity 2 refer to future time.
6. **Write the sentences again, using in each the word has or have and making necessary changes**

in the italicized words. Note: In #1, the letters showing past tense groups of words, A-L, outnumber the choices of sentences, A-J.

A. *Birds have sung in the leafy trees.*
B. *The artist has drawn pictures of strange scenes.*
C. *The bells have rung loud and clear.*
D. *The rain has come to the thirsty flowers.*
E. *We have seen ripe apples in the orchard.*
F. *The farmer boy has driven the cows to pasture.*
G. *The author has written a beautiful poem.*
H. *The cows have gone down to the river to drink.*
I. *The snow has fallen on the frozen ground.*
J. *The squirrel has eaten the sweet acorns from the oak trees.*

Lesson 63

The Comma in Address

A. "Mr. Brown, may we play baseball in your vacant lot?"
B. Yes, Harry, you may, if you will not be too noisy."
C. "May I play after school, Mother?"

1. **Who is addressed in sentence A? What punctuation mark is placed after the name?**
   Mr. Brown is addressed in sentence A. A comma is placed after his name.
2. **Who is addressed in sentence B? What punctuation marks are placed before and after the name?**
   Harry is addressed in sentence B. Commas are placed before and after his name.
3. **Who is addressed in sentence C? What mark is placed before the name? Note: The name of the person addressed is set off by a comma or commas.**
   Mother is addressed in sentence C. A comma is placed before the name.
4. **Write sentences in which the following are addressed: Mr. Davis, Cousin Clara, Grandfather, Rover, Dr. Andrews, Miss Taylor, Mother, Alfred, Baby.**
   Answers will vary.

Lesson 64

Oral Composition—A Story

1. **Complete a story from one of the following suggestions: tell your story to the class from an outline that you have made:**
   A. One day Frank met an old lady who was carrying a heavy basket. He—

B. Nellie could not learn her spelling lesson. The words were not difficult, but—

C. One morning, when James came downstairs, he found the kitchen full of smoke. He—

D. Helen received a camera for a birthday present. She went—

E. Near the foot of a high hill was a thick undergrowth of brush, and here a mother rabbit had made her home. Every evening—

Lesson 65
Selection for Study—"The Village Blacksmith"

1. **Describe the smith.**

   The smith is "a mighty man…With large and sinewy hands; And the muscles of his brawny arms Are strong as iron bands. His hair is crisp, and black, and long, His face is like the tan: His brow is wet with honest sweat, He earns whate'er he can, And looks the whole world in the face, For he owes not any man."

2. **Where was the blacksmith shop?**

   The blacksmith shop stood under a spreading chestnut tree in the village.

3. **What do you understand by the fifth and sixth lines of the second stanza?**

   "And looks the whole world in the face, For he owes not any man." Answers may vary.

4. **To what is the beat of the sledge compared in the third stanza?**

   The beat of the sledge is like the measured beat and rhythm of "a sexton ringing the village bell When the evening sun is low."

5. **Describe the picture in the fourth stanza.**

   "And the children coming home from school Look in at the open door; They love to see the flaming forge, And hear the bellows roar, And catch the burning sparks that fly Like chaff from a threshing floor." Answers may vary.

6. **Tell what you can of a blacksmith shop.**

   A blacksmith shop contained the tools to make and repair iron objects such as horseshoes, latches and hinges, farm tools and household utensils. A shop's major equipment included anvils, forges, bellows, and sledges. Shops were hot places to work because of the hot fires needed to heat the metal.

7. **Explain: A. anvil B. forge C. bellows D. sledge**

   A. The anvil in a blacksmith's shop is a heavy iron block on which the red hot iron is placed and hammered into shape.

   B. A forge is an open furnace in which the iron is heated. When it is red-hot, the iron is removed with tongs and placed against the anvil where it is hammered into the desired shape.

   C. A bellows is a wind-making machine used to intensify the fire needed to heat the iron in order to bend and form it. A bellows consists of a series of levers and valves that draw air into a chamber made of boards attached by leather sides. The air is expelled through a nozzle at the end and creates the draft that quickens the fire.

   D. The sledge used by a blacksmith is a heavy hammer.

8. **Describe the picture in the fifth stanza.**

   "He goes on Sunday to the church, And sits among his boys; He hears the parson pray and preach, He hears his daughter's voice, Singing in the village choir, And it makes his heart rejoice." Answers may vary.

9. **Tell what you think the last stanza means.**

   "Thanks, thanks to thee, my worthy friend, For the lesson thou hast taught! Thus at the flaming forge of life Our fortunes must be wrought; Thus on its sounding anvil shaped Each burning deed and thought." Answers may vary.

10. **What is the lesson that has been taught?**

    The lesson the blacksmith teaches us is that just as iron must be heated and beaten into shape, so the lessons we learn in life, though they may be hard to go through, shape us into better people.

11. **Use in sentences the following: "spreading chestnut tree," "sinewy hands," "evening sun," "flaming forge," "a night's repose."**

    Look for sentences that contain the following phrases: "spreading chestnut tree," "sinewy hands," "evening sun," "flaming forge," "a night's repose."

12. **Who wrote this poem?**

    Henry Wadsworth Longfellow wrote this poem.

13. **Can you tell the name of anything else this poet has written?**

    Included in this textbook are his poems "Daybreak" and "The Day is Done." Other famous works include: "Paul Revere's Ride," "The Song of Evangeline," "The Song of Hiawatha," "A Psalm of Life," "The Wreck of the Hesperus," "Woods in Winter," and "The Children's Hour," to name a few.

Extended Activity

This poem was written by Henry Wadsworth Longfellow, who along with William Cullen Bryant and John Greenleaf Whittier, were among the great American poets known as "The Fireside Poets." They lived and wrote in the 19th century. Research Longfellow using the Internet and/or an encyclopedia to answer the following questions.

1. **When was Longfellow born?**

   Longfellow was born February 27, 1807.

2. **Where was he born?**

   He was born in Portland, Maine.

3. **What did his father do for a living?**

   His father was a lawyer and congressman.

4. **How old was he when he published his first poem?**

   He was 13 when he published his first poem.

5. **What was the title of his first poem? His last poem?**

   The title of his first poem was "The Battle of Lovell's Pond." His last poem was "The Bells of San Blas" written just before he died at age 75.

6. **What other careers did Whittier pursue besides writing poetry?**

   Other careers Longfellow pursued besides writing poetry were teaching literature and languages at Bowdoin and Harvard. He published over 20 works including textbooks and travel books, along with volumes of poetry.

7. **Longfellow wrote several books and volumes of poetry. What was the title of his first volume of poems?**
The title of his first volume of poems was Voices of the Night.

8. **When did Longfellow die?**
Henry Wadsworth Longfellow died March 24, 1882.

Lesson 66
"Henry Wadsworth Longfellow"

1. **Tell the story of the chestnut.**

Extended Activity
Have the children research the story of the chestnut tree and
the chair on the Internet where they can see a photo
of the chair which resides at the Longfellow house in
Cambridge, MA. Longfellow enjoyed the poem so
much he wrote a poem for the children to say thank
you. The poem is entitled "From My Armchair" and
may be located on the Internet at www.everypoet.
com/archive/poetry/Henry_Wadsworth_Longfellow.
It is listed with Longfellow's complete poetical works
under the title "Ultima Thule."

Lesson 67
Singular and Plural Forms

Mr. Longfellow lived in Cambridge, and many of his poems were written about something
located near his home.

1. **In this sentence does the word home mean one home or more than one?**
In this sentence the word home means one home.

2. **Does the word poems mean one poem or more than one? Note: When a word means one, it
is said to be in the singular number. Note: When the word means more than one, it is said
to be in the plural number.**
The word poems means more than one.

3. **Write the plurals of the following words:**
A. **poem** *poems*
B. **table** *tables*
C. **poet** *poets*

    D. street *streets*

    E. house *houses*

    F. eye *eyes*

    G. tree *trees*

    H. chair *chairs*

    I. room *rooms*

    J. smile *smiles*

    K. spark *sparks*

    L. nickel *nickels*

4. How is the plural of most words formed?

The plural of most words is formed by adding an s.

5. Copy twenty words in the singular number from Lesson 66.

Words in the singular number from Lesson 66: study, house, room, man, table, mouth, smile, beard, poet, America, Cambridge, home, tree, smithy, shade, smith, work, poem, forge, street, chair, wood, city, day, friend.

6. Copy five words in the plural number from Lesson 65.

Words in the plural number from Lesson 65: hands, muscles, arms, bands, children, sparks, boys, fortunes. (Note: bellows may appear to be plural with the s, but as a tool it is singular.)

7. Write the singular of each of the following words:

    A. churches *church*

    B. porches *porch*

    C. birches *birch*

    D. benches *bench*

    E. arches *arch*

    F. ditches *ditch*

    G. brushes *brush*

    H. lashes *lash*

    I. crosses *cross*

    J. glasses *glass*

    K. sashes *sash*

    L. taxes *tax*

    M. foxes *fox*

    N. boxes *box*

    O. potatoes *potato*

    P. echoes *echo*

8. How was the plural of the words you have written formed?

The plural of the words were formed by adding es to the singular form of the word.

9. Notice the last two letters of each word included in the list.

Note: The plural form of words ending in ch, sh, s, z, or x is made by adding es to the word. Potato and echo require an es even though they end in a vowel.

Lesson 68
Selection for Study—"The Wind and the Moon"

1. **Why did the wind wish to blow out the moon?**

   "You stare In the air Like a ghost in a chair, Always looking what I am about—I hate to be watched; I'll blow you out."

2. **In the second stanza, what happened to the moon? Then what did the wind do?**

   "The Wind blew hard, and out went the Moon. So, deep On a heap Of clouds to sleep, Down lay the Wind, and slumbered soon, Muttering low, 'I've done for that Moon.'"

3. **In the third stanza, what did the wind see when he "turned in his bed"?**

   "She was there again! On high In the sky, With her one ghost eye, The Moon shone white and alive and plain."

4. **In the fifth stanza, what is meant by "thread"?**

   The thread is a moonbeam, the last glimmer of the Moon being blown away.

5. **What happened when the wind "blew a great blast"?**

   When the wind "blew a great blast," "the thread was gone. In the air Nowhere Was a moonbeam bare."

6. **Tell the story in the last three stanzas.**

   The Wind thought the Moon was gone, so he went to town and "leaped and helloed with whistle and roar." While the Wind was playing, the thread came back. She grew until she filled the night with her light. While the Wind bragged about the great power he had to blow the Moon "right out of the sky," the Moon "knew nothing about the affair; For high In the sky, With her one white eye, Motionless, miles above the air, She had never heard the Wind blare."

7. **Describe the sky as it appeared in the first, second, fifth, sixth, seventh, and ninth stanzas.**

   Assuming the sky refers to the interchange of the Wind and the Moon, the sky appears as follows: Stanza 1: "a ghost in a chair;" stanza 2: "deep on a heap of clouds;" stanza 5: "Nowhere was a moonbeam bare;" stanza 6: "a merry-mad clown;" stanza 7: "shone on her throne;" stanza 9: "high In the sky, With her one white eye, Motionless, miles above the air."

8. **In the first stanza, "stare," "air," and "chair" are said to "rhyme."**

   No answer needed.

9. **In the second stanza what words rhyme with the word "deep"?**

   In stanza two, deep rhymes with heap and sleep.

10. **Find words that rhyme in the other stanzas.**

    Words that rhyme stanza 1: stare air chair; stanza 3: high, sky, eye; stanza 4: puff, enough, snuff; stanza 5: air, where, bare; stanza 6: down, town, clown; stanza 7: shone, throne, alone; stanza 8: breath, faith, death (near rhyme); stanza 9: high, sky, eye.

11. **Use in sentences:**
    A. **slumbered**
    B. **ghost**
    C. **blast**
    D. **revels**
    E. **clown**

F. glimmering
G. motionless
H. silvery light
I. affair.

Sentences will vary but should reflect the following: A. slumbered B. ghost C. blast D. revels E. clown F. glimmering G. motionless H. silvery light I. affair

Lesson 69
Conversation—Clothing

1. Mention different materials that are used for clothing. Of what materials are the following made?
    A. shoes
    B. hats
    C. socks
    D. buttons
    E. gloves
    F. collars
    G. gingham
    H. overcoats
    I. raincoats
    J. ribbon
    K. mittens
    L. overshoes

2. Tell how these materials are obtained and through what changes they pass in the process of manufacture. Note: Materials used in clothing today include many natural as well as manmade substances. The items of clothing listed above can be made today from many different sources: a variety of animal skins and fur, leather, cotton, canvas, denim, felt, flannel, glass, lace, linen, muslin, nylon, plastic, polyester, rayon, satin, silk, terry, tweed, velvet, and wool to name a few.

Have students choose one item of clothing (see #1), its material (see #2), and then research the production of that material and piece of clothing. Students may present to the class an oral summary of their findings and make a collage that depicts their research.

Lesson 70
Conversation—Cotton

   A. Growing the cotton
   B. Picking
   C. Ginning
   D. Baling
   E. Shipping by boat or train
   F. At the mill
   G. Spinning into thread
   H. Weaving into cloth

1. Tell all you can about cotton; group your sentences in paragraphs.
Answers will vary.

Extended Activity

Make a collage showing as many items as you can that come from cotton.

Lesson 71
Composition—Cotton

1. Read again "The Story of the Flax," Lesson 40.
2. Using the outline given in Lesson 70, write the story of cotton.
3. Tell what happened to a single cotton plant.
4. After weaving into cloth tell of the transportation to a store in your city or town.
5. Tell the story of the cloth.
6. Who bought the cloth?

Lesson 72
Letter Writing

1. Imagine that you are visiting a cousin on a cotton plantation in the South.
2. Write a letter home, telling of your arrival and meeting your cousin.
3. Write about your cousin's home and surroundings, his pets, and the good times you are having there.
4. Ask some questions about your own home, and send messages to members of your family and your friends.

Lesson 73
Words that Rhyme

1. Write lists of words that rhyme with the following:
   grow
   kind
   ground
   talk
   part
   each
   tree
   brown
   sun
   ride
   hear
   nest
   high
   grand
   Answers will vary but must rhyme.

2. Read the poem, "The Barefoot Boy," lesson 35. Notice that the first line rhymes with the second. With what line does the third rhyme?
   The third line rhymes with the fourth line.

3. Write a stanza of four lines, making the first line rhyme with the second, and the third with the fourth.
   Answers will vary.

4. Let your stanza be about one of the following: a windy day, an oak tree, Christmas, football, a squirrel, a kitten, a bird, your schoolhouse.
   Answers will vary.

5. Write another stanza on any subject you wish.
   Answers will vary.

Lesson 74
Writing Sentences

Many hundreds of years ago, a Hebrew mother placed her baby boy in a tiny boat and hid him among the reeds by the river side.

1. In this sentence
   A. Read the words that tell when.
   The words that tell when are "many hundreds of years ago."

   B. Read the words that tell *who*.

The words that tell who are "a Hebrew mother" and "her baby boy."

2. **Read the words that tell two things that the mother did.**

The words that tell two things that the mother did are "placed her baby boy in a tiny boat and hid him among the reeds by the river side."

3. **Write groups of words that tell *when*: as, *last fall*.**

Answers may vary but may include words like: yesterday, tomorrow, next week, now, etc.

4. **Use some of these groups of words in writing sentences similar in form to the first sentence in this lesson. Let your sentences be about**
   A. an Indian boy
   B. a gray squirrel
   C. the king's daughter
   D. an angel
   E. a rich man
   F. George Washington
   G. an apple tree

Answers will vary but should include groups of words similar in form to the first sentence in this lesson showing when and using the above topics:

Lesson 75
Written Conversation

Nellie Taylor has moved into the house next to that of Bessie Brown. The two little girls are talking together.

1. **Write the conversation—Nellie asking questions about the school and neighborhood, which Bessie answers. Use the following form:**
Bessie: I am so glad you are going to live near me. Are you going to school Monday?
Nellie:—

Lesson 76
Letter Writing

A boy has failed to pass an examination and wishes to leave school.

1. **Write a letter urging him to try again.**
See the form for the letter in this book, in Lesson 28.
2. **Tell him of his need of an education, and offer to help him in making up the required work.**

Lesson 77

Possessive Form

    A. Butter is made from the milk of cows.
    B. Butter is made from cow's milk.
    C. The eggs of hens are good to eat.
    D. Hens' eggs are good to eat.
    E. The bees' cells are filled with honey.

1. **Read sentence A. Is the word *cows* singular or plural?**
The word cows *is plural.*

2. **In sentence B, how is possession shown?**
Possession is shown with the apostrophe after cows to show they possess the milk.

3. **In sentence C, is the word *hens* singular or plural?**
The word hens *is plural.*

4. **In sentence D, how is possession shown?**
Possession is shown with the apostrophe after hens to show they possess the eggs.

5. **In sentence E. how is possession shown?**
Possession is shown with the apostrophe after bees to show they possess the cells.

6. **The following words are in the possessive singular; change them to possessive plural:**
    A. **lion's** *lions'*
    B. **ant's** *ants'*
    C. **teacher's** *teachers'*
    D. **pupil's** *pupils'*
    E. **artist's** *artists'*
    F. **oak's** *oaks'*
    G. **wren's** *wrens'*
    H. **cricket's** *crickets'*
    I. **merchant's** *merchants'*
    J. **mother's** *mothers'*

7. **Use in sentences:**
    A. **all the birds' nests**
    B. **the bees' honey**
    C. **boys' voices**
    D. **squirrels' teeth**
    E. **cats' feet**
    F. **farmers' barns**
    G. **dogs' collars**
    H. **rabbits' ears**
    I. **butterflies' wings**
    J. **crickets' chirp**
Answers will vary but should include the above phrases in their sentences.

8. **Change the following sentences containing possessive forms:**

A. **The child listened for the music of the birds.** *A child listened for the birds' music.*

B. **The blossoms of the apple trees are sweet.** *The apple trees' blossoms are sweet.*

C. **The fierce roars of the lions frightened the other animals.** *The lions' fierce roars frightened the other animals.*

D. **The soft light of the moonbeams fell across the floor.** *The moonbeams' soft light fell across the floor.*

E. **The nest of the eagles was high up on the side of the mountain.** *The eagles' nest was high up on the side of the mountain.*

F. **Claws of cats are curved and long.** *Cats' claws are curved and long.*

Lesson 78
Conversation— The Dog Family

1. **Talk about the dog using the following outline:**

A. Covering of body

Most dogs have two coats of hair: an undercoat of shorter, fluffy hair to keep them warm and an outer coat of guard hairs to protect them from the weather.

B. Feet

Dogs' feet have cushioned pads which are covered with tough skin for protection. They have four toes on each foot and each toe has a blunt claw or toenail.

C. Teeth

Grown dogs have 42 teeth; they use the 12 front teeth to pick up their food, the 4 large fangs to rip up their food, and the other 26 teeth to crush and grind their food.

D. Food

Dogs need a balanced diet that provides both nutrients for their growth and calories for their energy. They should always have access to clean, fresh water.

E. Methods of hunting

Dogs use their keen sense of smell, their acute hearing ability and their whiskers to sense wind direction when they are hunting. They are able to track odors of their prey for many miles.

F. Habits

Dogs' habits are instinctual. They may turn around several times before laying down; they defend their territory and may bark or growl at anything that infringes on their territory.

G. Keen sense of smell

A dog's sense of smell is millions of times stronger than that of a human. It identifies objects by smell rather than sight. By sniffing objects a dog can identify an odor associated with its prey.

H. Varieties of dogs

Hundreds of varieties of dogs exist: purebred dogs have parents from the same breed; crossbred dogs have parents from two different breeds; mongrels have parents from a variety of breeds. The American Kennel Club has registered 128 breeds of dogs.

I. Use

Dogs serve many purposes. Besides providing companionship and affection for their owners, they may be used for hunting birds and other wild game, herding livestock on farms, as guard dogs, police dogs, guides for the blind and deaf, in rescue efforts, for competition at pet shows, and entertainment in circuses and movies.

J. Friendliness

Some breeds of dogs are more friendly than others. Dogs can quickly sense fear that may trigger their attack response. Most often, if you speak to a dog in a friendly manner, it will not attack.

K. Bravery

Many stories of brave dogs have appeared throughout history. Students may want to discuss movies they have seen or stories they have read that show bravery in dogs.

L. Intelligence

Dogs may vary in intelligence according to their breed. Most dogs can be taught to recognize and respond to a large number of commands and complicated behaviors. Some breeds require more patience from their owners than other breeds.

2. **When are animals said to belong to the same family? (See Lesson 44.)**

   Animals that are similar in general structure and habits are said to belong to the same family.

3. **The following animals belong to the dog family; compare those that you have seen with the dog using the points given in the outline:**

   A. wolf

   B. fox

   C. coyote

   D. hyena

   E. jackal.

   Responses will vary.

4. **Write ten statements about an animal of the dog family.**

   Responses will vary.

5. **Bring to class pictures of any of the animals mentioned in this lesson.**

   Responses will vary.

Lesson 79
Picture Study—
The Wounded Companion

1. **Describe the picture.**

   Answers may vary.

2. **To which boy do you think the dog belongs?**
   Answers may vary.
3. **Tell the story suggested by the picture.**
   Answers may vary.
4. **What is the artist's name?**
   The artist's name is John George Brown.
5. **Find another picture by the same artist in this book.**
   Another picture by the same artist can be found in Lesson 9 entitled "The Flower Girl." See Teacher Note in Lesson 9.

Lesson 80

Composition—"Story about Wool"

Frank Wentworth lived many years ago when this great country of ours was new. Winter was coming, and Mother Wentworth knew that Frank would need a heavy coat to keep him warm when the north wind piled the great snowdrifts high around the door.

1. **Copy the paragraph and complete the story, telling about**
   A. **Cutting the wool from the sheep**
   B. **Combing or carding it into long rolls**
   C. **Spinning it into yarn on the spinning wheel**
   D. **Dyeing it in the big kettle**
   E. **Weaving the yarn into cloth on the loom**
   F. **Making the cloth into a coat.**
2. **Let your story contain conversation between Frank and his mother concerning the work.**

Lesson 81

Correct Use of Words

A. "May I help you, Mother?"
B. "You may help cut the wool, Frank, but I doubt if you can spin it."
C. "I am sure I can spin it; please, let me try."

1. **Read the sentence that asks permission.**
   The sentence that asks permission: "May I help you, Mother?"
2. **Read the part of sentence B that grants the desired permission.**
   The part of sentence B that grants the desired permission: "You may help cut the wool, Frank."
3. **Read the parts of sentences B and C that relate to Frank's ability to spin.**
   The parts of sentences B and C that relate to Frank's ability to spin: "...but I doubt if you can

spin it." "I am sure I can spin it."

4. **Notice the use of *can* and *may*.**

   Note: May *means "permitted to" while* can *means "able to."*

5. **Write six sentences containing the word *may* in which you ask permission of your mother or teacher to do certain things.**

   Answers will vary but students should write six sentences containing the word may *in which they ask permission of their mothers or teachers to do certain things.*

6. **Write ten sentences containing the word *can* in which you ask different classmates concerning their ability to do certain things.**

   Answers will vary but students should write ten sentences containing the word can *in which they ask different classmates concerning their ability to do certain things.*

Lesson 82
Composition—
"Frisk and the Mirror"

One day Frisk saw himself in the mirror, which his mistress had been dusting. He thought he saw another dog. What do you think happened?

1. **Tell or write the story as if Frisk were telling it.**
   Begin the story in this way: This morning, when I went into the dining room, I was much surprised to see another dog standing in front of me.

Lesson 83
Picture Study—
Shepherd and Sheep

1. Describe the picture.
2. What time of year do you think it is? Give a reason for your answer.
3. What time of day do you think it is?
4. Which part of the picture interests you more, the sheep or the surroundings?
5. Does such a picture make you long to be in the woods?
6. What would you do if you had an afternoon to spend in such a place?
7. Of what use to a shepherd is a dog?
8. Tell any stories that you may have read about shepherd dogs.

Lesson 84
Correct Use of Words

    A. The shepherd *gives* food to the sheep.
    B. He *knows* the best pasture.
    C. The lambs *run* through the grass.
    D. Wolves *steal* some of the lambs.
    E. The shepherd *speaks* to his dog.
    F. He *takes* a lamb in his arms.

1. **Change the sentences so that they will refer to some time in the past.**
   Possible answers:
   A. *The shepherd gave food to the sheep yesterday.*
   B. *He knew the best pasture last summer.*
   C. *The lambs ran through the grass last spring.*
   D. *Wolves stole some of the lambs last week.*
   E. *The shepherd spoke to his dog last night.*
   F. *He took a lamb in his arms this morning*

2. **Change the sentences so that they will refer to some time in the future.**
   Possible answers:
   A. *The shepherd will give food to the sheep every day.*
   B. *He will know the best pasture each summer.*
   C. *The lambs will run through the grass in the morning.*
   D. *Wolves will steal some of the lambs while the dog sleeps.*
   E. *The shepherd will speak to his dog when the wolves are gone.*
   F. *He will take a lamb in his arms when it bleats.*

3. **Change the sentences, using in each the word has or have.**
   Use in each the word has or have:
   A. *The shepherd has given food to the sheep every day.*
   B. *He has known the best pasture each spring.*
   C. *The lambs have run through the grass every day.*
   D. *Wolves have stolen some of the lambs a few years ago.*
   E. *The shepherd has spoken to his dog while the sheep graze.*
   F. *He has taken a lamb in his arms when it gets tired.*

Lesson 85
Singular and Plural

Note: The plurals of some words are formed in irregular ways.

1. **Learn the following:**
Singular:
- A.   mouse
- B.   ox
- C.   goose
- D.   foot
- E.   man
- F.   woman
- G.   tooth
- H.   child

Plural
- A.   mice
- B.   oxen
- C.   geese
- D.   feet
- E.   men
- F.   women
- G.   teeth
- H.   children

Note: The following words have the same form for both singular and plural: *sheep, deer, moose*

2. Copy, from Lesson 40, ten words that are plural; change them to the singular number.

flowers *flower*

wings *wing*

clouds *cloud*

men *man*

roots *root*

fibers *fiber*

threads *thread*

dresses *dress*

rags *rag*

rollers *roller*

sheets *sheet*

words *word*

Lesson 86

A Legend about King Solomon— "King Solomon and the Bees"

1. **Why did the Queen of Sheba travel far to see Solomon?**
The Queen of Sheba traveled far to see Solomon because she wanted "to see the splendors of his

court, and bring some fitting tribute to the mighty king."

2. **What had she heard with regard to the great Hebrew king?**

   With regard to the great Hebrew king she heard "What flowers of learning graced the royal speech; What gems of wisdom dropped with every word; What wholesome lessons he was wont to teach In pleasing proverbs." She had also heard "How through the deepest riddles he could spy; How all the curious arts that women boast Were quite transparent to his piercing eye."

3. **How did she test his wisdom?**

   She tested his wisdom by holding "before the monarch's view, In either hand, a radiant wreath of flowers; The one, bedecked with every charming hue, Was newly culled from nature's choicest bowers; The other, no less fair in every part, Was the rare product of divinest art. 'Which is the true and which the false?' she said."

4. **What was the result of the test?**

   "While thus he pondered, presently he sees, Hard by the casement—so the story goes—A little band of busy bees, Hunting for honey in a withered rose. The monarch smiles and raised his royal head; 'Open the window!' was all he said. The window opened at the king's command; Within the room the eager insects flew, And sought the flowers in Sheba's dexter hand! And so the king and all the courtiers knew That wreath was nature's."

5. **Write the story of "King Solomon and the Bees," using the following words:** *monarch, tribute, proverbs, rumor, piqued, transparent, radiant, culled, garlands, amazement, trivial, perplexed, withered, baffled.*

   Answers will vary.

6. **Arrange your story in paragraphs, and let it contain at least two direct quotations.**

   The story should be written in paragraphs and contain two direct quotes.

Lesson 87

Composition—A Story

1. **Tell the fable of "The Hare and the Tortoise."**
2. **Write a similar story about two boys: Frank, who learns everything easily, and Carl, who has to work hard to learn his lessons. A prize has been offered for the pupil who spells the most words correctly. Show how Carl won the prize.**
3. **Let your story contain some direct quotations.**

Lesson 88

Selection for Study—"Daybreak"

1. **Give the meaning of "mariners," "chanticleer," "clarion," "belfry," "proclaim."**

   The definitions are: mariners are seamen or sailors; chanticleer is a rooster; clarion is a trumpet;

belfry is a bell tower; proclaim is to announce.

2. **What effect does the wind have on the mists?**

     The wind asks the mists to "make room for me!"

3. **Who or what is meant by "it" in the second stanza?**

     "It" in the second stanza refers to the wind.

4. **What words might have been used in place of "landward" in the third stanza?**

     Toward land or on land are words that might have been used in place of "landward" in the third stanza.

5. **Explain "leafy banners" in the fourth stanza.**

     "Leafy banners" in the fourth stanza refers to the trees and their leaves.

6. **Explain the sixth stanza.**

     The sixth stanza suggests the wind is telling the rooster to crow; the dawn is here.

7. **What do you understand by the last stanza?**

     Answers may vary. The "churchyard" may refer to the cemetary in which nothing moves. The wind says, "Not yet. In quiet lie."

8. **Use in sentences: "hailed," "landward," "leafy," "banners," "fields of corn."**

     Answers may vary.

9. **To what different things did the wind speak?**

     The wind spoke to the mists, the mariners, the people on land, the forest, a bird, a rooster, fields of corn, bell in the tower, and the churchyard.

10. **How many different quotations are there in the poem?**

     There are nine different quotations in the poem.

11. **What contraction do you find?**

     In stanza six is the contraction o'er which means over

12. **Find examples of the person or thing addressed.**

     Examples of the person or thing addressed: mists, the mariners, the people on land, the forest, a bird, a chanticleer, fields of corn, bell in the tower, and the churchyard.

13. **Who wrote this poem?**

     Henry Wadsworth Longfellow wrote this poem. See the extended activity for Lesson 65 for more information on the author.

Extended Activity

Words at the end of two or more lines of poetry that rhyme are said to have end rhyme. Rhymes can be organized in patterns called rhyme schemes: lines that rhyme are assigned the same letters of the alphabet beginning with A. Example:

Twinkle Twinkle little star (A)
How I wonder what you are. (A)
Up above the world so high, (B)
Like a diamond in the sky. (B)

The rhyming words are *star* and *are*, *high* and *sky*, so the rhyme scheme is AABB.

Identify the rhyme scheme of this poem by Henry Wadsworth Longfellow.

AA BB CC DD EE FF GG HH II JJ.

Find the rhyme scheme of the poem in Lesson 86.

ABABCC DEDEFF GHGHII JKJKLL MNMNOO PQPQRR STSTUU VWVWXX

Lesson 89
Dictation

1. **Write from dictation the first four stanzas of "Daybreak," Lesson 88.**

    A wind came up out of the sea,
    And said, "O mists, make room for me!"
    It hailed the ships, and cried,
    "Sail on, Ye mariners, the night is gone!"
    And hurried landward far away,
    Crying, "Awake! It is the day!"
    It said unto the forest, "Shout!"
    Hang all your leafy banners out!"

Lesson 90
Exclamations

The wind said unto the forest, "Shout!"
It called to the ships, "Awake! The night is gone!"
The sailors shouted, "Hurrah! The day is come!"

1. **Where are exclamation points (!) placed in these sentences?**

    Exclamation points are found after "Shout!" "Awake! The night is gone!" and "Hurrah! The day has come!"

2. **How many exclamations can you find in the poem, Lesson 88?**

    There are 11 exclamations in the poem in Lesson 88: me! gone! Awake! day! Shout! out! sing! near! morn! bell! and yet!

3. **Write exclamations which you might use**
    A. **If you had lost some money**
    B. **If you had found it again**
    C. **If you had received a gift**
    D. **If you heard something that greatly surprised you**
    E. **If you were hurt**
    F. **If you wished someone to keep quiet**

G. If you had won a game
H. If you had lost a game
I. If you were in need of help
J. If you were tired
K. If you were given a holiday.

Answers may vary.

Lesson 91
An Autobiography

Note: An autobiography is an account of one's life written by oneself.
1. Use the following outline in writing your autobiography:
   A. Name
   B. Birthplace
   C. Date of birth
   D. Residence
   E. School life
   F. Name of school
   G. Name of teacher
   H. Grade
   I. Studies
   J. Occupations outside of school
   K. Favorite games or sports
   L. Favorite books
   M. Pets
   N. Friends
   O. Interesting or exciting events in your life
   P. Plans for the future
   Q. Education
   R. Business

Extended Activity

After the students have written their autobiography, have them design a scrapbook consisting of one page per outline topic including pictures and memorabilia associated with that topic.

A. Name: refer to the Extended Activity in Lesson 1 for the first page in the scrapbook. Students can use the meanings of their names and a piece of art that depicts their names from that assignment.
B. Birthplace: design their birth announcements; include photos of their birthplace/hospital photos/family tree
C. Date of birth: research the headline news, movies, famous characters on that date
D. Residence: photo of current home/family members

E. School life: photos/clippings

F. Name of school: photos/school mascot

G. Name of teacher: photo/what they remember about that teacher

H. Grade: copy of report cards

I. Studies: favorite classes/why

J. Occupations outside of school: extracurricular activities

K. Favorite games or sports: photos

L. Favorite books: design miniature characters or book covers of their favorites

M. Pets: photos

N. Friends: photos and special memories

O. Interesting or exciting events in your life: photos of family vacations/special events

P. Plans for the future: mini collage of their dreams for the future

Q. Education: schools of choice/school colors/preferred field of study

R. Business: mini collage of the business they hope to pursue.

The scrapbook rubric, page 222, may assist the teacher in evaluating the scrapbook holistically, as well as assisting the students in knowing how they will be graded.

Lesson 92
"Story of a Meadowlark"

Once upon a time, a child sat under an oak tree near a stream of water. She seemed very sad, for now and then a tear rolled down her face and fell upon the grass. Presently, where the tears had fallen, something moved. The child turned and beheld at her side a beautiful meadowlark.

1. Complete the story.
2. What was the meadowlark's first question?
3. What was the little girl's answer?
4. What did the meadowlark do to help the child?
5. Think of your story and make an outline that you can use in telling it.
6. What exclamations might the child use when she sees the meadowlark?
7. What exclamations might the meadowlark use when she hears the sad story of the little girl?
8. What exclamations might the child use to show her happiness after the meadowlark had helped her?
9. Use in your story: A. Quotation marks B. Possessive form

Lesson 93
Composition— Two Squirrels

1. Write or tell a story about two little squirrels that lived in an old elm tree.

   Answers may vary,

2. Include in your story some incident that might happen in the life of a squirrel

   Answers may vary.

3. What enemies has a squirrel?

   Squirrels' enemies include people, cats, dogs, hawks, owls, snakes, and foxes among other types of wildlife.

4. What narrow escape might a squirrel have?

   Answers may vary.

Lesson 94
Conversation—Gnawers or Rodents

1. Talk about the squirrel from the following outline:

   A. Size

   Squirrels vary in size depending on the type of squirrel: red squirrel, gray squirrel, or flying squirrel. They range in size from 10-28 inches long. Their tails make up about half their length. They can weigh as little as three ounces or as much as three pounds.

   B. Covering of body

   Squirrels are covered with fur which is longer in winter than in summer to protect them from the cold.

   C. Color

   Squirrels may be reddish brown, gray, or black. Some may have white fur on their underparts.

   D. Feet

   Squirrels have very strong feet that help propel them from branch to branch. They also use their front feet as hands for cracking open their food.

   E. Teeth

   Squirrel teeth are continually being sharpened as they gnaw their food. Their teeth never stop growing so gnawing prevents the teeth from becoming too long.

   F. Food

   Foods include berries, nuts, seeds, corn, grains, mushrooms.

   G. Provisions for winter

Squirrels are busy all summer gathering and storing food for winter when the food supply is covered with snow. They store their food in holes in the ground, trees, or in their nests and find it again by using their sharp noses.

H. Habits

Squirrels are famous for their whisking tails, their chattering and chirping when they are upset, and their excellent climbing and leaping ability.

2. **Why is the squirrel called a gnawer?**

The squirrel is called a gnawer because he gnaws his food. Since the teeth never stop growing, gnawing keeps them short and sharp.

3. **When are animals said to belong to the same family?**

Lesson 44: Animals that are similar in general structure and habits are said to belong to the same family.

4. **Tell what you can of the:**
   A. **beaver**
   B. **rabbit**
   C. **mouse**
   D. **hare**
   E. **chipmunk**
   F. **porcupine**
   G. **guinea pig**
   H. **rat**
   I. **prairie dog**
   J. **woodchuck**

Assign the animals to students for research. After they have gathered their information, the students may share their findings with the class so all animals are researched.

Lesson 95
Correct Use of Words

A. Tom and Henry are both tall, but I believe Henry is the taller.
B. There are several tall boys in the class, but Frank is the tallest.

1. In sentence A how many boys are compared?
    In sentence A two boys are compared; Tom and Harry.
2. What is added to tall to indicate comparison?
    Er is added to tall to indicate comparison.
3. In sentence B, where more than two are compared, what is added to tall?
    In sentence B, where more than two are compared, est is added to tall.

Note: When words are long they are usually compared by prefixing *more* and *must; as,* beautiful, *more* beautiful, *most beautiful.* Note: Some words are compared irregularly; *as, good, better, best.*

1. Fill in the blanks in the following sentences with words chosen from the list on page 100:
    A. I have only a little money and she has _more_.
    B. Which is the _younger_ of the two boys?
    C. There are many pretty pictures in the room; which do you think is the _prettiest_?
    D. This is a _good_ apple, but that one is _better_.
    E. You took the _best_ apple in the basket.
    F. Sugar is _sweet_, but honey is _sweeter_.
    G. This is an amusing story, but that one is _more amusing_.
    H. Today is cold, Saturday was _colder_, and last Friday was the _coldest_ day of this month.
    I. Which of the two babies is the _older_?
    J. Which of the three babies is _oldest_?
    K. This orchard has a great many trees, but the orchard across the street has _more_.
    L. All the trees have apples on them, but this one has _most_.
    M. Which tree in the orchard is _farthest_ from the road?
    Answers may vary but should show the correct comparison.

Word List

little, less, least   old, older, oldest   good, better, best
pretty, prettier, prettiest   large, larger, largest   sweet, sweeter, sweetest
cold, colder, coldest   amusing, more amusing, most amusing   young, younger, youngest
many, more, most   far, farther, farthest

Lesson 96
Conversation—Money

1. **Name different kinds of money.**

   US money includes pennies, nickels, dimes, quarters, half dollars, dollar coins and paper bills.

2. **Of what is a penny made?**

   Pennies used to be made of copper, but are now made of copper-coated zinc or tin.

3. **Of what is a nickel made?**

   Nickels contain a mixture of nickel and copper.

4. **Name some money that is made of silver.**

   When this book was first printed, dimes, quarters and half-dollars were largely made of silver. Few coins are made of silver today except for the American Silver Eagle, a dollar coin used as a collector's item. Dimes and quarters from before 1965 and half-dollars from before 1971 have been removed from circulation because of the value of silver. Copper and nickel have replaced silver in minting dimes, nickels, and half-dollars.

5. **Of what is a quarter made?**

   Today's quarter is made of copper and nickel.

6. **Why is a quarter smaller than a silver dollar?**

   A quarter is smaller than a silver dollar because it is less in value.

7. **Why are the edges of some coins notched?**

   The edges of coins were first notched around the edge to keep people from shaving off the gold or silver from the coin, devaluing it. Today the notches help blind people distinguish between coins.

8. **In what is the right to coin money vested?**

   In the Constitution of the United States of America, Article I, Section 8, Powers of Congress include the power "To coin Money, regulate the Value thereof…and all other Powers vested by this Constitution in the Government of the United States." http://www.usconstitution.net/const. html

9. **What is the place where money is coined called?**

   The US Department of the Treasury manufactures money: Bureau of the Mint makes coins and the Bureau of Engraving and Printing produces paper money. Mints are located in Denver, CO and Philadelphia, PA.

10. **Examine a piece of money.**

11. **Tell what printing and pictures you find.**

    Answers may vary.

12. **Explain the meaning of the pictures.**

    Answers may vary.

13. **Examine and describe a piece of paper money.**

    Answers may vary.

Lesson 97
Composition—"History of a Dime"

One morning in winter, a shining dime came from the mint and began its journey in the world. It went first to a bank, where—

1. Complete the story, telling of the different people who used the dime. Trace it until it is finally lost in a lake or river.

Lesson 98
Picture Study—
Return of the Fishing Boats

1. Look carefully at the picture, then close your eyes and try to see it.
   Answers will vary.
2. Does the picture suggest any body of water that you have seen?
   Answers will vary.
3. Have you seen sailboats? If you have, tell something about them.
   Answers will vary.
4. What time of the day do you think it is?
   Answers will vary.
5. Where have the boats been?
   Answers will vary.
6. Can you think of a story suggested by the picture?
   Answers will vary.
7. Suppose a boy twelve years old were on the boat, what story might he tell?
   Answers will vary.
8. Do you think this picture could be used to illustrate any poem in this book?
   Lesson 88 is a poem about the wind who in stanza two "hailed the ships and cried, "Sail on, Ye mariners, the night is gone!" Lesson 99: "Sweet and Low" Lesson 178: "Old Ironsides." Lesson 249: "Landing of the Pilgrim Fathers." Lesson 282: "Columbus."
9. What part of the poem suggests the picture?
   Answers will vary.

Lesson 99
Selection to be Memorized— "Sweet and Low"

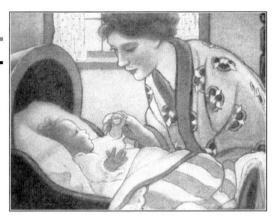

1. **Do you like the poem? Why?**
    Answers will vary.
2. **Who is supposed to be saying or singing it?**
    The mother is supposed to be saying or singing it.
3. **What picture does the poem suggest?**
    Answers will vary.
4. **What lines suggest that the father may be out on the sea?**
    Lines 5: "Over the rolling waters go," 7: "Blow him again to me;" 10 and 12: "Father will come to thee soon;" and 13: "Father will come to his babe in the nest," suggest that the father may be out on the sea.
5. **What do you understand by "rolling water"?**
    "Rolling water" suggests the wave action of the sea.
6. **Name the words that describe "moon."**
    The words that describe "moon" are dying and silver.
7. **Explain "dying moon."**
    A "dying moon" may mean night is almost over and the moon is about to disappear.
8. **Which lines end in words that rhyme?**
    Stanza 1: lines 1, 3, 5, and 6; stanza 2: lines 9, 11, 13, and 14 end in words that rhyme.
9. **Which lines end in the same word?**
    Stanza 1: lines 3 and 6 "blow;" stanza two: lines 10 and 12 "soon" end in the same word.
10. **Explain the marks of punctuation in the last line of the poem.**
    The marks of punctuation in the last line of the poem are used as commas in direct address: "Sleep, my little one, sleep, my pretty one, sleep."
11. **Who wrote this poem?**
    Alfred Tennyson wrote this poem.
12. **Memorize the poem.**
13. **Write the stanza from memory.**
    Sweet and low, sweet and low, Wind of the western sea; Low, low, breathe and blow, Wind of the western sea! Over the rolling waters go, Come from the dying moon, and blow, Blow him again to me; While my little one, while my pretty one, sleeps."
14. **Which words in the first stanza rhyme with "low"?**
    In the first stanza "blow" and "go" rhyme with "low."
15. **Which words in the second stanza rhyme with "rest"?**
    In the second stanza breast, nest, and west rhyme with "rest."

Lesson 100
Summary—Continued from Lesson 51

To Remember

Correct the following sentences by adding quotation marks.
1. **Susan is working hard in school this year said her teacher.**
   "Susan is working hard in school this year," said her teacher.
2. **Hurry I must get you to school in twenty minutes the bus driver said sharply.**
   "Hurry!" I must get you to school in twenty minutes!" the bus driver said sharply.
3. **I think that the best time of year to play baseball is in the spring laughed Jon.**
   "I think that the best time of year to play baseball is in the spring," laughed Jon.
4. **Mom asked did you clean your room this morning?**
   Mom asked, "Did you clean your room this morning?"
5. **Last week George said I'll return your baseball bat tomorrow; however, a week later he still has not returned it.**
   Last week George said, "I'll return your baseball bat tomorrow;" however, a week later he still has not returned it.
6. **Can you believe that we have only three weeks until school is out for the summer Patty cried?**
   "Can you believe that we have only three weeks until school is out for the summer?" Patti cried.
7. **Certainly I will explain the math problem to you. I know you will understand it Mrs. Norman said.**
   "Certainly I will explain the math problem to you. I know you will understand it," Mrs. Norman said.
8. **Father said why don't you run to the freezer and bring us each a popsicle?**
   Father said, "Why don't you run to the freezer and bring us each a popsicle?"
9. **When Sally gets her allowance she shouts when can I go shopping?**
   When Sally gets her allowance she shouts, "When can I go shopping?"
10. **This math is too complicated. I need a math whiz to explain it wailed Sam.**
    This math is too complicated. I need a math whiz to explain it," wailed Sam.

Multiple Choice: Check the correct answers.
11. a. **Help. I'm drowning.** *b. Help! I'm drowning!* c. **Help? I'm drowning?**
12. *a. Hurry! We'll be late!* b. **Hurry. We'll be late.** c. **Hurry we'll be late?**
13. *a. This dog's fur is black.* b. **This dogs fur is black.** c **This dogs' fur is black.**
14. a. **Those girl's hair are all short.** *b. Those girls' hair are all short.* c. **Those girls hair are all short.**
15. a. **Don't touch that stove. It's hot.** b. **Don't touch that stove. It's hot?** *c. Don't touch that stove! It's hot!*
16. *a. My bike's back tire is flat.* b. **My bikes' back tire is flat.** c. **My bikes back tire is flat.**
17. *a. Wait for me! I'm hurrying!* b. **Wait for me? I'm hurrying!** c. **Wait for me. I'm hurrying.**
18. a. **Mothers apple pie is my favorite dessert.** b. **Mothers' apple pie is my favorite dessert.**

c. Mother's apple pie is my favorite dessert.

19. *a. All my friends' names begin with the letter* M. **b. All my friend's names begin with the letter** *M.* **c. All my friends names begin with the letter** *M.*

20. **a. Disneys rollercoasters are world famous.** *b. Disney's rollercoasters are world famous.* **c. Disneys' rollercoasters are world famous.**

21. **a. Will you Mary bring me my shirt!** *b. Will you, Mary, bring me my shirt?* **c. Will you, Mary bring me my shirt?**

22. **a. Jim fill the dogs dish.** *b. Jim, fill the dog's dish.* **c. Jim, fill the dogs dish.**

23. **a. How old are you Tom. b. How old are you, Tom.** *c. How old are you, Tom?*

24. **a. What Sarah shall we do about your grades!** *b. What, Sarah, shall we do about your grades?* **c. What, Sarah, shall we do about your grades.**

25. **a. Will you please mow the grass Danny? b. Will you please mow the grass, Danny.** *c. Will you please mow the grass, Danny?*

True or False

26. **Words in the singular form the possessive by adding the apostrophe and s.**

    True—Words in the singular form the possessive by adding the apostrophe and s.

27. **Words in the plural, ending in s, form the possessive by adding an apostrophe before the s.**

    False—Words in the plural, ending in s, form the possessive by adding an apostrophe after the s.

28. **Words in the plural refer to one object.**

    False—Words in the plural refer to two or more objects.

29. **Direct quotations are enclosed in commas.**

    False—Direct quotations are enclosed in quotation marks.

30. **The name of the person addressed is separated from the rest of the sentence by a comma.**

    True—The name of the person addressed is separated from the rest of the sentence by a comma.

Part Two

Lesson 101
Selection for Study—"The Story of a Seed"

Note: Sometimes a direct quotation is divided by other words. As, "For me," replied the first, "I mean to be a rose."

1. **Observe carefully the punctuation of the divided quotation.**
   No response required.

2. **In this lesson find exclamations, contractions, divided quotations.**
   Exclamations: "Oh, Dear!" "I am growing! I am growing!" "And what a delicious breath it was!" "But, alas!;" Contractions: don't, It's, It's, It's; Divided quotations: "For me," replied the first, "I mean to be a rose." "Oh, dear!" cried the first. "I have had some water. I never knew until it was inside me. I am growing! I am growing! Good-bye."

3. **Tell "The Story of the Seed."**
   Answers will vary.

4. **Use in sentences:** *wearisome, patiently, delicious, refreshing, inclined, dismay, yielded, straightway.*
   Sentences will vary.

Extended Activity

In Lesson 35, Extended Activity B, the students learned that point of view is the position or angle from which a story is written or told. What point of view does the writer of this story take? What words or phrases does the writer use to show point of view?

The writer uses the third person omniscient point of view. Sentences that show third person omniscient point of view are:

"For somehow when it had said that, it felt as if all the words in the world were used up."

"…till at last it felt that it was in the open air;"

"It meant to see the sky the first thing…But somehow or other—though why it could not tell—it felt very much inclined to cry." "It felt yet more inclined to hang down its head and cry."

"I will be a Star of Bethlehem, at least,' said the flower to itself. But its heart felt very heavy…"

"It half closed its leaves in terror and the dismay of loneliness. But that instant it remembered what the other seed used to say, and it said to itself, 'It's all right; I will be what I can.'"

Lesson 102
Dictation

1. **Write from dictation the first twelve lines of "The Story of the Seed," Lesson 101.**

First twelve lines:

Long, long ago, two seeds lay beside each other in the earth, waiting. It was cold and rather wearisome, and, to pass away the time, the one found means to speak to the other.

"What are you going to be?" said the one.

"I don't know," answered the other.

"For me," replied the first, "I mean to be a rose. There is nothing like a splendid rose. Everybody will love me then."

"It's all right," whispered the second; and that was all it could say. For somehow when it said that, it felt as if all the words in the world were used up. So they were silent again for a day or two.

Lesson 103
Divided Quotations

1. **Change the following to divided quotations:**
   A. The first replied, "I mean to be a rose. There is nothing like a splendid rose."

   "I mean to be a rose," the first replied. "There is nothing like a splendid rose."

   B. "I'm growing! Good-bye," the seed replied.

   "I'm growing!" the seed replied. "Good-bye."

   C. The seed said to itself, "It's all right; I will be what I can."

   It's all right," the seed said to itself. "I will be what I can."

2. **Write quotations, each of which shall be divided by one of the following expressions:**
   A. replied the soldier
   B. shouted the north wind
   C. said the barefoot boy
   D. I answered
   E. laughed Harry
   F. the girl said
   G. called the captain
   H. said the little red hen
   I. he said to himself.

   Answers will vary but should reflect the above phrases in divided quotations.

Lesson 104
Divided Quotations

1. Write this story, changing as much of it as possible to direct quotations.
2. Let some of the quotations be divided by such expressions as, said the fox, the fox begged, etc.
3. Add other remarks that the fox might have made.
4. After each remark of the fox refer in some way to the crow.
5. Tell what the crow may have thought as she flew homeward.

Lesson 105
Indirect Quotations

A. The fox told the crow he had heard that her voice was very beautiful.
B. The fox said, "I have heard that your voice is very beautiful."
C. The fox begged for one little song.
D. "Won't you please sing one little song for me?" begged the fox.

1. **Which of these sentences contain direct quotations?**
   Sentences B and D contain direct quotations.
2. **Which do not contain the exact words of the speaker? Note: Sentences A and C are called *indirect quotations* because they give the thought of the speaker, but not his exact words.**
   Sentences A and C do not contain the exact words of the speaker.
3. **Copy, from Lesson 88, a sentence containing a direct quotation; change it to an indirect quotation.**
   Lesson 88 sample direct quotation: "O mists, make room for me!" Sample indirect quotation: The wind told the mist to make room for him.
4. **Copy, from Lesson 56, two sentences containing direct quotations; change them to indirect quotations.**
   Lesson 56 sample direct quotation: The teacher said, "Someone is at the door." Sample indirect quotation: The teacher told the students that someone was at the door. Sample direct quotation: Tom said, "It is not I." Sample indirect quotation: Tom said it wasn't him.
5. **Copy, from Lesson 101, four sentences containing direct quotations; change them to indirect quotations.**
   Lesson 101 sample direct quotations: "What are you going to be?" said the one. "I don't know," answered the other. "For me," replied the first, "I mean to be a rose. There is nothing like a splendid rose. Everybody will love me then." "It's all right," whispered the second.
   Sample indirect quotations: The first seed asked the second seed what she was going to be. The second seed said she didn't know. The first seed said she'd like to be a rose so everybody would love her. The second seed decided that would be all right.

Lesson 106

Composition—A Story

As Paul Carter was going on an errand one day, he found a pocketbook by the side of the walk.

1. Write the story, mentioning:
   A. The contents of the pocketbook
   B. What Paul was tempted to do
   C. What he decided to do
   D. How he returned the pocketbook to the owner.
   If possible, let your story contain indirect quotations and direct quotations; let one or more of the direct quotations be divided.

Lesson 107

Conversation—The Body

1. **What holds the body erect?**
   The skeleton, made up of about 200 bones, forms the framework that keeps the body erect.
2. **What moves the body?**
   The skeleton and the muscles work together to move the body.
3. **What is the outer covering of the body called?**
   The outer covering of the body is called the skin, or epidermis. It protects the inner tissues from bacteria found in the world around us.
4. **What organ pumps the blood through the body?**
   The heart pumps the blood through the body.
5. **How does the blood reach all parts of the body?**
   The blood reaches all parts of the body through the circulatory system.
6. **Where are the lungs located?**
   The lungs are located behind the rib cage.
7. **How are the lungs and heart protected?**
   The heart and lungs are protected by the ribs.
8. **Of what use are the lungs?**
   The lungs are part of the respiratory system which provide the body with oxygen and remove carbon dioxide.
9. **Of what advantage are the joints?**
   Moveable joints such as knee and elbow joints help us move; fixed joints such as the skull do not move but protect the organs of the body.
10. **Compare the elbow joint with the wrist joint. Which joint moves only backward and forward?**

The elbow joint allows us to turn our hands up and down and rotate our upper arms. The wrist joint can move both backward and foreword and sideways.

11. **Compare the wrist joint with the other joints of the body.**

The ankle joint allows the foot to move sideways, up and down. The knee joint works a little like a hinge allowing the leg to swing from side to side, front to back.

12. **Of what use are the fingernails?**

Fingernails protect the tips of our fingers and allow us to pick up tiny objects, open knots, and accomplish a myriad of other tasks.

13. **Where is food digested?**

Food is digested in the stomach.

14. **What part of the eye has the power of sight?**

The retina is the part of the eye that has the power of sight.

15. **In how many directions can you look without turning your head?**

You can see straight ahead, from side to side, and up and down without moving your head.

16. **Of what use are the eyebrows?**

The eyebrows keep moisture such as sweat and rain from entering our eyes.

17. **Of what use are the eyelids?**

The eyelids are lined with conjunctiva which lubricates the eyes, keeping them from drying out.

18. **Where is the voice produced?**

The voice is produced in the voice box or larynx

19. **Of what use is the tongue?**

Besides helping us taste and chew our food, it also helps us form the sounds of words.

20. **Where is the palate?**

The palate is the roof of our mouth.

21. **Describe the mouth.**

The mouth includes lips which help us drink and take in food, teeth to help us grind and crush our food, salivary glands which help the food begin to digest, and the tongue which helps us taste, eat, and swallow.

22. **Where is the brain located?**

The brain is located in the head above the spinal cord.

23. **How is it protected?**

It is encased in the skull.

24. **Of what use are the nerves?**

Nerves regulate the body systems and help us adjust to our environment.

25. **Name the five senses.**

The five senses are sight, sound, smell, taste, and touch.

26. **Which sense is the most important?**

Answers will vary.

The questions above are designed for discussion. Answers may vary but may include the above overview.

Lesson 108
Debate

The sense of sight is more important than the sense of hearing.

1. Let two pupils debate the question, one taking the affirmative side and the other the negative. Note: The speaker for the affirmative should tell of the benefits that sight gives, the work that could not be done except by means of the eyes and the many pleasures it brings.
2. State arguments that may be presented by the negative side and answer them. Note: The speaker for the negative should tell of the benefits of hearing and its pleasures.
3. Reply to the arguments given by the speaker for the affirmative and show any mistakes he may have made in reasoning.
4. Let the class decide which pupil has presented the stronger argument.
5. The pupils who take part in the debate should make outlines of their speeches.

Note: As a rule the strongest arguments should be placed last.

Extended Activity

Have the students complete the graphic organizer to prepare for their argument. Refer to Lesson 25, "Extended Activities," for additional activities on this topic.

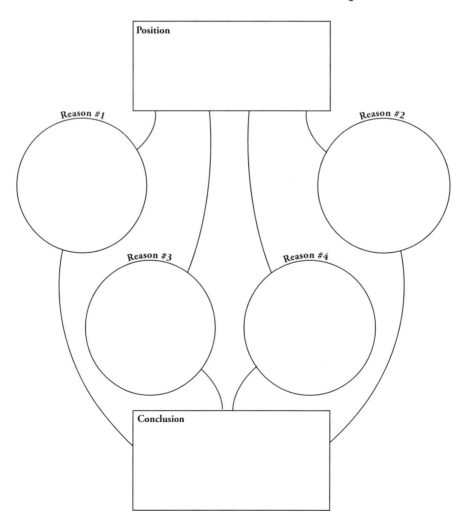

Lesson 109
Letter Writing—Review

1. Write the heading that you would use if writing a letter from your home today.
2. Write the heading that you would have used for sending a letter from some city near your home last Christmas.
3. Write the heading that you might use for sending a letter from London on your next birthday.
4. Write the salutations that you would use in addressing your mother; your cousin; your uncle; your teacher; a classmate.
5. Write a complimentary close for each of these letters.
6. Write a note asking a classmate to go home from school with you.
7. Tell about some pet, game, or new book that you would like to show.
8. Write an answer to the note telling why you cannot go to his home today. Ask your friend if he would like to read the book you received for your birthday recently.

Teacher Note (see notes from Lesson 28)

An outline of the friendly letter shows five basic parts:

The heading includes two lines for the writer's address and the date in the upper right-hand corner of the letter.

The salutation or greeting appears at the left-hand margin two lines below the heading and begins with *Dear* followed by the name of the person being addressed and a comma.

The body is the main part of the letter and includes the ideas or information you wish to tell your friend. Skip a line after the salutation and between each paragraph.

The complimentary closing follows the body and begins two lines below the body and just to the right of the middle of the letter. The first word is capitalized and the closing ends with a comma.

The signature is written beneath the closing and is usually just your first name.

Lesson 110
Homonyms

Note: Words that are alike in sound but different in meaning are called homonyms.
1. **Find the meaning of the following homonyms and use each in a sentence:**
   Sentences using each of the homonyms will vary.
   A. steal, steel
   steal: to take what does not belong to you; steel: heavy metal
   B. knot, not
   knot: formed by tying strings or ropes; not: a negative of a word
   C. feet, feat

feet: measurement or what we walk with; feat: an act of skill

D. beet, beat

beet: a plant; beat: rhythm or to hit

E. ate, eight

ate: past tense of eat; eight: number

F. sun, son

sun: a star around which the planets revolve; son: male offspring

G. no, know

no: the negative of a choice; know: understand

H. hour, our

hour: relates to time; our: belonging to us

I. would, wood

would: desire, wish; wood: made from trees

J. lye lie

lye: material coming from wood ashes; lie: to rest or tell an untruth

K. fore, four

fore: forward, in front of; four: a number

L. meet, meat

meet: to encounter; meat: solid food

2. **Fill the blanks in the following sentences with words from the list above:**
   A. **The bridge was ninety _feet_ long and was constructed of _steel_ and iron.**
   B. **The athlete performed a dangerous _feat_.**
   C. **We _ate_ sugar that was made from the sugar _beet_.**
   D. **I will _meet_ you there in an _hour_.**
   E. **Soap is made from _wood_ ashes and _lye_.**
   F. **The hail _beat_ the blossoms from the fruit trees.**

Lesson 111
Picture Study—
Departure of the Pilgrims

1. **Tell the story of the Pilgrims.**
   Pilgrims who chose to leave Holland joined with other families in England and sailed to America in 1620 on the Mayflower. For 65 days 102 men, women, and children sailed across the Atlantic Ocean in rough seas until they landed on Cape Cod in November. When they arrived in America, the Pilgrim leaders wrote and signed the Mayflower Compact, the first agreement that arranged for self-government in America.

2. **Why had they left their homes in England to go to Holland?**

They left their homes in England to go to Holland because of religious persecution and political unrest. Many of the Pilgrims belonged to a religious group who called themselves Separatists since they separated from the Church of England for religious beliefs. They were hunted down and persecuted for their faith, so they fled to Holland.

3. **How were they treated in Holland?**

The Dutch treated them well, allowing them to practice their faith and start their own small businesses. They lived in Holland for 11 years.

4. **Why did they wish to go to America?**

They decided to leave Holland for America since many of them feared their children would become more Dutch than English. Because they were not citizens of Holland, they were limited in their ability to buy land and have skilled trades. Also, war was breaking out in Europe and the Pilgrims wanted a place of safety to practice their religion and self-government.

5. **Describe the picture.**

Departure of the Pilgrim Fathers from Delft Haven *by Charles West Cope, a painter of historical events, shows the Pilgrims boarding the ship in Holland for their new home in America.*

6. **Tell something of the occupants of the boat.**

Answers may vary.

7. **Do they seem glad or sorrowful?**

Answers may vary.

8. **Describe the people on the shore.**

Answers may vary.

9. **Tell anything you can concerning the voyage and the early days in America.**

Answers may vary.

Answers to all above will vary but should reflect the brief overview above.

Lesson 112
Conversation—Foods

Note: A list of articles of food arranged in the order in which they are to be served at a meal is called a menu.

1. **Write a menu for a Thanksgiving dinner.**
2. **Mention the source of each article of food.**
3. **Make a list of the countries that contributed the dinner.**
4. **Tell about the transportation of articles.**
5. **Tell through what process each article had to pass before it was ready to be eaten.**
6. **Mention some of the people who aided in its preparation.**
7. **Classify foods under these heads:**
   A. **animal**
   B. **vegetable**
   C. **mineral**

Teacher Note

Encourage the students to make an outline before writing. They should develop one paragraph per topic.

Suggested outline:
Introduction
Menu and Source of Food
Countries of Food Origin
Transportation of Food
Food Process
People Involved in Preparation.

See the essay rubric, page 220, for the grading criteria.

Lesson 113
Composition—A Loaf of Bread

1. Write the history of a loaf of bread.
2. Begin with the wheat that the farmer sowed. Use the following outline:
   A. Sowing the wheat
   B. The wheat field
   C. The rain
   D. The sunshine
   E. Cutting the wheat
   F. The threshing
   G. The mill
   H. The grinding
   I. The flour
   J. Transportation of the flour
   K. Sale of the flour in the store
   L. Making the bread

Lesson 114
"Thanksgiving"

1. Talk about the meaning of this poem.
   Possible answer: The poem recognizes God as the giver of all food for both humans and creatures.
2. Name the things mentioned in the poem which God has given to man for food.

Things mentioned in the poem which God has given to man for food: wheat, yellow corn, fish, flesh, fowl, fruit.

3. **Mention other things that you have reason to be thankful for.**

   Answers will vary.

4. **With what kind of letter does God begin?**

   God begins with a capital letter.

5. **Find in the poem other words referring to God.**

   Other words referring to God: His, He, He, His, He.

6. **With what kind of letters do these words begin?**

   These words all begin with capital letters since they refer to God.

Lesson 115
Singular and Plural

Singular: A. wolf B. shelf C. wife D. calf
Plural: E. wolves F. shelves G. wives H. calves

1. **Study the words. Which of the words end in singular?**

   A. wolf B. shelf C. wife D. calf

2. **Which ends in fe?**

   The word wife ends in fe.

3. **In forming the plural, f or fe is changed to what letters?**

   In forming the plural, f or fe is changed to ves.

4. **Write the plural of the following:**

   A. knife *knives*

   B. life *lives*

   C. self *selves*

   D. half *halves*

   E. thief *thieves*

   F. beef *beefs or beeves*

   G. loaf *loaves*

   H. sheaf *sheaves*

5. **Copy the following sentence (Number 6), filling the blanks to make a rule for this formation of the plural:**

6. **Most words ending in f or fe form the plural by changing** *f* **or** *fe* **to** *ves*.

Lesson 116
Conversation—
Cud Chewers

1. **Talk about the cow, using the following outline:**
    A. Size
    Height is about five feet; weight is from 900 to 1200 pounds.
    B. Covering of body
    Most breeds have short hair that lengthen in winter for protection from the cold.
    C. Feet
    Cows' hooves (also hoofs) are cloven or divided.
    D. Teeth
    Grown cattle have 32 teeth but they do not have cutting teeth in the front of their upper jaws, so they tear the grass by moving their heads instead of biting it. They chew their cud with their back teeth called molars.
    E. Food
    Cows eat corn, silage, clover hay, and pasture grass.
    F. Habits
    Cows are known for the common habit of chewing their cud. Cattle are ruminants which means they have four stomach compartments. They chew their food two separate times: the first time they chew and swallow their food; the second time they bring it back up and chew it again. The second chewing is called a cud.
    G. Use—milk, meat, hide, hair, etc.
    Besides milk, meat, hide and hair, cattle provide humans with butter, ice cream, cheese, yogurt, leather, glue, and soap to name a few.
    H. Means of protection
    Cattle may protect themselves by using their hooves for kicking and their horns for butting and goring.
2. **Why is the cow called a cud chewer?**
    Cattle are called cud chewers because that is the way they digest their food.
3. **Tell what you can of the following cud chewers, stating in what respects they are like cows:**
    A. goat
    B. giraffe
    C. antelope
    D. deer
    E. sheep
    F. buffalo
    Besides all chewing the cud, they all have cloven or divided hooves.
4. **Name some animals that belong to the cat family.**

See Lesson 44, Cat family: A. lion B. panther C. leopard D. puma E. tiger F. wild cat G. jaguar H. lynx.

5. **Name some animals that belong to the dog family.**
   See Lesson 78, Dog family: A. wolf B. fox C. coyote D. hyena E. jackal.
6. **Name some animals that are rodents.**
   See Lesson 94, Rodents: A. beaver B. rabbit C. mouse D. hare E. chipmunk F. porcupine G. guinea pig H. rat I. prairie dog J. woodchuck.

Lesson 117
Picture Study—
The Deer Family

1. **Describe the picture, "The Deer Family."**
   Sir Edwin Henry Landseer painted this picture entitled The Deer Family.
2. **Which is the father deer?**
   The large deer with antlers is the father deer.
3. **Tell what you can of the habits of deer.**
   Like cows, deer have more than one stomach and chew their cud. They are shy creatures, running from perceived danger. They have antlers on their heads.
4. **What do they eat?**
   They eat twigs, bark, leaves, grass, and tender shoots of trees and plants.
5. **Where are they found? Did you ever see one?**
   There are over sixty kinds of deer and they are found all around the world in hot and cold climates, mountains and plains.
6. **Read the first and second paragraphs in this lesson and complete the following sentences:**
7. **"Landseer" begins with a capital letter because** *it is the surname of the painter.*
8. **There is a period after 1802 because** *it is the end of the sentence.*
9. ***London* begins with a capital letter because** *it is the proper name of a place.*
10. ***When* begins with a capital letter because** *it is the first word in the sentence.*
11. **There is a comma after *bears* because** *it is the first in a series of items.*

Lesson 118
Correct Use of Words

    A. Sweet blossoms *grow* on the apple trees.
    B. The sun *shines* upon them.
    C. The birds *begin* to build a nest.
    D. They *choose* a place in a tall tree.
    E. They *bring* feathers to line the nest.
    F. They *fly* to the garden for bugs.
    G. The wind *blows* loud and shrill.
    H. It *breaks* the branches from the tall tree.
    I. It *shakes* the tree and the nest falls to the ground.

1. **Change these sentences so that they will refer to some time in the past. Change the italicized words.**

    A. Sweet blossoms grew on the apple trees.
    B. The sun shone upon them.
    C. The birds began to build a nest.
    D. They chose a place in a tall tree.
    E. They brought feathers to line the nest.
    F. They flew to the garden for bugs.
    G. The wind blew loud and shrill.
    H. It broke the branches from the tall tree.
    I. It shook the tree and the nest fell to the ground.

2. **Rewrite the sentences so that they will refer to some time in the future. Change the italicized words if necessary.**

    A. Sweet blossoms will grow on the apple trees.
    B. The sun will shine upon them.
    C. The birds will begin to build a nest.
    D. They will choose a place in a tall tree.
    E. They will bring feathers to line the nest.
    F. They will fly to the garden for bugs.
    G. The wind will blow loud and shrill.
    H. It will break the branches from the tall tree.
    I. It will shake the tree and the nest will fall to the ground.

3. **Rewrite the sentences, using in each the word has or have. Change the italicized words.**

    A. Sweet blossoms have grown on the apple trees.
    B. The sun has shone upon them.
    C. The birds have begun to build a nest.
    D. They have chosen a place in a tall tree.
    E. They have brought feathers to line the nest.
    F. They have flown to the garden for bugs.

G. *The wind has blown loud and shrill.*
H. *It has broken the branches from the tall tree.*
I. *It has shaken the tree and the nest has fallen to the ground.*

Lesson 119
Selection for Study—"The Windflower"

1. The windflower is another name for the anemone (a-nem-o-ne). It is one of the earliest flowers of the spring; have you seen it?
    Answers will vary.
2. Explain the meaning of the poem.
    Answers will vary but the meaning of the poem may reflect that each of us has a place and purpose. We are all here for a reason.
3. Look in the dictionary for the meaning of *boisterous, fragile, raiment.* Note: Notice that "windflower" is composed of two words, *wind* and *flower.* Such a word is called a compound word. Note: Some compound words are written with a hyphen between the two words, as, good-bye.
    boisterous: violent, blustery, stormy
    fragile: frail, tender, easily broken
    raiment: garments, clothing.
4. Find in the poem other compound words that are written without a hyphen. Note: The names of numbers under one hundred that are expressed by two words are written as compound words, as thirty-five, sixty-four.
    Other compound words that are written without a hyphen: roadsides, snowflakes, sometimes, snowdrifts.
5. Copy ten compound words from your reader or other books. Notice whether the words are written with or without the hyphen.
    Ten compound words from your textbook:
    Lesson 3: nearby, someone, something
    Lesson 6: overlook, lonesome, knee-deep
    Lesson 26: Sunday, sometimes, everybody, butterflies, honeydew, sunshine, good-bye
    Lesson 35: barefoot, turned-up, strawberries, sunshine, million-dollared, woodchuck

Lesson 120
Prose Study—"A Plant"

1. Write a story of "The Child and the Plant." Begin it in this way: A child found a seed that was apparently as lifeless as a grain of sand—

Answers will vary.

2. **What were some of the secrets of the plant?**

Some secrets of the plant: no name, no bloom, it was a "green and living thing unlike the seed, unlike the soil, unlike the air, secrets that baffle the wisest men."

3. **What was the lesson that the plant taught?**

The lesson that the plant taught: "It is worth while to have a plant."

4. **Why is it "worth while to have a plant"?**

It is "worth while to have a plant" because it teaches us about nature, how things grow, and what they need to survive.

5. **Find the meaning of baffle, neglected, apparently.**

The meaning of baffle: puzzle, confuse; neglected: failed, left undone, unfinished; apparently: seemingly, at first sight.

6. **Tell the history of the plant.**

Answers will vary.

7. **Use some of the expressions from the prose study above.**

Answers will vary.

Extended Activity

Have the students plant a flower seed in a container and care for it as the poem suggests providing light, water, and care. Watch its progress.

Lesson 121
Conversation—Flowers

1. **Write answers to the following, each sentence to contain a series of words and but one connecting word with each series.**

   A. Name some flowers that grow wild.

   Wild flowers may include daisies, black-eyed Susans, bluebells, and buttercups.

   B. Name some flowers that bloom earliest in the spring in your neighborhood.

   Spring flowers may include daffodils, tulips, violets, and lilacs.

   C. Name some flowers that bloom in the fall.

   Fall flowers may include asters, chrysanthemums, and goldenrod.

   D. Name some flowers that grow from seeds.

   Flowers that grow from seeds are sweet peas, sunflowers, nasturtiums, and marigolds.

   E. Name some flowers that grow from bulbs.

   Flowers that grow from bulbs are tulips, gladiolus, begonias, and Easter lilies.

   F. Name some flowers that grow on vines.

   Flowers that grow on vines include bittersweet, morning glories, honeysuckle, and clematis.

   G. Name some flowers that grow on small plants.

   Flowers that grow on small plants include lilies of the valleys, petunias, and pansies.

   H. Name some flowers that grow on bushes and shrubs.

Flowering bushes and shrubs may include roses, lilacs, forsythia, and hydrangeas.

I. Name some flowers that grow on trees.

Magnolias, dogwoods, and horse chestnuts are flowering trees.

J. Name some flowers that are fragrant.

Roses, honeysuckle, lavender, and lilacs are fragrant.

K. Name some flowers that grow well in gardens.

Garden flowers include dahlias, iris, peonies, and hollyhocks.

L. What flowers do you like best?

Answers will vary.

2. **Write a short description of your favorite flower.**

Answers will vary.

Have students research the flowers in their region to answer the questions, since flowers bloom at different times in different climates.

Lesson 122
Composition— "The Monarch Butterfly"

A beautiful orange and black butterfly flew slowly over the meadow. Near a milkweed stalk it paused and lighted on one of the tender green leaves. After a while it flew away, but on the milkweed it had left a number of tiny eggs…

Finish the story. Tell of the hatching of one of the eggs, the caterpillar, its growth and food, the chrysalis, and the butterfly.

Extended Activity

Have the students draw pictures of each of the stages of the butterfly.

Lesson 123
Dictation

1. **Find the meaning of the following words and use them in sentences: universal, verdure, foliage, rustic, moist.**

Sentences will vary.; meaning of the following words: universal, recognized everywhere; verdure, rich green color of plants; foliage, plants; rustic, country, rural; moist, damp or dewy.

2. **What pictures does the paragraph suggest?**

   The picture suggests a countryside rich with color and plants of all sorts.

3. **In the third sentence, with what are the fields of England contrasted?**

   The fields of England are contrasted with other lands "white with dust."

4. **How could the hedges, trees, and flowers suggest the patterns of a carpet?**

   The hedges, trees, and flowers suggest the patterns of a carpet with their varying shades of color and shape.

5. **Write the paragraph from dictation.**

   See the book for dictation passage.

6. **Complete the following sentences:**

   A. "No" begins with a capital letter because *it is the first word in the sentence*.

   B. "England" begins with a capital letter because *it is the name of a country*.

   C. There is a period after "verdure" because *it is the last word in the sentence*.

   D. *Beautiful* and *green* describe "carpet."

   E. There is a comma after "hedges" because *it is an item in a series of words*.

   F. *Rustic* describes houses.

   G. *Wild* describes roses.

   H. There are an apostrophe and s after Stoddard because *the lectures belong to Stoddard*.

   I. "Stoddard" begins with a capital letter because *it is the name of a person*.

Lesson 124
Selection for Study—
"October's Bright Blue Weather"

1. **Explain what is meant by the first stanza.**

   The first stanza suggests that even if you took all the bright colors of the sun, skies, clouds, and flowers of June together, they could not compare with the color of "October's bright blue weather."

2. **Why are apples compared to jewels?**

   Apples are compared to jewels as "red apples lie in piles like jewels shining."

3. **What flowers are mentioned in this poem?**

   Flowers mentioned in this poem are goldenrod and gentians.

4. **What seeds are referred to in the fifth stanza?**

   Seeds referred to in the fifth stanza are the "white-winged seeds."

5. **What fruits are mentioned?**

   Fruits mentioned are grapes and apples.

6. **Why does it speak of satin burrs?**

The poem speaks of satin burrs falling from chestnut trees. They may look like satin from a distance, but the burrs of chestnut trees are prickly.

7. **Write a description of a picture that you would paint, if you were an artist, to illustrate this poem. Tell what you would have for the principal object, what you would place in the foreground, and what in the background. Begin your description thus: If I were painting a picture to illustrate this poem, I would—**

Answers will vary.

Lesson 125
Correct Use of Words

A. Don't you like the cold weather?
B. I don't like it very well.
C. Sam likes it; he doesn't mind the cold.

1. **What contractions are used in the sentences?**
The contractions don't *and* doesn't *are used in the sentences.*

2. **For what words do they stand? Note: Use *don't* only in the place of *do not*. Use *doesn't* only in the place of *does not*.**
Don't stands for do not and doesn't stands for does not.

3. **Copy the following sentences, using the contractions in place of *do not* and *does not*:**
   A. Bees do not work in winter
   Bees don't work in winter..
   B. A bee does not have time to play.
   A bee doesn't have time to play.
   C. Do you not like October?
   Don't you like October?
   D. The leaves do not remain on the trees all winter.
   The leaves don't remain on the trees all winter.
   E. The water in the brook does not sing as it did last summer.
   The water in the brook doesn't sing as it did last summer.
   F. The goldenrod does not blossom until late in the summer.
   The goldenrod doesn't blossom until late in the summer.
   G. Some birds do not go south for the winter.
   Some birds don't go south for the winter.

4. **Write three questions beginning with don't.**
   Answers will vary.

5. **Write three questions beginning with doesn't.**
   Answers will vary.

Lesson 126
Picture Study—*The Balloon*

This picture was painted by a French artist, Julien Dupre, and represents country life in France.

1. **Look at the picture and tell what you think the people are doing.**
   The people are watching the balloon in the distant sky.
2. **What do you suppose they are saying?**
   They may be talking about the balloon floating high above the land on which they are working so hard and how amazed they are at men flying, a new development at the time the painting was made.
3. **What were they doing before they saw the balloon?**
   Before they saw the balloon they were cutting the grass to make hay for their animals.
4. **What time of year is it?**
   It is probably summer.
5. **Give the reason for your answer.**
   Summer is when the crops are ready to cut for haymaking.
6. **Compare this method of haying with that employed on a farm in the United States.**
   Haymaking in the United Sates today would not require a lot of manual labor. Tractors, wagons, mowers, rakes and balers would all take the place of hand tools.
7. **Describe the background of the picture. What kind of trees do you see?**
   The trees are tall slender trees with shorter trees at their base.
8. **Write a short description of the picture.**
   Answers will vary.

Possible answers above.

Lesson 127
Composition

1. **Read again the poem, "October's Bright Blue Weather." Choose another month or season, and write a short article in which you try to prove that it is the most delightful time of the year.**

Extended Activity

Create a visual aid to go with your article that supports your belief that it is the most beautiful time of year.

Lesson 128
Conversation—Ships of the Air

1. **Tell what you can of airships and balloons.**
    Airships are also known as blimps, zeppelins, or dirigibles. They use a light gas for lifting power and can be steered in any direction. In WWI they were used as bombers; in WWII they protected ships from submarine attacks. Today they are largely used for advertising or research. Balloons rise and float in the air with the help of hot air or gas. They are largely used for sport ballooning and research.

2. **What causes the balloon to rise?**
    Hot air or lighter-than-air gas inside the balloon causes it to rise.

3. **How is the balloon affected by the wind?**
    The wind can blow the balloon in any direction. It cannot be steered, but the pilot can control the vertical movement of the balloon, thus rising or falling to find air currents blowing in the direction the pilot wishes to take.

4. **Can it sail against the wind?**
    A balloon cannot sail against the wind.

5. **What is the motive power of an airship?**
    The motive power of an airship is a light gas and the use of engines, propellers, and instruments that help the pilot move the airship through air.

6. **Can it sail against the wind?**
    The airship can sail against the wind.

7. **If you have seen an airship, describe it.**
    Answers will vary.

8. **Bring pictures to class.**

Lesson 129
Composition—A Trip in an Airship

1. Imagine yourself in an airship taking a trip over some country that you have studied recently in geography.
2. Tell of your start, how you felt as the airship went higher, what you saw as you looked over the sides.
3. Describe the mountains, rivers, cities, and people.
4. Stop at the place that interests you most.

Extended Activity

Have the students create an airship from paper or cardboard. Then have them write the composition as journal entries as shown in Lesson 145, using the outline to describe their trip.

Lesson 130
Abbreviations

1. **Why are words sometimes abbreviated?**
   Words are abbreviated to save time and space when writing.
2. **Learn the abbreviations.**
Note: Many state abbreviations use the first letter and the second or last letter as an abbreviation. States which begin with the same letters such as A, M, or N have a variety of letters in their abbreviations. If the states have two words, they use the first letters of each word as their abbreviations.
3. **Write them from dictation.**
   Dictate using the list from the book.

Lesson 131
Reproduction—A Fable

1. **Write this fable in dialogue form. Add to the conversation anything that will increase the interest. Begin it in this way:**
   Monkey: Here is a good fire. Let us sit by it.
   Cat: I like to sit by a fire.

Lesson 132
Composition

1. **Tell or write one of the following stories:**
   A. **Little Red Riding Hood**
   B. **Puss in Boots**
   C. **Cinderella**
   D. **Jack and the Beanstalk**
   E. **The Sleeping Beauty**
   F. **Diamonds and Toads**
   G. **The Fisherman and His Wife**
   H. **The Tinder Box**
   I. **Beauty and the Beast**
   J. **The Ugly Duckling**
   K. **Why the Sea is Salt**
   L. **The Discontented Pine Tree**
If you do not know any of these, tell or write some other story.

Lesson 133
Selection for Study—"The Greek Myth—Echo"

1. Tell the story of *Echo*.

Note: In the second paragraph the words "the Greek mythical queen of the heavens" explain who Juno was. Such a group of words is called an *explanatory expression*.

Answers will vary.

2. How is the explanatory expression separated from the rest of the sentence?

The explanatory expression is separated from the rest of the sentence with a comma.

3. Find explanatory expressions in Lessons 1, 21, and 28.

Explanatory expressions in Lessons 1: "Pharaoh, the king of the country;" 21: "the wren, the smallest, the least powerful of birds;" and 28: "Your friend, Charles White."

Lesson 134
Explanatory Expressions

1. Use the following in sentences:

Answers will vary but should show commas around the explanatory expressions. Examples may include:

A. Jack, the boy who climbed the beanstalk

Jack, the boy who climbed the beanstalk, brought his mother riches.

B. June, the month of roses

My favorite month is June, the month of roses.

C. Cotton, the principal product of the Southern States

Cotton, the principal product of the Southern States, is used for making clothes.

D. Mr. Carter, our new neighbor

Have you met Mr. Carter, our new neighbor?

E. Sir Edwin Landseer, the artist

Sir Edwin Landseer, the artist, painted a picture entitled The Deer Family.

F. Henry Wadsworth Longfellow, the best-loved poet of America

Henry Wadsworth Longfellow, the best-loved poet of America, wrote the classic poem entitled "The Village Blacksmith."

2. Place an explanatory expression after each of the following, and use in sentences:

A. George Washington

George Washington, our first president, was famous for chopping down the cherry tree.

B. The President of the United States of America

The President of the United States of America, Abraham Lincoln, is featured on our penny.

C. Cinderella

Cinderella, the poor stepdaughter, won the prince's love with her beauty.

D. Electricity

Electricity, an important form of energy, must be used with care.
E. The Panama Canal
The Panama Canal, the passage between the Atlantic and Pacific Oceans, was completed in 1914.
F. My friend
My friend, the one with the broken leg, gave me a new baseball and mitt for my birthday.

Lesson 135
Selection to be Memorized

1. **Write the selection from memory.**
   Refer to the memorization rubric, page 218.
2. **Bring leaves from different kinds of trees.**
   Answers will vary.
3. **Name them and tell which trees are favorites as shade trees.**
   Answers will vary.
4. **Name some trees that are valuable for timber and for fuel.**
   Answers will vary.
5. **At what season are trees the most beautiful? 1.**
   Answers will vary.

Extended Activity

Factual statements are true and can be proven from data. Opinion statements are feeling-based and cannot be proven. Question 5 asks, "At what season are trees the most beautiful?" That is an opinion statement since not everyone may agree on what season the trees are most beautiful.

Decide if the following statements are facts or opinions. If you said the statement is an opinion, underline the words or expressed feelings that make it an opinion statement.
1. **Columbus sailed to America in 1492.**
   Fact
2. **He was the greatest explorer of all time.**
   Opinion
3. **He was the oldest of five children.**
   Fact
4. **He was the most handsome of his brothers.**
   Opinion
5. **Columbus spent lots of money to tackle that voyage.**
   Opinion
6. **When he landed in the Bahamas, he thought he landed in the Indies near China.**
   Fact

7. The Indians <u>were thrilled</u> to see Columbus and his men.
   Opinion
8. Columbus was a <u>cruel</u> taskmaster.
   Opinion
9. On his second voyage he discovered Jamaica.
   Fact
10. On his fourth voyage, one-third of the people on the ships were boys between twelve and eighteen.
    Fact

Lesson 136

Singular and Plural

A. pony B. story C. lady D. sky E. ponies F. stories G. ladies H. skies

1. Study the words.
2. With what letter does each word in the singular end?
   Each word in the singular ends with a y.
3. Is the letter before the last letter a vowel or a consonant?
   The letter before the last letter is a consonant.
4. What change was made in forming the plural?
   Changing the y to i and adding es was made in forming the plural.
5. Write the plural of the following words:
   A. balcony
      balconies
   B. family
      families
   C. country
      countries
   D. daisy
      daisies
   E. baby
      babies
   F. cherry
      cherries
   G. study
      studies
   H. city
      cities
   I. sky
      skies

J. enemy
   enemies

6. Copy the following sentence, filling the blanks to make a rule for this formation of the plural:

Note: Words ending in *y* preceded by a <u>consonant</u> form the plural by changing *y* to *i* and adding <u>*es*</u>.

Lesson 137
Picture Study—
A River Scene

1. Here is a copy of one of his pictures. Notice how beautifully the trees have been painted.
   No response needed.

2. Did the artist wish the landscape, or the people, to be the more prominent?
   The artist wished the landscape to be the more prominent since the people are only a minor part of the picture.

3. Can you think of any reason why there is little ground and much sky in the picture? Which would make the better background for beautiful trees?
   Perhaps the reason there is little ground and much sky in the picture is because the sky would make the better background for beautiful trees.

4. What can you see in the distance?
   You can see buildings in the distance.

5. Does the picture suggest morning or evening?
   The picture may suggest evening because of the direction of the shadows.

6. Would such a place attract you? What would you do if you were there?
   Answers will vary.

7. Can you find a quotation that this picture would illustrate?
   Answers will vary.

Possible responses above.

Lesson 138
Dictation

Jean Corot, the artist, once said: "After one of my excursions I invite nature to come and spend a few days with me. Pencil in hand, I hear the birds singing, the trees rustling in the wind; I see the running brooks and the streams charged with a thousand reflections of sky and earth—nay, the very sun rises and sets in my studio."

1. **Explain the meaning of the paragraph.**
    Answers will vary.
2. **If a picture were made to illustrate it, what would the picture contain?**
    Answers will vary.
3. **Write the quotation from dictation.**

Lesson 139
Selection for Study—"The Song of the Brook"

1. **What is meant by the first line of the poem?**
    "I come from haunts of coot and heron." The first line of the poem suggests the brook has come from where the water birds and herons live.
2. **Explain the second line.**
    "I make a sudden sally." The second line suggests the brook makes a turn.
3. **Why does the poet use the word "chatter" in the third stanza? Suggest other words that might have been used instead.**
    The poet may use the word "chatter" in the third stanza to indicate the noise made by the brook as it flows over the rocks. Other words that might have been used: splash, gurgle, jabber, gush.
4. **What is meant by "brimming river" in the fifth stanza?**
    "Brimming river" in the fifth stanza may suggest the river is almost overflowing its banks.
5. **What season does this poem suggest?**
    This poem may suggest a summer season with its references to "lawns and grassy plots...sweet forget-me-nots."
6. **What is the meaning of the seventh stanza?**
    The seventh stanza may suggest that the brook flows on forever; it never goes away.
7. **Name some of the places through which the brook passed.**
    Some of the places through which the brook passed: among the fern, down a valley, between the ridges, by twenty thorps, a little town, half a hundred bridges, over stony ways, into eddying bays, by field and fallow, fairy foreland, by lawns and grassy plots, hazel covers, forget-me-nots, among skimming swallows, against sandy shallows to the brimming river.
8. **Which stanza suggests the prettiest picture?**
    The prettiest picture is an opinion. Answers will vary.
9. **Would *A River Scene,* by Corot, fit a part of this poem? Describe some other picture of a river or stream.**
    Answers will vary.
10. **Have you seen a brook like this? Describe it.**
    Answers will vary.
11. **Memorize the stanza you like best, and also the last stanza.**
    Refer to the memorization rubric, page 218.

Lesson 140
Composition

1. The Missouri River has its source in the mountains of Yellowstone National Park. With the aid of a map, trace a drop of water from Yellowstone National Park to the Gulf of Mexico. Begin your story in this way: "The Story A Drop of Water Told" For days I floated high above the earth in a soft fleecy cloud. Then the air became colder, and I fell down from the blue sky to the side of a mountain in a wonderful park.
   Answers will vary.
2. Read again "The Song of the Brook," Lesson 139. If possible use some of the following expressions in your story: "over stony ways," "brimming river," "grassy plots," "sandy shallows," "down a valley."
   Answers will vary.
3. Use other expressions from the poem.
   Answers will vary.

Teacher Note
Refer to the short story rubric making sure to look for the following expressions: "over stony ways," "brimming river," "grassy plots," "sandy shallows," "down a valley."

Lesson 141
Business Letters

Note: The part of the letter between the heading and the salutation is called the address. It consists of the name and place of business of the person of the firm to whom the letter is written.
1. Write the letters from dictation.

Lesson 142
Letter Writing

1. Write to the publishers for a copy of this book or some other book that they publish. State that you enclosed a money order in payment.
2. Write a reply stating that your order has been received and that the book has been sent.

Teacher Note
Books available from this publisher and an address can be found at the back of this book.

Lesson 143
Autobiography of a Book

1. Trace a book from the time it left the printers with its clean, fresh pages and stiff, strong back. Tell who bought the book, how it was treated, and what different people read it.
2. Imagine that you are the book, and write its autobiography, as you wrote your own.

Teacher Note
Reference Lesson 91 for the autobiography definition and outline. An autobiography is an account of one's life written by oneself.

Lesson 144
Correct Use of Words

1. What is a homonym? (See Lesson 110.)
   Homonyms are words that are alike in sound but different in meaning.
2. **Find the meanings of the following homonyms, and use each in a sentence.**
   Note: some words may have multiple meanings. Allow the students to look up the words and identify the meanings or forms they are least familiar with. Possible answers:
   A. do, dew, due
   do: perform, bring about; I will do my homework.
   dew: moisture that falls on cool objects at night; The dew dripped from the spider web this morning.
   due: owed as a debt or obligation; My homework assignment is due tomorrow.
   B. grate, great
   grate: scratch or grind; I grate my nails on the rough cement.
   great: large; A great big tree stands in my front yard.
   C. dear, deer
   dear: precious; Ellie is my dear friend.
   deer: wild animal; Deer are cud-chewing creatures.
   D. nose, knows
   nose: the part of the face that contains the sense of smell; My nose tells me Mother is baking brownies for dessert.
   knows: understands; My dog knows how to do tricks.
   E. to, two, too
   to: in the direction of; I am going to school.
   two: number; My little sister will be two on her birthday.
   too: in addition or excessive; My math homework is too (excessive) hard, too (also).
   F. week, weak

week: a seven-day cycle; I'll be out of school in two weeks.

weak: lacking strength; I felt weak when I saw the snake crawling toward me.

G. right, write

right: showing direction; Turn right at the next corner.

write: to form words; I did write a letter to Lost Classics Book Company in Lesson 142.

H. rein, rain

rein: a strap attached to a bit used to control an animal; I pulled on the rein to stop the horse.

rain: moisture falling from the clouds; I hope it won't rain during the parade.

I. sew, sow, so

sew: to fasten with stitches; My mother will sew the hole in my jeans.

sow: to plant; The farmer sows his seeds in the spring.

so: with the result; I study hard so I can get a good grade.

J. bee, be

bee: an insect; A honey bee is valuable insect to agriculture.

be: exist, live; I want to be a fireman when I grow up.

K. fir, fur

fir: type of tree; We decorated a fir tree for our Christmas tree last year.

fur: animal pelt; My kitten's fur is thick and soft.

L. new, knew

new: unused; My new shoes hurt my feet.

knew: past tense of know, understood; I knew I would get an A in science.

Lesson 145

A Diary

Note: People often keep a record of the events of each day. This record is called diary.

1. **Keep a diary for a week. Put down every day the events that interest you, or that you would like to remember.**

   Allow students to share one diary entry they especially enjoyed writing.

2. **Complete the following sentences:**

   A. There is a period after Sept. because *it is an abbreviation for September*.

   B. There is an apostrophe in it's because *it is an abbreviation for it is*.

   C. Mother's is written with an apostrophe and s because *the birthday belongs to Mother*.

   D. Anna begins with a capital letter because *it is the name of a person*.

   E. Cousin begins with a capital letter because *it is used as part of Louisa's name*.

Lesson 146
Longfellow's Diary

1. **Find in the dictionary the meaning of the word "tessellated."**

   "Tessellated" is having a checkered appearance. Thus. "The tessellated (or checkered) shadow of the honeysuckle lies motionless upon my study floor, as if it were a figure in the carpet."

2. **Read the description several times. Notice the beginning and the close.**

   Note the length of the final sentence. "The birds are caroling in the trees, and their shadows flit across the window as they dart to and fro in the sunshine, while the murmur of the bee, the cooing of the doves from the eaves, and the whirring of the little hummingbird that has its nest in the honeysuckle, send up a sound of joy to meet the rising sun."

3. **Using this as a model, describe an autumn day, a spring day, or a winter day.**

   Answers will vary.

Lesson 147
Selection for Study—"The Cloud"

1. **What does the cloud do for the flowers?**

   Line 1: The cloud brings "fresh showers for the thirsting flowers;" Line 3: the cloud bears "light shade for the leaves;" Line 5: from the cloud's "wings are shaken the dews that waken the sweet buds."

2. **Explain the third line of the first stanza.**

   Third line of the first stanza: "I bear light shade for the leaves when laid In their noonday dreams."

3. **What things are mentioned in the third and fourth stanzas that the cloud does?**

   In the third and fourth stanzas the cloud wields "the flail of the lashing hail, And whiten the green plains under, And then again I dissolve it in rain, And laugh as I pass in thunder. I sift the snow on the mountains below, And their great pines groan aghast; And all the night 'tis my pillow white, While I sleep in the arms of the blast."

4. **Explain the meaning of "flail," "dissolve," "groan," "aghast," "blast."**

   The meaning of flail: a hand instrument used to cut grain when it is ripe; dissolve: cause to disintegrate or disappear as the cloud dissolves the hail; groan: to utter a deep sigh, to moan; aghast: frightened, scared; blast: a violent storm.

5. **What is the meaning of the second line of the fourth stanza?**

   The second line of the fourth stanza: "And their great pines groan aghast."

6. **What is the meaning of the third and fourth lines of the fourth stanza?**

   The third and fourth lines of the fourth stanza: "And all the night 'tis my pillow white, While I sleep in the arms of the blast."

7. **Which lines in each stanza of this poem rhyme?**

Lines in each stanza of this poem that rhyme: the second and fourth lines in each stanza rhyme.

8. **Find two words in the first line that rhyme.**

   Two words in the first line that rhyme: showers and flowers.

9. **Find two words in the third line that rhyme. Note: Such words are called *interior* rhyme.**

   Two words in the third line that rhyme: shade and laid.

10. **Find other interior rhymes in this poem.**

    Other interior rhymes in this poem: Stanza 2: shaken and waken, rest and breast; Stanza 3: flail and hail, again and rain; Stanza 4: snow and below, night and white.

11. **Find other poems containing interior rhymes.**

    Answers will vary.

12. **Write a stanza of four lines in which the first and third, or the second and fourth lines rhyme.**

    Answers will vary.

13. **Let your poem be about one of the following: A. A brook or river B. A valley C. The picture, *A River Scene*, Lesson 137 D. A snowstorm E. Some part of the description by Longfellow, Lesson 146.**

    Answers will vary.

14. **Write another stanza, choosing any subject you wish.**

    Answers will vary.

Lesson 148
Dictation—"A Dry Season"

It is a long time since much rain fell. The ground is a little dry; the road is a good deal dusty. The garden bakes. Transplanted trees are thirsty. Wheels are shrinking and tires are looking dangerous. Men speculate on the clouds; they begin to calculate how long it will be, if no rain falls, before the potatoes will suffer; the oats, the grass, the corn—everything!

—Henry Ward Beecher

1. **Write the paragraph from dictation.**

Lesson 149
Composition

1. **Study the paragraph quoted in Lesson 148. Notice the form of the description. Write a paragraph entitled "A Wet Season." Begin the paragraph in this way: Rain rain, rain! All day and night it rained steadily. It—**

Lesson 150

Summary—Continued from Lesson 100

To Remember

Words that are alike in sound but different in meaning are called homonyms.

The name of God and all words referring to the Deity should begin with capital letters.

An explanatory expression should be separated from the rest of the sentence by commas.

Use don't only in place of do not. Use doesn't only in place of does not.

Words ending in *y* preceded by a consonant form the plural by changing *y* to *i* and adding *es*.

Words ending in *f* or *fe* form the plural by changing *f* or *fe* to *ves*.

Extended Activity

The following test may be assigned to the students as a review of the skills covered in Lessons 101-149.

Complete each sentence with the correct pair of homonyms. Choose from these homonyms: band, banned; knight, night; road, rode; tense, tents; seem, seam; wait, weight; cents, sense; pain, pane; horse, hoarse; prince, prints

1. The *knight* rode through the *night* to rescue the princess.
2. I was *hoarse* from yelling at the *horse*.
3. I felt *pain* when I cut my finger on the broken window *pane*.
4. The *band* was *banned* from playing at the game.
5. My friend uses good *sense* when he spends fifty *cents*.
6. John *rode* his skateboard down the *road*.
7. Sewing the *seam* would *seem* like a good thing to do when you rip it.
8. I can't *wait* until my *weight* goes down!
9. Colorful *prints* of the noble *prince* decorated the walls.
10. We were very *tense* when the bear sniffed around our *tents*.

Write a homonym that goes with each of the following words:

11. we'd *weed*
12. meat *meet*
13. flee *flea*
14. bare *bear*
15. pail *pale*
16. here *hear*
17. blew *blue*
18. seen *scene*
19. some *sum*
20. whole *hole*

The following lines of poetry are taken from Edward Everett Hale's poem "Thanksgiving." Rewrite the following sentences correctly.
21. **Praise god for wheat, so white and sweet.**
    Praise God for wheat, so white and sweet.
22. **Praise god for yellow corn, with which his waiting world is fed.**
    Praise God for yellow corn, with which His waiting world is fed.
23. **Praise god for fish and flesh and fowl, he gave to man for food.**
    Praise God for fish and flesh and fowl, He gave to man for food.
24. **Praise god for every creature which he made, and called it good.**
    Praise God for every creature which He made, and called it good.
25. **Praise god, his children all, to whom he gives their daily bread.**
    Praise God, His children all, to whom He gives their daily bread.

Place commas in the following sentences where they are needed.
26. **My dog the one with the curly tail can roll over and beg for a bone.**
    My dog, the one with the curly tail, can roll over and beg for a bone.
27. **My favorite month is February the month of love.**
    My favorite month is February, the month of love.
28. **Corn the principal crop of the Midwest is exported around the world.**
    Corn, the principal crop of the Midwest, is exported around the world.
29. **Mr. Wendell our next door neighbor bought a brand new boat.**
    Mr. Wendell, our next door neighbor, bought a brand new boat.
30. **"The Song of the Brook" was written by Alfred Tennyson a famous English poet.**
    "The Song of the Brook" was written by Alfred Tennyson, a famous English poet.

Complete the sentences with the correct contraction don't or doesn't.
31. **Cats often (<u>*don't*</u> doesn't) like baths.**
32. **(Don't <u>*Doesn't*</u>) your cat hate them, too?**
33. **My friend (don't <u>*doesn't*</u>) give her cat a bath.**
34. **She (don't <u>*doesn't*</u>) think the cat needs it.**
35. **I (<u>*don't*</u> doesn't) agree with her.**

Write the plural forms of the following words:
36. **canary** *canaries*
37. **enemy** *enemies*
38. **berry** *berries*
39. **scarf** *scarves*
40. **cliff** *cliffs*
41. **spy** *spies*
42. **pony** *ponies*
43. **giraffe** *giraffes*
44. **knife** *knives*
45. **shelf** *shelves*

46. **cherry** *cherries*
47. **story** *stories*
48. **dolly** *dollies*
49. **elf** *elves*
50. **wharf** *wharves*

Lesson 151
Correct Use of Words

Teacher's Note
The pronoun *I* is used as a subject of a sentence, and *me* is used as an object.

1. **Use the following in sentences:**
   Answers will vary. Below are example sentences.
   A. he and I
   He and I went swimming at the lake.
   B. she and I
   She and I jumped off the diving board.
   C. you and I
   You and I are good friends.
   D. from you and me
   Sally took swimming lessons from you and me.
   E. by you and me
   The turtle swam by you and me.
   F. with you and me
   Thomas will go swimming with you and me.
   G. to him and me
   Thomas gave sunscreen to him and me.
   H. with them and me
   Tomorrow James will go swimming with them and me.
2. **When you speak of yourself and one or more others, whom do you mention last?**
   When you speak of yourself and one or more others, you mention yourself last.

Lesson 152
Picture Study—
Two Mothers

Teacher's Note

Elizabeth Gardner Bouguereau was the first American artist to study at the Paris Salon of the French Academy of Art and the first American woman to be awarded a medal by the Academy. She did much to further female artists in France, opening the doors for women artists to have studios. Her painting was realistic and she often painted animals and children. Elizabeth Gardner was born in New Hampshire (1837-1922), but lived most of her life in France.

1. **What do you see in the picture?**
    A mother and daughter are in the picture. Because of the pots on the wall it looks as if they are in a kitchen. The two are looking at a mother hen and her chicks.

2. **Why is the picture called "Two Mothers"?**
    The picture is titled "Two Mothers" because a human mother and her child are illustrated with a hen and her chicks. A hen is a mother too.

3. **How does the mother care for her little girl?**
    The mother cares for the little girl by feeding her, teaching her and keeping her safe.

4. **How does the hen care for her chicks?**
    The hen keeps her chicks safe, warm and well fed.

5. **Does the hen seem to talk to her chickens?**
    Yes, the hen seems to talk to her chicks by making certain sounds.

6. **How does she warn them of danger?**
    The hen warns her chicks of danger by making clucking noises and pecking at a predator.

7. **How does she feed them?**
    A hen feeds her chicks by finding grains and small insects and putting them into the chick's mouth until the chick is able to eat on its own. Usually a chick just hatched will feed for two days on the yolk from inside its egg.

8. **What do you think the child is saying?**
    The child might be saying something about the chicks or asking a question about the chicks since it appears she and her mother are looking at them.

Lesson 153
Composition—An Important Event

1. **Do you read the newspapers?**

    Answers will vary. Discuss with students different ways we receive news today. Many people read the news online or watch twenty-four hour news on cable television. News stations such as CNN and FOX provide news as it happens. Discuss how this is different from reading the news the next day.

2. **Study carefully the form in which an important piece of news is presented. Does the article give the opinion of the writer or merely state facts? Notice the headlines. What do they contain?**

    Most news articles should not express the opinion of the writer. A news article will give the most pressing details first – who, what, why, when and where – then depending on space allowed in the paper the article will give more details. Headlines contain the subject of the article. Titles are very important because most people scan the newspaper and only read those articles that most interest them. Therefore, titles need to provide information as well as catch the reader's attention.

3. **Imagine that you are a newspaper reporter and write an article about the most important even of the past month. Give headlines.**

    Answers will vary. For additional practice, use the following historical events and have students create catchy headlines for them or do more research on one of the events and write a newspaper article for it. If students have access to publishing software, allow them to design their newspaper using the computer.

    A. President Lincoln was shot at the Ford's Theater by John Wilkes Booth. Lincoln died April 15, the day after he was shot.

    B. During colonial times before the Revolution, the Stamp Act was passed (1765) requiring that all bills, notes and other documents be written on stamped paper which had to be purchased by the English government. This led to much discontent by the colonists who cried, "No taxation without representation."

    C. In 1861 a convention of delegates from the seceded states met in Montgomery, Alabama. These delegates formed a new government called the Confederate States of America and they elected Jefferson Davis as President.

    Use newspaper article rubric, page 224, for evaluation of students' article.

4. **Was the event of importance to your neighborhood alone, or to the state and country?**

    Answers will vary.

Lesson 154
Selection for Study—"The Tree"

1. **Write the first stanza of the poem from memory.**

    Verify the correctness of the student's answer with the poem or if the student memorized the stanza and presented it orally, refer to the memorization rubric, page 218.

2. **With what kind of letter does the word "Tree" begin? Note: when animals or objects are represented as talking and acting like people, they are said to be "personified." The name of anything personified should begin with a capital letter. When something is personified it is treated like a proper noun.**

   The word Tree *begins with a capital letter.*

3. **Find in the poem other objects that are personified.**

   Other objects that are personified are the Frost and the Wind because they are given the human quality of speech—"…said the Frost" "…said the Wind."

4. **Find in the poem an example of the possessive singular.**

   An example of the possessive singular is "Tree's." Possessive singular means that the noun is singular and something belongs to it. In this poem the early leaf-buds belong to the Tree. Refer to Lesson 37.

5. **Write lists of the words that rhyme.**

   Words that rhyme are: alone-grown, down-crown, sung-swung-hung, see-thee, glow-now-low.

Lesson 155
Composition

Tell the story of an oak desk in your schoolroom. Begin your story in this way: Once upon a time a tiny acorn fell to the ground near the foot of a great mountain.

Tell about—
  A. **The growth of the oak tree**
  B. **The cutting of the tree**
  C. **Hauling the log to the river**
  D. **Floating down the river to the mill**
  E. **Sawing the log**
  F. **The making of the desk**
  G. **Selling the desk**
  H. **What has happened to it since it came to your school**
  I. **Descriptions of the woods where the tree grew**
  J. **The river**

   In creating this story, have students complete the story map, page 225.
   For each part of the plot the student should include the appropriate information from the list above.
   Use the short story rubric, page 219, to evaluate student's writing.

Lesson 156
Composition—A Story

1. Complete the story, telling how Carl warned the train, why the engineer did not at first see him, what the passengers said, and what they did for him.
   Use the short story rubric, page 219, to evaluate this assignment. Students can also tell the story orally.

Extended Activity
Have students create a comic strip with 6 blocks. Students should illustrate each part of the story in each block and write a caption under each. Have students title their work.

Lesson 157
A Dialogue

1. Write a dialogue that might have taken place between the two, in which Mr. Evans asks questions concerning Carl's home and finds out that the boy longs for a chance to go to school. Begin the dialogue this way:

   Mr. Evans: My boy, you have done a brave deed. Had it not been for you many of us would have lost our lives. Where is your home?
   Carl: _____.

Teacher Note
Explain to students that until about the beginning of the 1900s not all children went to school. Many children who were poor or who lived in agricultural areas worked instead of attending school. Wealthy children were tutored. For example, Theodore Roosevelt was sent to Europe to be tutored and earn some of his education. The first public high school opened in 1821, and in 1827 Massachusetts passed a law stating that towns with more than 500 families had to have a public high school open to all students. It wasn't until 1918 that compulsory education laws were finally passed in all states.

Lesson 158
Letter Writing

1. Write a letter which Carl might have sent to his mother, telling about his new home and his school.
   Refer to Lesson 27 for proper format for a letter.

Lesson 159
Formation of Sentences

A. A brave boy saved the train.

B. He lived in the little house on the side of the mountain.

C. A brave boy who lived in a little house on the side of the mountain saved the train.

(Notice that the two sentences above were joined by the word *who*.)

1. Combine the sentences of each of the following groups by using the word *who*.

A. The passengers crowded about the boy.

B. They had been saved.

The passengers who had been saved crowded about the boy.

A. A rich man took the boy to his home.

B. The rich man was on the train.

A rich man who was on the train took the boy to his home.

A. The artist was Jean Corot.

B. He painted beautiful pictures of trees.

The artist was Jean Corot who painted beautiful pictures of trees.

A. The people are called Eskimos.

B. They live in the far north.

The people who live in the far north are called Eskimos.

A. The fisherman came home before the storm.

B. He had been out to sea.

The fisherman who had been out to sea came home before the storm.

A. The people saw a balloon high in the air.

B. They were working in the fields.

The people who were working in the fields saw a balloon high in the air.

A. The man waited to see what would happen.

B. He placed the stone in the road.

The man who placed a stone in the road waited to see what would happen.

A. The boy found a sack of gold.

B. He moved the stone from the road.

The boy who moved the stone from the road found a sack of gold.

Teacher Note

The phrases that begin with *who* are called *dependent clauses*. Dependent clauses contain a subject (who) and a verb, but they cannot stand along. Dependent clauses must be connected to an independent clause (complete sentence).

Lesson 160
Composition—A Story

1. Write a story about a man who is rich but who has no little boys or girls in his home. As he passes down the street on a cold night, he sees a poor little ragged boy gazing wistfully into a shop window filled with toys.
2. Tell what the man did for the boy.

Use the short story rubric, page 219, to evaluate this story.

Extended Activities

Have students write this story in the form of a play. Use dialogue. Refer to lessons 52 and 56. Perform the play.

Lesson 161
Letter Writing

1. Write to W. A. King, a real estate dealer in Erie, PA, telling him that you expect to move to that city and wish to rent a house.
   Refer to Lesson 27 for letter writing and use the letter writing rubric, page 221, for evaluation. Have students research Erie, PA on the Internet or in an encyclopedia or almanac. Erie, PA, is an industrial city in northwest Pennsylvania. It was named after the Great Lake, Erie. Being the fourth largest city in Pennsylvania, Erie is known for the manufacturing of plastics, steel, and iron. It also has manufacturing for locomotive building. Tourism has become increasingly important to the economy of the city.
2. Tell him the size of the house that you will need, and what rent you are willing to pay.
   Have students list what rooms they would want in a house and research how much the average rent for a house that size would be. There are many web sites listing houses for rent in Erie, PA. An extended activity would be to have students draw a floor plan of a house.
3. Write the reply, in which the real estate dealer describes a house which he has for rent, and states the price.
   Refer to Lesson 27 for letter writing and use the letter rubric, page 221, for evaluation. Students can make up an address for Mr. W. A. King.

Lesson 162
Picture Study—
Summer Evening

1. **What in the picture suggests the title?**
   The title is Summer Evening *and the shadows in the lake suggest the sun is setting.*
2. **Have you seen places in the country similar to this?**
   Answers will vary.
3. **Which part of the picture is the center of interest?**
   The woman carrying a jug is the center of interest.
4. **Does the dress of the woman tell anything about her?**
   The dress the woman is wearing is not ornate. It looks as though she is a working woman, carrying water back to her cottage in a village.
5. **What do you see on the other bank of the river?**
   On the other bank of the river are two other women who are gathering water from the lake.
6. **What is in the far distance?**
   In the far distance is a building that looks like it is probably a farm or a home.
7. **If you were to add to the picture, what would you put to the right? In front? To the left?**
   Answers will vary.
8. **Write a short description of a summer evening.**
   Answers will vary. Suggest students go outside in early evening and write their observations.

Extended Activity

Based on students' answers for question #8, have students draw their picture with the additions.

Lesson 163
Study of Words

1. **Make a list of twelve or more words that tell of size, weight, height, or depth; as gigantic, extensive, tiny.**
   Have students come up with words on their own, then have students use a thesaurus to add words they do not know. Example words—enormous, huge, colossal, gargantuan, broad, wide, ample, spacious, expansive, petite, miniscule, infinitesimal.
2. **Which words in your list describe the following:**
   A. mountain
   Mountains will be described in terms of size and height—enormous, gargantuan, or tall.
   B. river
   Rivers will be described in terms of length or depth—extensive, elongated, tapered, shallow, or deep.

C. tree

Trees will be described in terms of height or width—refer to A. mountain.

D. plain

Plains would be described in terms of width—spacious, expansive, open, or broad.

E. flower

Flowers will be described like trees, only flowers are small so words such as petite, or little are more appropriate than words that describe something large.

F. man

A man can be described in terms of height, width and weight. Words that describe a heavy man are portly, obese, plump or stout. Words that describe a thin man are lean, emaciated, skeletal, or undernourished.

G. valley

A valley would be described similar to a plain.

H. cloud

A cloud will be described in terms of weight—fluffy, light, feathery or downy.

3. **Write sentences containing the various words on your list.**

   Answers will vary. Verify that students have written a sentence containing a complete subject and predicate.

Lesson 164

Selection for Study—"Woodman, Spare That Tree"

Teacher Note

George Pope Morris (1802-1864) was born in Philadelphia, Pennsylvania. He had a distinguished career as an editor, founding the *New York Mirror*. He published many poems during his life.

1. **Describe a picture that would illustrate the first stanza of the poem.**

   In the first stanza students may picture a tall, leafy tree with a man standing next to it. The man is talking to a woodsman.

2. **Why does the author wish to protect the tree?**

   The author wishes to protect the tree because "in [his] youth it sheltered [him]" and his forefather "placed it near his cot."

3. **Read the lines that show why the tree was dear to the poet.**

   Lines that show why the tree was dear to the poet are: "I sought its grateful shade," "my sisters played" under the tree, and "My mother kissed me here; My father pressed my hand."

4. **Explain the first and second lines of the fourth stanza.**

   "My heartstrings round thee cling, close as thy bark, old friend" is a simile. The speaker's feelings for the tree are close to his heart as bark is close to the tree.

5. **Find in the poem examples of the following:**

A. Person spoken to

Person spoken to in stanza one, the first and seventh lines: "Woodman spare that tree!"; "There woodman, let it stand"; in stanza two, the fifth line: "Woodman, forebear thy stroke"; and in the sixth line of the fourth stanza: "And, woodman, leave the spot."

B. Contractions

Contractions—I'll, o'er, I've

C. Possessive form

Possessive form—forefather's hand, his cot, thy stroke, its earthbound ties, its grateful shade, my hand, my heartstrings, thy bark, thy branches, thy axe

D. Plurals formed by adding *s* to the singular

Plurals formed by adding s *to the singular—ties, sisters, heartstrings*

E. Plurals formed by adding *es* to the singular

Plurals formed by adding es *to the singular—skies, branches*

Extended Activity

Have students define the following words—

    bough—*a branch of a tree (noun)*

    forefather—*an ancestor (noun)*

    renown—*fame (adjective)*

    hew—*to strike with an ax (verb)*

    forebear—*withhold, restrain (verb)*

    idle—*passing time doing nothing (adjective)*

Have students rewrite the poem using more vernacular vocabulary. After students have rewritten the poem, have them analyze whether the poems have the same tone or emotion. Which version sounds more poetic?

Lesson 165

Composition—A Plea For Life

Have students plan their essay before they begin to write.

Use the diagram on the next page to help the students plan their essays.

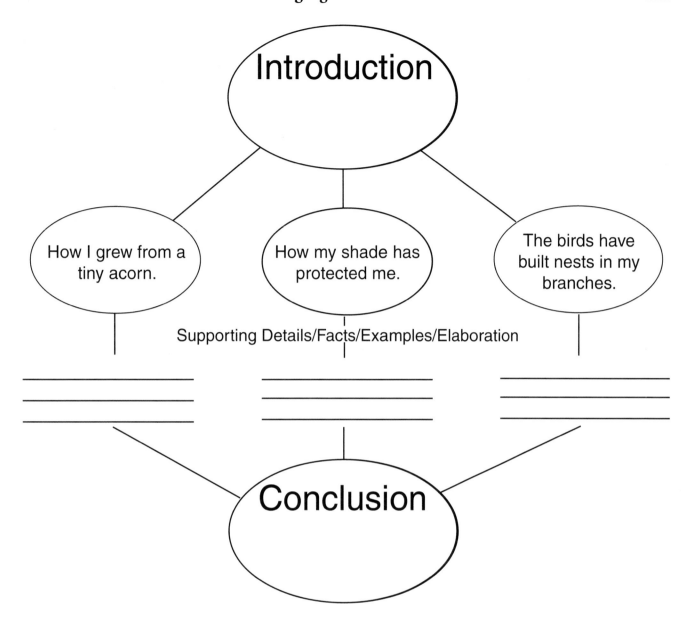

Lesson 166

Review—Singular and Plural

Copy the following words, and write after each its plural form.

loaf *loaves*	**knife** *knives*	**brush** *brushes*	**goose** *geese*
fox *foxes*	**crow** *crows*	**field** *fields*	**sky** *skies*
sheep *sheep*	**branch** *branches*	**lady** *ladies*	**family** *families*
man *men*	**word** *words*	**cow** *cows*	**ox** *oxes*
calf *calves*	**echo** *echoes*	**basket** *baskets*	**storm** *storms*
insect *insects*	**worm** *worms*	**deer** *deer*	**wolf** *wolves*
city *cities*	**robin** *robins*	**bench** *benches*	**meadow** *meadows*
bough *boughs*	**baby** *babies*	**church** *churches*	**farmer** *farmers*
child *children*	**country** *countries*	**eagle** *eagles*	**thief** *thieves*

box *boxes*	**arch** *arches*	**sister** *sisters*	**century** *centuries*
potato *potatoes*	**fairy** *fairies*	**cricket** *crickets*	**mouse** *mice*
daisy *daisies*	**wife** *wives*	**woman** *women*	**man** *men*

paragraph *paragraphs*

Lesson 167
Kinds of Sentences

A. Do not cut down that great tree.
B. It has stood for many years
C. Birds have built their nests in its branches.
D. Do you not see how strong it is?
E. Will you not stop and rest in its shade?
F. Put away your axe.
G. The tree is saved!
H. Long live the great tree!

1. **Which of these sentences ask questions?**
Note: A sentence that asks a question is called an **interrogative sentence**.
   D and E ask questions and are interrogative sentences.
2. **Which sentences command or request?**
Note: A sentence that commands or requests is called an **imperative sentence**.
   A and F make commands and are imperative sentences.
3. **Which sentences exclaim?**
Note: A sentence that exclaims, or is introduced by what or how (not asking questions), is called an **exclamatory sentence**.
   G and H exclaim and are exclamatory sentences.
4. **Which sentences state something?**
Note: A sentence that states something is a **declarative sentence**.
   B and C make a statement and are declarative sentences.
5. **Write three declarative sentences about the picture on page 147.**
   Answers will vary. Examples of declarative sentences for the picture on page 147:
   Three girls are standing on the shore.
   A boat is ready to leave the shore.
   Clouds are gathering in the sky.
6. **Write three interrogative sentences about the picture on page 103.**
   Answers will vary. Examples of interrogative sentences about the picture on page 103:
   How many fish have the fishermen caught?
   Where are the fishermen going?
   What kind of sailboat are the fishermen sailing?
7. **Write three exclamatory sentences suggested by the picture on page 82.**

Answers will vary. Examples of exclamatory sentences suggested by the picture on page 82:

The dog is hurt!

The poor dog!

The boy is helping the dog!

8. **Write three imperative sentences that command.**

Answers will vary. Have students think of commands their parents give them or commands they make to their younger siblings. Examples of imperative sentences that make a command:

Take out the garbage.

Slow down!

Do your homework.

9. **Write three imperative sentences that make requests.**

Answers will vary. Examples of imperative sentences that make a request:

Help your brother pick up his toys.

Please, feed the dog.

Please, call your friend on his birthday.

Lesson 168
Letter Writing

1. **Write one of the following letters, and the reply.**
   A. Henry Andrews, who lives at Hickory Grove, Iowa, R. D. 4, writes to Barnett Bros., 854 State Street, Chicago, IL, asking the cost of a box of tools; he states what he wishes the box to contain.
   B. Mrs. Ethel Edwards, who lives at Forestville, ME, writes to Cooper Dry Goods Co., Portland, ME, asking the price of a set of furs; she states what kind of furs she prefers.
   Note: In the reply to this letter the salutation should be *Dear Madam*.

Use the letter writing rubric, page 221, for evaluation. Have students address an envelope (outlines on page 226) to go with the letter. Students can also go online to find out about tools, tool prices, furs, and fur prices. R. D. stands for Rural Delivery and ME is the postal abbreviation for Maine.

Lesson 169
Selection for Study—"Legend of the Arbutus"

1. **Tell the story of the "Legend of the Arbutus."**
   The question is asking students to summarize the story. A summary is a short version of a longer piece that captures the most important parts of the original. A summary tests a student's understanding of the original and a student's ability to state the main idea. As much as possible

a summary should be written in the student's own words.

Example summary of the "Legend of the Arbutus": In the Northland there was an old man who lived in a wigwam. It was very, very cold. One day a beautiful woman entered the wigwam. The old man told the woman he was Winter and that when he nodded his head snow fell and it becomes bitter cold. The woman said she was Spring and that when she nodded her head the gentle breezes blow and the earth is glad. As the woman was talking the old man disappeared and where he had lain was a mass of leaves from which pink and white flowers emerged. The flower was the arbutus. The woman said to the flower that whoever picks it will know that winter has ended and spring is near.

2. **Make a list of the pictures that might be used to illustrate this story. Write a short description of one of them.**

   Answers will vary. As an extended activity have students find a picture of an arbutus and a wigwam. Have students draw their pictures.

3. **Find in the story four different ways in which capital letters are used.**

   Capital letters are used in four different ways: to begin a sentence, to name a person (Winter, Spring), to name a place (the Northland), and to title a story ("Legend of the Arbutus").

Lesson 170
Conversation—The Post Office

1. **What is done to the envelope at the post office, before the letter is sent?**

   When letters arrive at the post office they are sorted according to the Zip Code. Every area is assigned a number which is referred to as the Zone Improvement Plan or Zip Code. Letters are dumped into a Dual Pass Rough Cull System (DPRCS) which automatically sorts the mail. Items of unusual size are removed from this system and sorted manually. Letters are then sent to a central sorting office then shipped to its destination.

2. **Why must every envelope bear a stamp?**

   Postage stamps are evidence that a person has pre-paid for postal services. Other ways of paying for sending letters and packages are to mail items in pre-paid postage envelopes or to mail items that have been marked through a postage meter.

3. **What are the duties of a postman? How does he carry the mail? At what time of the year are his burdens the heaviest?**

   A postman's duty is to deliver the mail. Some postmen carry mail in a bag and walk to each house or business in a selected area. These postmen usually work in highly populated areas. A rural postman usually delivers the mail while driving a vehicle. A postman's burdens are usually the heaviest during holiday times, such as Christmas, when it is tradition to send cards and gifts.

4. **If the postman cannot find the person to whom the letter belongs, what is done with it?**

   If the postman cannot find the person to whom the letter belongs, it is returned to the sender;

therefore, it is important to put a return address on all items sent. If the letter is not returned to the sender, the sender can request that the letter be traced. Today everything is computerized so that all the Post Office has to do is input a tracking number and the letter can be retrieved. If a letter does not have a return address nor a tracking number, the letter is considered a "dead letter" and is sent to a location where the postman opens the letter and from the contents tries to identify an address at which to send the letter.

5. **Tell what you can about rural delivery.**

   Rural delivery is the delivery route in which the population is less than a city and one in which the postman has to cover more miles. The postman who delivers to rural areas typically drives and is usually not required to wear a uniform.

6. **Tell what you can about parcel post.**

   Parcel Post is a method of mailing packages. This method is often inexpensive and slower than other methods of mailing. Parcel post is most often used when mailing heavy packages up to 70 pounds.

7. **What do you understand by special delivery?**

   Special delivery refers to letters and packages that have special importance, and which may require special handling, such as fragile contents, etc.

8. **What does it cost to send a letter by special delivery?**

   Delivery rates vary and change occasionally. Have students refer to the United States Postal Service web site to get the answer to this question (www.usps.com) or students can contact their local post office.

9. **How may money be sent safely by mail?**

   Money can safely be sent by mail. Usually it is best to not mail cash, but rather a check so that in the event something does happen the person can cancel the check. A person can also purchase insurance for letters and packages of special value. A person can send the letter Certified Mail. If a letter is Certified, the receiver must sign for the letter and then the sender is notified that it was received.

10. **What do you understand by registered mail?**

    Registered Mail is an item that when sent has its details recorded to track its location. Registered Mail ensures and gives proof of delivery.

11. **Trace a letter sent from your home to 654 Broadway, New York, NY.**

    Today, the United States Postal Service and other mail delivery companies offer tracking service. Depending on how one mails an item, it can be given an identification number. With this number a person can track the progress of an item as it is enroute to its destination. Customers can go online and enter the I.D. number and the computer will inform the sender of the item's progress. According to the USPS regular mail cannot be tracked. Tracking information is available up to two years. After 90 days, the information is archived. For more information, students can access the USPS web site.

12. **At least how many people would have to handle it before it reached its destination?**

    Because of computerization and the invention of the DPRCS, approximately three to four people handle a letter.

Lesson 171
Description—A Postage Stamp

1. **Examine different kinds of postage stamps.**
    (See below.)
2. **Describe one of them. Tell what pictures and printing you find on it. Tell why you think the picture was chosen.**
    1-2. Students can refer to the web site of the United States Postal Service (www.usps.com) to see pictures of different stamps and to get the background of why a particular stamp was chosen.
3. **If you have any foreign stamps, compare them with those of the United States.**
    Answers will vary. If a student does not have a foreign stamp, many web sites show pictures and give explanations of foreign stamps. Have students research these web sites.

Extended Activity
Have students design their own postage stamp. Have them write a letter or give a speech persuading the United States Postal Service to adopt the stamp and put it into circulation.

Lesson 172
Titles

A. The children sang, "Home Sweet Home."
B. *Black Beauty* is the story of a horse.*
C. The subject of his composition was "Happy Days on the Farm."
D. Do you read *The Daily News*?*

1. **A. What book is named in these sentences?**
    Black Beauty *is the title of a novel and should be underlined or italicized.* *
    B. What composition?
    "Happy Days on the Farm" is a composition.
    C. What song?
    "Home Sweet Home" is a song.
    D. What newspaper?
    The Daily News *is a newspaper title.* *
2. **What marks enclose titles of poems, books, etc., when they are used in a sentence?***
    Marks that enclose titles of poems, short stories, etc. are quotation marks.
3. **Do all the words in every title begin with capital letters? Note: Titles of poems, books, etc. when used in a sentence are sometimes italicized.***
    No, not all words in a title are capitalized. Small, common words such as a, an, the, of *and* for *are typically not capitalized, unless they are the first word of the title.*
4. **Write sentences containing the name of—**

A. a song

B. a poem

C. a book you have read

D. a book you wish to read

E. a newspaper

F. a subject for a composition.

Answers will vary. Please check to see that each was correctly punctuated according to the teacher's note.

Teacher Note*

Practice has changed since the original release of the textbook in 1914. Specifically: titles of short stories, songs, compositions, newspaper articles, and poems are put inside quotation marks. Titles of books, newspapers, plays, movies, paintings, ships, and CDs are either underlined or put in italics.

Lesson 173
Letter Writing

A. George Randall, Fremont, VA, writes to Mr. W. T. Blair of the Public Library of Richmond, VA, asking for a list of ten books suitable for boys to read. (Such a letter should enclose a stamp for the answer.)

B. Edith Randall writes for a similar list of books for girls.

1. Write one of the letters, and a reply.

Use the letter writing rubric, page 221, to evaluate students' work. To find information on books for boys and girls, students can go to their public or school library and request the information from the librarian. Many web sites offer suggested lists of books for boys and girls. Students can do a search by typing "list of books for boys/girls".

Lesson 174
Selection to be Memorized

Neither a borrower nor a lender be;
For loan oft loses both itself and friend,
And borrowing dulls the edge of husbandry.
This above all: to thine own self be true,
And it must follow, as the night the day,
Thou canst not then be false to any man.
—William Shakespeare

1. How does a loan often lose "both itself and friend?"

A loan is when a person borrows money from someone. It is wise to not borrow money. Borrowing money often results in the loss of the money because it can be hard to repay, and the loaner will often have hard feelings towards the borrower if the money is not repaid.

2. **Explain the third line.**

"Borrowing dulls the edge of husbandry." Husbandry is the management of resources. If one has to borrow then he probably has not managed his resources well, and without working in exchange for money that management can be dulled.

3. **Tell what you think the poet meant by the last two lines.**

The last two lines, "And it must follow, as the night the day,/Thou canst not then be false to any man." refer to the line above: "to thine own self be true." If a person is true and honest to himself, then he will be true and honest to others. This follows naturally just as the night follows the day.

4. **Memorize the poem.**

(See below.)

5. **Write the poem from memory.**

Use the memorization rubric, page 218, to evaluate student's ability to memorize this poem.

Teacher Note

This poem is an excerpt from Shakespeare's *Hamlet*. Polonius offers these words of advice to his son who is ready to leave for France.

Lesson 175
Formation of Sentences

A. Two children went out to play in the new-fallen snow.
B. It was a cold winter day.
C. The sun shone after a long storm.
One cold winter day, when the sun shone after a long storm, two little children went out to play in the new-fallen snow.

1. **Notice that the three short sentences were combined into one long one. Which form do you like better?**

Students should like the combined sentences better. Combining sentences make the flow of ideas smoother than short, choppy sentences. Combining sentences demonstrates more mature writing.

2. **Combine each of the following groups into a single sentence; change some of the words if necessary:**

A. The south wind came to see what the storm had done. The south wind lives in the land of summer.

The south wind, who lives in the land of summer, came to see what the storm had done.

B. He blew his soft breath against the snowflakes. The snowflakes disappeared.

When he blew his soft breath against the snowflakes, they disappeared.

C. The elm tree stood by the gate. The elm tree shook its branches. The elm tree said, "I think spring has come; I must wake my buds."

While the elm tree stood by the gate shaking its branches, it said, "I think spring has come; I must wake my buds."

D. The seeds had slept all winter under the dead leaves. The seeds heard the south wind calling. The seeds said, "It must be time to rise; we hear the sounds of spring."

The seeds, who had slept all winter under the dead leaves, heard the south wind calling and said, "It must be time to rise; we hear the sounds of spring."

E. The robin had been in the Southland. The robin heard the call of spring. The robin said, "I must go north again; it is time to build my nest."

The robin, who had been in the Southland, heard the call of spring and said, "I must go north again; it is time to build my nest."

3. **Write five groups of short sentences and change each group to a single sentence.**

Answers will vary. Teachers may use these additional sentences for students to combine:

A. The robin built a nest. He built it in the oak tree. The robin lives in my back yard.

The robin who lives in my backyard built a nest in the oak tree.

B. I heard the robin sing. The robin sang, "Let the soft rain fall and let the flowers bloom." The robin sat in the oak tree.

I heard the robin who sat in the oak tree sing, "Let the soft rain fall and let the flowers bloom."

C. The robin needed to feed her young. The robin went to look for food. The robin found worms.

The robin, who needed to feed her young, went to look for food and found worms.

Lesson 176
Picture Study—
Return of the Mayflower

1. **Tell what you can about the Pilgrims.**

Pilgrims came to America for many religious reasons. One of these reasons was their desire to escape the persecution they endured because of their religious beliefs. Pilgrims were the early settlers of the Plymouth Colony in Massachusetts. They are known for having established a government document named the "Mayflower Compact" and for celebrating the first Thanksgiving.

2. **What was the name of the ship in which they came to America?**

The name of the ship in which they came to America was the Mayflower.

3. **This picture represents the return of the ship to England.**

4. **Describe the picture.**

The picture shows pilgrims standing on the shore watching the Mayflower *sail off into the distance.*

5. **Which are the principal figures?**

The principal figures are the man and woman standing in the foreground.

6. **What do you think must have been the feelings of the people who remained in America?**
Since America was largely an uncivilized land, the pilgrims were probably worried about the work of establishing a new community. They would have to find resources for food and shelter. However, the pilgrims were persistent people and were probably excited about their new freedom and opportunity.

Teacher Note

George Henry Boughton (1834-1905) was born in England but grew up in Albany, New York. As an adult he lived mostly in London. He painted many pictures that were popular in both England and America.

Lesson 177
Letter Writing

Write a letter to a cousin in England. Tell of the new country, the Indians, the hunting and fishing, and an incident that might happen in a child's life.
While this assignment asks students to write a letter, the content of that letter is descriptive. Teachers can choose to use the letter writing rubric, page 221, or the short story rubric, page 219, to evaluate the writing. Refer to students' work in Lesson 22. Students may need to gather information about Pilgrims. They may search the Internet or reference the following:
A First Book in American History *by Edward Eggleston—Chapter V "Captain John Smith", Chapter VII "The Story of Pocahontas", Chapter IX "Captain Myles Standish", Chapter X "Myles Standish and the Indians."*
A History of the United States and Its People *by Edward Eggleston—Chapter VII "The Coming of the Pilgrims" and Chapter XII "How the Indians Lived."*
Mary of Plymouth, *while historical fiction, is a letter home from Plymouth in book form and may be useful as a reference to life in the fledgling colony.*

Lesson 178
Selection for Study

1. **What is the meaning of "aye" and "ensign"?**
"Aye" is a word of confirmation and often means yes. An "ensign" is a flag or banner. Sometimes it can be an emblem.

2. **Explain the third and fourth lines of the first stanza.**

    The lines "And many an eye has danced to see/ That banner in the sky" refer to the many people who looked to the banner flying on the Constitution. It is almost as if the banner flying on the ship had become a tradition.

3. **To what does the seventh line refer?**

    The seventh line is a metaphor. The author is comparing the power, speed and light, of the Constitution *to a meteor. As a meteor blazes across the sky, the* Constitution *blazes across the ocean.*

4. **What is the meaning of "vanquished foe"?**

    "Vanquished" means defeated and a "foe" is an enemy, therefore a "vanquished foe" is the defeated enemy who surrendered or "knelt" to the ship.

5. **In the third stanza explain "shattered hulk."**

    The "shattered hulk" is the ruined, old or damaged body of the ship.

6. **What did the poet think should be done with the ship?**

    The poet thinks the ship ought to continue to be used until it "sink(s) beneath the wave... and there should be her grave" rather than taking it out of service and destroying it.

7. **Account for uses of the apostrophe in the poem.**

    The apostrophe is used several times in this poem. It is used to show possession- "cannon's roar," "heroes' blood," "victor's tread," and it was used to show a contraction—"o'er."

Extended Activity

This poem was written by Oliver Wendell Holmes; who along with Henry Wadsworth Longfellow, John Greenleaf Whittier, and William Cullen Bryant; was another great American Fireside poet. Research Holmes using the Internet and/or an encyclopedia to answer the following questions.

1. **When was Holmes born?**

    Holmes was born on August 29, 1809.

2. **Where was he born?**

    He was born in Cambridge, Massachusetts.

3. **What was his father's occupation?**

    His father was a clergyman and the author of the Annals of America.

4. **Where did Holmes attend school?**

    Holmes studied at Phillips Andover Academy and graduated from Harvard. He also studied in Paris.

5. **What was his area of study?**

    Holmes studied medicine and anatomy.

6. **What poem first brought him prominence?**

    The poem that first brought him prominence was "Old Ironsides."

7. **What are some titles of his other famous poems? Choose one of these and copy it.**

    Some of his other famous poems are "The Chambered Nautilus," "The Height of the Ridiculous," and "The Deacon's Masterpiece."

8. **Tell something of his personality.**

    Holmes was known for his wit and positive disposition.

9. **What character created by Sir Conan Doyle was patterned after Holmes?**

Sir Conan Doyle is rumored to have been inspired to create Dr. Watson, Sherlock Holmes's friend, after Oliver Wendell Holmes.

10. **When did Holmes die?**

Holmes died on October 7, 1894.

Lesson 179
Study of Words

The word *plot* means nearly the same as plan.

Note: Words that have the same meaning are called synonyms.

1. Find in Column B a synonym for each word in column A; write the words in pairs, thus, plot—plan.

A.	B.
lessen	high
generous	sure
grand	busy
ancient	joy
industrious	old
courageous	misfortune
famous	magnificent
lofty	scold
splendid	quiet
scheme	celebrated
disaster	bold
happiness	superb
certain	liberal
censure	plot
silent	diminish

lessen	*diminish*
generous	*liberal*
grand	*magnificent*
ancient	*old*
industrious	*busy*
courageous	*bold*
famous	*celebrated*
lofty	*high*
splendid	*superb*
scheme	*plot*
disaster	*misfortune*
happiness	*joy*

certain   *sure*
ensure   *scold*
silent   *quiet.*

Lesson 180
Description of an Old Mill

1. **Does this description present a picture to you?**

    The description should present at least two vivid pictures to the student. The first picture is described in the first paragraph—the location of the mill. The second picture is described in the third paragraph—the interior of the mill.

2. **After reading the description could you recognize the old mill if you were to pass it?**

    Students should be able to recognize the old mill if they were to pass it.

3. **Notice that in the first sentence the most important part is placed last. Rearrange the sentence so that this part shall be first. Do you like it as well? The first part of the sentence tells two things about the location of the mill.**

    The first sentence reads: "Near the waterfall where two roads meet, stands an old saw mill." The sentence rearranged reads: "An old saw mill stands near the waterfall where two roads meet." Answers will vary according to which sentence students like better. Both sentences have the same meaning.

4. **Use the following groups of words as parts of sentences; let the first part of each sentence answer the question where. Write two or more statements about the location of each object that you are describing.**

    A. …stood a cherry tree covered with blossoms.

    B. …was a ship that had fought many battles.

    C. …sat an old man

    D. …a mocking bird had build its nest.

    E. …lived a gray squirrel.

    F. …was a row of stately birches.

    Answers will vary. Example sentences:

    A. In the center of the park stood a cherry tree covered with blossoms.

    B. In the harbor was a ship that had fought many battles.

    C. On the park bench sat an old man.

    D. Within the thick branches of the cherry tree a mocking bird had built its nest.

    E. Near the garden lived a gray squirrel.

    F. Down Central Avenue was a row of stately birches.

Extended Activity

Have students draw the mill, or have students plot the location of the waterfall, sawmill, hill, little river, and oak tree according to the written description.

Lesson 181
Composition—A Description

1. Read again the description of an old mill given in Lesson 180.
2. Use the following outline in describing one of the buildings in the list below:
   A. Location
   B. Surroundings
   C. Material of which it is built
   D. Age
   E. Size
   F. Interior
   G. Incidents connected with the history of the building
   H. Adaptation to purpose it serves
   I. Improvements that might be made
   Church, Library, Post Office, School, Store, Factory, Railroad Station, Old Farmhouse
3. In some of your sentences place the important part last.

Use the essay rubric, page 220, to evaluate this descriptive essay.

Have students plan their essay before they begin to write. Encourage students to group A-H into four paragraphs (Paragraph 1 could be A-E, Paragraph 2 could be F, Paragraph 3 could be G-H, and Paragraph 4 could be I.) After students plan, have them write a rough draft of the essay. In the rough draft, have students underline their sentences that have the important part first. Analyze the number of sentences that have the important part first and then as students rewrite their final copy, have them vary their sentences by inverting several of them, putting the important part last.

Lesson 182
Description of a Person

1. Make an outline for the description of a person.
2. Use your outline in describing one of the following:
   A. a tramp
   B. an engineer
   C. a baby
   D. a policeman
   E. a blacksmith
   F. your mother

To outline begin by brainstorming. Take those ideas and organize related ideas together. Then to create an outline, ideas need to be organized from general to specific. The most general ideas will be labeled with a Roman numeral. As ideas begin to get more specific move to a capital letter, a number, then a lower case letter.

For example:

Vehicles
    I. Ford
       A. SUVs
          1. Explorer
          2. Expedition
       B. Cars
          1. Mustang
          2. Taurus
    II. Chevrolet

Notice that the roman numerals, capital letters and numbers are lined up evenly and that each is indented. The first word after the letter or number is to be capitalized.

Students may prefer to organize their essay using other graphic organizers besides the formal essay. Typically in a five paragraph essay, students should have an introduction, three main points regarding the topic, and a conclusion. Refer to Lesson 165 for an alternative to organizing an essay.

Lesson 183
Selection to be Memorized

1. **What are the eyes of the night?**
   The eyes of night are the stars. The poem states there are "thousands" of them.
2. **What is the eye of day?**
   The eye of day is the sun. The poem states that there is but "one."
3. **Explain the fifth line.**
   The fifth line means that the mind can think and dream a "thousand" things.
4. **Memorize the poem.**
   Use the memorization rubric, page 218, to evaluate.
5. **Write the poem from memory.**
   Compare the poem on page 101 with what the student wrote.

Lesson 184
Correct Use of Words

1. **What are synonyms?**
   Synonyms are words that mean the same. For example, chubby, fat, and obese all mean someone who is overweight.
2. **What are homonyms?**
   Homonyms are words that sound the same but have different spellings and different meanings. The words in #3 are homonyms.

3. **Use the following homonyms in sentences:**
   Answers will vary. Example sentences:

   A. there, their
   There are three birds in the nest. Their mother has gone to look for food.

   B. herd, heard
   The herd was moved to the other pasture. I heard that coyotes have been stalking them.

   C. flour, flower
   Flour was the main ingredient in the cake recipe. I cut a flower to put in the vase.

   D. sea, see
   The sea was churning with rough waves. I see the storm approaching.

   E. here, hear
   The children are here in the play room. I hear them laughing.

   F. by, buy
   I will go by the store on my way home. I will buy a loaf of bread.

   G. hare, hair
   The hare hid in the garden. His hair was soft brown.

   H. sent, cent, scent
   I sent my aunt a card. The postage used to cost a cent. My card had a floral scent.

   I. fair, fare
   I went to the county fair. The fare to enter was three dollars.

   J. o'er, oar
   The ship sailed o'er the sea. The man used an oar to move his little fishing boat.

   K. be, bee
   I hope to be an environmentalist some day. I will study the bee.

   L. stair, stare
   I tripped on the stair of my front door. I saw my guest stare at my misfortune.

   M. vale, veil
   The storm ripped through the vale. The lady wore a veil to the funeral.

Lesson 185

Letter Writing

Tom Evans writes to his uncle, George A. Evans, a rich man, calling attention to the condition of a poor family in the neighborhood.

1. **Write a letter, telling about the family and their needs.**
   Answers will vary. Use the letter writing rubric, page 221, to evaluate this assignment.

Lesson 186
Composition—A Story

Early one morning, Harry Ford heard a noise on the back porch. He opened the door and there on the steps was a poor little dog that held up a lame foot and cried pitifully.

1. Finish the story. Tell how Harry took care of the dog, what tricks he taught his pet, and what games they played together.
2. Let the last part of the story tell of something that the dog did for Harry, or for some other member of his family.

Have students plan their story before they begin to write. Have students utilize the story map, page 225.

To evaluate this assignment use the short story rubric, page 219.

Lesson 187
An Imaginary Diary

1. Review Lesson 145.
2. Write a diary of a Maltese kitten, for one week. Include something about
   A. The kitten's home,
   B. Its master or mistress,
   C. Other pets in the family,
   D. Some incident that might happen to a kitten.

When students write the diary, verify that the student included a date for each entry using the correct abbreviation for the month. Also, check that the student included information about A-D in the diary. The teacher may want to instruct the student to have at least four entries in the diary.

Lesson 188
Picture Study—
The Spinner

Students will need to use an encyclopedia or search the Internet for information to answer the following questions.

1. **Describe the picture.**

   The picture is of an old woman bending over a spinning wheel. It appears as if she is threading the distaff.

2. **Tell what you can of the process of spinning and weaving used in early days.**

   Spinning is the process of twisting wool fibers into a yarn. The spinner used to be spun by hand. Later the wheel could be spun by foot or electricity.

3. **How was the spindle used?**

   The spindle is the part of the spinning wheel that is used to add twist to the fiber and hold the fiber together. The spindle is usually stabilized by a weight.

4. **Of what use was the distaff?**

   The distaff is the tool designed to hold the unspun fibers.

5. **Tell something of the manufacture of woolen goods at the present time.**

   Answers will vary. Modern manufacturing of woolen goods is fairly simple and provides for mass production of goods. First, when the wool arrives at the factory, it is sorted according to quality and length. The wool then goes through several stages of cleansing. The wool is first washed and dried then machines pick out burrs and other impurities. The wool is washed again in a process called carbonizing. This process takes out the vegetable matter. Once this is completed the wool is put into another machine that oils the wool. Oiling allows the wool to work easily in the spinning machines and prevents fibers from flying about. Finally the wool is carded and put on the spinning machines.

6. **Does the picture interest you?**

   Answers will vary.

7. **Compare it with *The Gleaners*, page 210. In what ways are the pictures similar?**

   The Gleaners is a picture of three women picking wheat. In both pictures a woman is bending over her work. (See extension activity.)

8. **Why do you suppose an artist chose such a subject for a painting?**

   Answers will vary. It is probable that the artist admired the necessity of spinning as well as the art of spinning.

9. **If the spinner had been a young woman, would the picture have been more pleasing?**

   Answers will vary. Today students might respond that to see a young woman spinning would seem out of place, since spinning is a rare craft.

10. **Do such pictures make you feel more kindly toward the aged and poor?**

    Answers will vary. Hopefully, students will appreciate the work ethic and knowledge of crafts such as spinning old people possess.

11. **Mention subjects that might be used for pictures that you have suggested.**

    Answers will vary.

12. **Describe one of the pictures that you have suggested.**

    Answers will be dependent on how students respond to #11.

Teacher Note

Nicolas Maes (1634-1693) was a Dutch painter. The style of his early works strikingly resemble that of Rembrandt. Maes often painted domestic life. His favorite subjects were women

spinning, weaving, reading the Bible, or preparing a meal. Later in life he focused on painting portraits. His work can be seen in museums all over the world.

Extended Activity

The Spinner and *The Gleaners* have some things in common. Compare and contrast the two paintings. Take into consideration the tone, subject, shading, background and artists. Use the Venn Diagram, page 227, to show what they have in common and how they are different.

Lesson 189
Selection for Study

1. **What is the meaning of "inherit," "heritage," "sinewy," "benign"?**
   Inherit—(verb) to receive from an heir; heritage—(noun) something that comes to a person by reason of birth; sinewy—(adjective) vigorous or tough; benign—(adjective) a kindly disposition.
2. **What are the things that a rich man's son inherits?**
   A rich man's son inherits "lands," "piles of brick and stone and gold," and "soft white hands."
3. **Why do these things bring him cares?**
   These things bring him cares because "the bank may break, the factory burn" and "a breath may burst his bubble shares."
4. **What does a poor man's son inherit?**
   A poor man's son inherits "stout muscles and a sinewy heart, a hardy frame" and "a hardier spirit."
5. **Tell in your own words the substance of the fourth stanza.**
   The fourth stanza explains that by working hard and learning to be patient, one develops "courage if sorrow come[s]."
6. **Explain, "A patience learned of being poor."**
   "A patience learned of being poor" means that if one is poor he must wait to attain the things he wants. Being poor requires that one must save and plan.
7. **In the fifth stanza, what toil may the rich man's son possess?**
   In the fifth stanza a rich man's son can toil by giving to charity.
8. **What is meant by the second line of the sixth stanza?**
   The line "There is worse weariness than thine" means that one should not despair over his condition because there are others who live in a more desperate state.
9. **Explain the fifth line of the sixth stanza.**
   The line "And makes rest fragrant and benign" means that the harder one works the more he can enjoy his sleep in peace and take pride in his labors.
10. **How might a rich man benefit your town or city by charity?**
    Answers will vary. In some towns a man may give money to help the schools, help feed the poor, help house the poor. There are many charitable organizations. Have students research those organizations that exist in their town.

11. **Would the giving of a playground or park be charity?**

    The giving of a playground or park is charitable because it not only makes the town beautiful, but provides a place for children and families to play.

12. **Which is better charity, to give a poor man a sum of money or to give him an opportunity to work at good wages? If you were poor which would you prefer?**

    Answers will vary. Students should recognize that there is value in working; therefore it would be a better charity to give a poor man the opportunity to work.

Extended Activities

1. Have students research charitable organizations in their town. Have them find a way that they could volunteer their time to help one of these charities. Students could also form a fund-raiser in which the money would be donated to a charity. Common types of charities students participate in are food and clothing drives. Students could also donate items to organizations such as Goodwill.

2. Have students discuss their generation's attitude towards work. What does the popular media say about hard work? Is there conflict between the message in this poem and the message espoused from their friends and community.

3. This poem was written by James Russell Lowell, who along with John Greenleaf Whittier and William Cullen Bryant, was another great American Fireside Poet. Research Lowell using the Internet and/or an encyclopedia to answer the following questions.

    A. **When was Lowell born?**

    Lowell was born February 22, 1819.

    B. **Where was he born?**

    He was born in Cambridge, Massachussetts.

    C. **What was his father's occupation?**

    His father's occupation was a clergyman.

    D. **Where did Lowell attend school?**

    Lowell attended Harvard.

    E. **What was his area of study?**

    He studied law.

    F. **When was his first poem published?**

    His first poem was published in 1841 at the age of 22.

    G. **What poem first brought him prominence?**

    A poem that brought him prominence was "The Cathedral."

    H. **What are some titles of his other famous poems? Choose one of these and copy it.**

    Some of his other poems were: "Fireside Travels" and "Among My Books."

    I. **Tell something of his personality.**

    Lowell was considered gentle and concerned about political affairs.

    J. **When did Lowell die?**

    Lowell died August 12, 1891.

Lesson 190
Selection to be Memorized

1. Which people do you think are happier, those who have regular work to do, or those who spend their time in pleasure? Think of someone who seems to be very happy. Why is he happy? Do you think the very rich are any happier than other people?

   Answers will vary. Students are to realize that money alone does not make one happy.

2. Memorize the paragraph by Charles Kingsly.

   Use the memorization rubric, page 218, to evaluate students' recitation of this paragraph.

3. Write the paragraph from memory.

   Compare students' writing to the paragraph.

Lesson 191
Composition

1. Write a composition, stating what characteristics you like in a boy or girl, and what traits you do not like.
2. In your composition you may refer to—

   A. Qualities of mind,

   B. Disposition

   C. Habits

   D. Personal appearance, including neatness.

   Use the short story rubric, page 219, to evaluate this assignment.

Lesson 192
Quotations

1. Bring to class quotations and stories to illustrate the following topics: *politeness, industry, truthfulness, kindness to animals.*

Lesson 193
Selection to be Memorized—"Today"

1. What lesson do you think the author meant that this poem should teach?

This lesson should teach that a day comes and it goes and one cannot get it back. One should use his time wisely.

2. **What do you understand by "useless" day? How might such a day be spent?**
   A "useless" day is one in which nothing is accomplished. A day might be spent reading, studying, playing and sharing time with others, working for wages, or giving to charity.

3. **Use in sentences:**
   Answers will vary.
      A. eternity
      B. aforetime
      C. behold
      D. dawning

4. **Memorize the poem.**
   Use the memorization rubric, page 218, to evaluate this assignment.

Lesson 194
Composition

1. **Write a composition with two parts. In Part One, tell how a boy or girl let a day "slip useless away."**
   (See below.)

2. **In Part Two, tell how a boy or girl did not let the day "slip useless away."**
   This assignment is best suited for two paragraphs; however, a story could be written about both parts. To make this assignment suitable for a large class, assign half the class Part One and the other half of the class Part Two. Have students read their compositions out loud. Discuss the differences between the stories.

Lesson 195
Summary—Continued from Lesson 150

Teacher Note
Titles of books, plays, newspapers, and paintings should be underlined or italicized. Titles of articles, poems, songs and short stories are put inside quotation marks.

Multiple Choice. Choose the correct answer.
1. *a. Sally and I went to the store.* **b. Me and Sally went to the store. c. Sally and me went to the store**

2. **a. After the movie, Tom, me, and Jane went to the pizza parlor.** *b. After the movie, Tom, Jane, and I went to the pizza parlor.* **c. After the movie, me, Tom, and Jane went to the pizza parlor.**

3. For the given word, choose the letter of its synonym:
   Honesty: a. dishonest, *b. sincerity,* c. trickery
   Benign: *a. caring,* b. cruel, c. malevolent
   Sinewy: a. puny, b. frail, *c. strong*

4. Underline the part of the sentence that illustrates personification: The *Sun smiled* upon the children.

5. Circle the word that should be capitalized: Honesty and *integrity* are friends of those who wish to be respected.

6. Identify each sentence as interrogative, imperative, exclamatory or declarative.
   a. The boy designed a kite. *declarative*
   b. Will the wind carry it to the skies? *interrogative*
   c. Run faster to pull it off the ground. *imperative*
   d. His design works! *exclamatory*

7. Rewrite each sentence making the appropriate changes in punctuation.
   a. Thomas Carlyle wrote the poem titled today.
   Thomas Carlyle wrote the poem titled "Today."
   b. The boy enjoyed the novel Little Men
   The boy enjoyed the novel, Little Men.
   c. I subscribe to the New Yorker, a monthly magazine.
   I subscribe to the New Yorker, *a monthly magazine.*
   d. My favorite Christmas song is Joy to the World.
   My favorite Christmas song is "Joy to the World."

Part Three

Lesson 196

"A Story about George Washington"

1. **What lesson do you think the author meant that this story should teach?**

   This story teaches that helping others is a virtue.

2. **Read the lines that show General Washington was ready to help his men and share their hardships.**

   General Washington was ready to help his men and share in their hardships. The lines that tell us this are: "At this moment Washington ran to them, and with his great strength gave them the needed help," and "Next time you have a log too heavy for your men to lift, send for me."

3. **What do you think must have been the feelings of the soldiers that General Washington helped?**

   The soldiers must have felt deep gratitude. The story says, "The grateful men thanked the stranger."

4. **What good qualities did General Washington show?**

   General Washington showed good qualities in this story. As a leader he was willing to do that which his men had to do.

5. **Why did the corporal not help the soldiers?**

   The corporal did not help his men because he thought he was better than his men, and as a corporal he didn't need to do the manual labor his men had to do.

6. **Make an outline of this story.**

   Answers will vary, but an outline of this story should be similar to the following:

   I. Setting—Cold weather, Washington traveling to visit a camp he ordered to be fortified

   II. The corporal and his men were building a breastwork of logs in which the men had difficulty lifting the logs.

   III. Washington stops to help the men.

   IV. Washington asks the corporal why he didn't help his men, then reveals who he was.

7. **Tell the story from your outline.**

   Answers will vary. Make sure that students follow the story chronologically and put it in their own words. Students' summaries should be no longer than a paragraph (6-8 sentences).

Lesson 197
Subject and Predicate

A. The moon is very beautiful
B. Its soft yellow light brightens the earth.

1. **What object is spoken about in the first sentence?**
   The moon is the object spoken about in the first sentence.
2. **What is said about the moon?**
   The moon is beautiful.
3. **What is spoken about in the second sentence?**
   The soft yellow light is what is spoken about in the second sentence.
4. **What is said about its soft yellow light?**
   What is said about the light is that it brightens the earth.
5. **What is the subject, and what is the predicate of the second sentence?**
   The light is the subject and brightens is the predicate of the second sentence.
6. **Write sentences, using the following as subjects:**
   A. The Panama Canal
   B. A range of high mountains
   C. The governor of our state
   D. The great Mississippi River
   Answers will vary. Students need to add predicates to the subjects given. For example:
   A. The Panama Canal contains many gates.
   B. A range of high mountains is in North Carolina.
   C. The governor of our state is running for a second term.
   D. The great Mississippi River ends in Louisiana.
7. **Write sentences, using the following as predicates:**
   A. is the largest state in the Union
   B. spins a web from which silk is made
   C. is made from the sap of a tree
   Answers will vary. Students need to add subjects to the predicates given. For example:
   A. Alaska is the largest state in the Union.
   B. A spider spins a web from which silk is made.
   C. Syrup is made from the sap of a tree.

Lesson 198
Selection for Study

1. **Compare this paragraph with "October's Bright Blue Weather," Lesson 124. Find references in the poem similar to those in the paragraph.**

Both "October's Bright Blue Weather" and the passage by Henry Ward Beecher are about the autumn. Both mention apples: "when on the ground red apples lie" and "apples drop in the stillest hours." Both selections also mention leaves falling to the ground: "Bright leaves sink noiseless in the hush of woods" and "Leaves begin to let go."

2. **Explain: "Swing in long waverings," "the winds rake them," "are tranquil," "gorgeous apparel."**

   The phrase "swing in long waverings" describes the listless falling of leaves to the ground. "The wind rakes them" describes the movement of the leaves on the ground when the wind blows. It is as if the wind is raking the leaves. "Are tranquil" means that the night is calm and peaceful. "Gorgeous apparel" describes autumn as a colorful time when the leaves turn from green to reds, oranges, and yellows.

3. **Write the quotation from dictation.**

   Compare students' work with the passage.

Lesson 199
Review

1. **Complete the following sentences by referring to the quotation from Henry Ward Beecher in Lesson 198:**

   A. There is an exclamation point after October, because *it is an exclamatory sentence*.

   B. There is a period after pods, because *it is a declarative sentence*.

   C. There is an apostrophe and s after year, because *it shows possession—work belongs to the year*.

   D. There is comma after sayeth, because *it introduces a direct quote*.

   E. There are quotation marks around *it is good*, because *"it is good" is a direct quotation*.

   F. *It* begins with a capital letter because *the first word of a direct quotation begins with a capital letter*.

2. **Copy the following sentences, and draw a line under the subject of each:**

   A. Ripened *seeds* shake in their pods.

   B. *Apples* drop in the stillest hours.

   C. *Leaves* fall to the ground.

   D. The *days* are calm.

   E. The *nights* are tranquil.

   F. The year's *work* is done.

   G. *She* walks in gorgeous apparel.

3. **Draw two lines under the predicate of each sentence (The students may use two lines to differentiate the subject from the predicate in the same sentence. The predicate is underlined with a *single line* in the answers below.)**

   A. Ripened seeds *shake* in their pods.

   B. Apples *drop* in the stillest hours.

   C. Leaves *fall* to the ground.

D. The days <u>are</u> calm.

E. The nights <u>are</u> tranquil.

F. The year's work <u>is</u> done.

G. She <u>walks</u> in gorgeous apparel.

Lesson 200
Selection to be Memorized

1. **What colors would be used in painting the picture suggested by the poem? Describe the picture.**
   Students should suggest that colors used in painting a picture suggested by the poem are reds, yellows, and oranges, and possibly dark greens and browns. This poem is about autumn. Have students paint an autumn picture or find one to illustrate this poem.
2. **Memorize the poem.**
   Use the memorization rubric, page 218, to evaluate this assignment.
3. **Write the poem from memory.**
   Compare the poem students write with the poem by William Herbert Carruth.

Lesson 201
Letter Writing

1. **Write a letter asking a friend to take dinner with you and go for a ride next Saturday. State at what time you will have dinner, and when you expect to return from the ride.**
   (See below.)
2. **Write a letter answering the invitation. If it is possible to accept, state why.**
   Use the letter writing rubric, page 221, to evaluate this assignment.

Lesson 202
Picture Study—
The Gleaners

The Gleaners **was painted by Jean Francois Millet, an artist who loved the peasant people of France.**

1. **The picture shows a broad wheat field where there had been a plentiful harvest. Three women**

have come to the field to pick up the stray pieces of wheat that the reapers have left. The artist has tried to portray the pathos of the poor peasant woman's life of toil and privation. Has he succeeded in his attempt?

Pathos means sorrow or misery. Students should answer that yes the artist has been successful in portraying the women's pathos.

2. **What colors do you think the artist used in painting the picture?**

Because the women are in a wheat field and because they are poor, the artist probably used dull colors such as browns, golds and grays.

3. **Notice that the figures of the women seem to stand out from the page. This effect was obtained by the skillful use of light and shade. Find the places where the light is strongest and where the shade is heaviest.**

Light is strongest in the sky and on the side of the ladies where the sun is shining on them. The sun is lowering towards the west, so the sun only reflects on that side of the ladies. The dark shades are most prevalent on the right side of the picture and on the ground.

4. **Describe the background of the picture. In what ways does it suggest that the owner of the field was a man of wealth?**

In the background are large and numerous stacks of wheat, suggesting a plentiful harvest.

5. **What part of the picture suggests poverty?**

The fact that the women are bending and have rags wrapped around their waists to carry the left over wheat suggests poverty. Also, the women are wearing work bonnets.

6. **Does the picture make you feel sad, or glad?**

Answers will vary. Most likely the picture will make the students feel sad. The mood of this picture is dismal.

Lesson 203
Compound Subject and Predicate

A. Men and women work in the fields, in France.
B. The reapers cut the grain and carry it to the barn.

1. **The first sentence has two subjects; name them.**
In the first sentence the subjects are men and women.
2. **What is the predicate of the first sentence?**
The predicate of the first sentence is work.
3. **What is the subject of the second sentence?**
The subject of the second sentence is reapers.
4. **Name the two predicates in the second sentence?**
The predicates in the second sentence are cut and carry.

Note: When two or more simple subjects are united they fom a compound subject.
Note: When two or more simple predicates are united they form a *compound predicate*.

5. **Name the subjects and predicates in the following sentences and tell which are compound:**

A. Bushes and trees were covered with soft white snow. *Bushes, trees—were covered*

B. Apples, peaches, and pears grew in the orchard. *Apples, peaches, pears—grew*

C. The farmer plowed the ground and planted the seed. *farmer—plowed, planted*

D. The great trees and the sparkling brooks made the meadow beautiful. *trees, brooks—made*

E. New York and Chicago are large cities. *New York, Chicago—are*

F. The women gathered the grain and ground it into flour. *women—gathered, ground*

G. The rain watered the thirsty fields and made them fresh and green again. *rain—watered, made*

H. Millet and Corot were great artists. *Millet, Corot—were*

I. The leaves let go of the branches and floated gently to the earth. *leaves—let go, floated*

J. History and geography are very interesting studies. *history, geography—are*

Extended Activities

Subject—What the sentence is about

Predicate—Tells something about the subject

When two or more simple subjects are united (connected by a conjunction such as *and, but,* or *or*), they form a compound subject.

When two or more simple predicates are united (connected by a conjunction such as *and, but,* or *or*), they form a compound predicate. Predicates are verbs. When identifying the predicate be sure to include the main verb and all its helpers.

Part I.

Directions: Have the students create a blank chart like the one below and have them write the subject(s) and predicate(s) of each sentence.

A. Bushes and trees were covered with soft white snow.

B. Apples, peaches, and pears grew in the orchard.

C. The farmer plowed the ground and planted the seed.

D. The great trees and the sparkling brooks made the meadow beautiful.

E. New York and Chicago are large cities.

F. The women gathered the grain and ground it into flour.

G. The rain watered the thirsty fields and made them fresh and green again.

H. Millet and Corot were great artists.

I. The leaves let go of the branches and floated gently to the earth.

J. History and geography are very interesting studies.

	Subject(s)	Predicate(s)
A.	*Bushes, trees*	*were covered*
B.	*Apples, peaches, pears*	*grew*
C.	*farmer*	*plowed, planted*
D.	*trees, brooks*	*made*
E.	*New York, Chicago*	*are*
F.	*women*	*gathered. ground*
G.	*rain*	*watered, made*
H.	*Millet, Corot*	*were*

| I. | *leaves* | *let go, floated* |
| J. | *History, geography* | *are* |

Part II.
Directions: Write a sentence using a compound subject and a sentence using a compound predicate.
    Answers will vary.

Lesson 204
Selection for Study—"July"

1. **What is meant by the first and second lines of the first stanza?**
   The first and second lines of the first stanza mean that the cardinal and the butterfly can be seen fluttering during the month of July.
2. **How could the cobweb pull "the cornflower's cap awry"?**
   The spiders spin cobwebs atop the corn bending them over.
3. **Why is the word "flame" used in the third stanza?**
   Flame denotes the color red, and some poppies are red in color. The flower looks like a flame.
4. **Explain lines three and four of the third stanza.**
   Lines three and four of the third stanza read: "And the silver note in the streamlet's throat/ Has softened almost to a sigh." This means that the stream makes low, sweet noises. The water running down the stream almost sounds like someone sighing.
5. **How many pictures do you find in this poem?**
   Students should be able to identify a picture in each of the stanzas. For example, in "tangled cobweb pulls the cornflower's cap awry" students should be able to see cobwebs atop a corn plant.
6. **Which part do you like best?**
   Answers will vary.
7. **Memorize the two stanzas that mean the most to you.**
   Use the memorization rubric, page 218, to evaluate this question.

Lesson 205
Transposed Order

    A. The ripe nuts fall to the ground.
    B. To the ground fall the ripe nuts.

1. **What is the subject of the first sentence? (Notice that in the second sentence the subject is placed after the predicate.)**
   The subject of the first sentence is nuts.

Note: When the subject of a sentence is placed after the predicate, the sentence is said to be in transposed order.

2. Name the subject in each of the following sentences; then reconstruct the sentence, placing the subject before the predicate:

A. In the tranquil waters of the lake are reflected a few late flowers.

Subject—flowers; A few late flowers are reflected in the tranquil waters of the lake.

B. Calm and quiet are the days.

Subject—days; The days are calm and quiet.

C. In their pods shake the ripened seeds.

Subject—seeds; The ripened seeds shake in their pods.

D. Through the leafless branches may be seen the stars.

Subject—stars; The stars may be seen through the leafless branches.

E. Finished is the work of the year.

Subject—work: The work of the year is finished.

F. So still are the hours that time forgets them.

Subject—hours: The hours are so still that time forgets them.

G. On the far horizon is a faint haze.

Subject—haze: A faint haze is on the far horizon.

H. Over upland and lowland grows the goldenrod.

Subject—goldenrod: The goldenrod grows over upland and lowland.

I. Near the waterfall stands an old mill.

Subject—mill: An old mill stands near the waterfall.

3. Name the subject in each of the following sentences; then reconstruct the sentence, placing the subject after the predicate.

A. Lilies tall lean over the wall.

Subject—Lilies: Over the wall lean tall lilies.

B. Poppies flame in the rye.

Subject—Poppies: In the rye flame poppies.

C. The little birds have flown from the nest.

Subject—birds: From the nest have flown the little birds.

D. The heat floats like mist.

Subject—heat: Like a mist floats the heat.

E. The streamlet's music is like a sigh.

Subject—music: Like a sigh is the streamlet's music.

Note: It is often best to rearrange the words of the predicate when reconstructing the sentence.

Lesson 206
Conversation—The School

Talk about the following:

1. The number of school buildings in your city, town, or district.

Answers will vary depending on where students live.

2. **How are schools supported?**

Public schools are supported by taxes. The taxes people pay on their property (land or house) goes to public schools. Schools can receive tax money through the Federal government, the state government, and/or the local government. Some schools also apply for grants to help pay for special programs and field trips. Private schools are supported through tuition, money parents privately pay to the school. Private schools often have fund raisers to help with school supplies, textbooks, and building costs.

3. **Expense of maintaining schools.**

Some expenses of maintaining a school are busses (maintenance and gas), electricity, telephone and T.V. cable lines, teacher salary, and lunchroom expenses.

4. **What are the duties of the board of education?**

Some of the duties of the board of education are to develop policy, hire and fire teachers, monitor curriculum and technology, maintain buildings, and develop budgets.

5. **Has your state a compulsory school law?**

All 50 states have a compulsory school law.

6. **What are the advantages of such a law?**

Answers will vary.

7. **What higher schools or colleges are near you?**

Answers will vary.

8. **Where is your state university?**

Answers will vary.

9. **Tell what you can about the state university.**

Answers will vary.

Offered above is some information that might help facilitate conversation.

Extended Activity

As an extension to Lesson 206, have students log onto a university web site to gather specific information regarding curriculum and entrance requirements. Students could also write questions based on #1-9 and interview a school principal.

Lesson 207
Debate

A boy or girl who has received a high school education is better fitted for business life than the pupil who goes to work after completing only the elementary course.

1. **Debate the subject. Read suggestions regarding a debate, Lesson 108.**

Have students complete the following chart before they begin their debate. Students can go on-line and find information about salary comparisons based on education.

	Pros	Cons
High School		
Elementary		

Lesson 208
Selection for Study—"The Invention of Printing"

Topics for Conversation

1. **Tell what you can of the way in which books were made, before the invention of printing.**

   Based on the reading selection pages 217-218 students should be able to recall that books were hand written before the invention of printing. These books took much time to write and were very costly; therefore only the very rich had access to them.

2. **Compare opportunities for education that people have now, with those that people had seven hundred years ago.**

   Most people today have the opportunity to become educated and literate. Because printing is inexpensive and books are easy to obtain, even the poorest people can learn to read. Most people who lived seven hundred years ago were not formally educated. Those that were often were taught in the Church and they would study grammar, rhetoric, logic, Latin, astronomy, and mathematics.

3. **Tell what you can of typesetting and modern methods of printing.**

   After a book manuscript is edited, it is then set to type. Most typesetting is done by phototypesetting machines. With today's technology, typesetting and printing a large number of books in little time is very easy.

Extended Activities

1. **Take students to a newspaper office to tour how the papers are printed.**
2. **Have students create their own book. Students can bind their books in numerous ways.**

They can make an accordion book or a flap book.

Accordian Book:

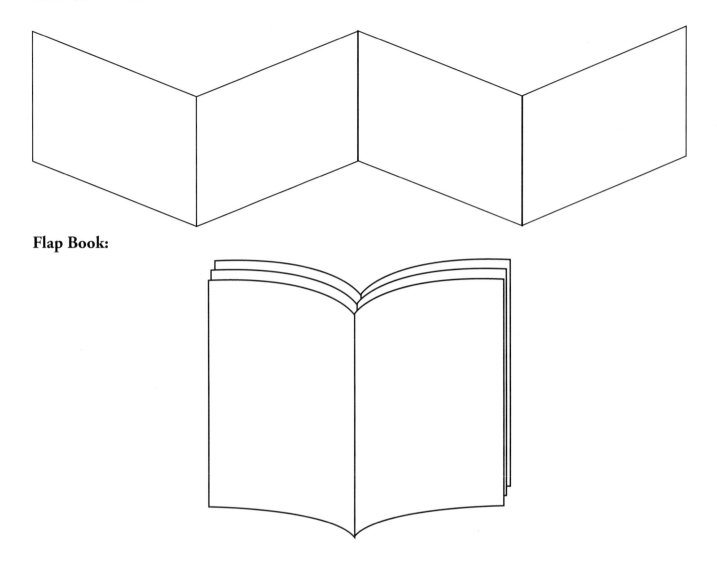

Flap Book:

Lesson 209
Composition

1. Clip news items from papers. Read to the class those which you think are best. Observe the form in which they are written.
   Answers will vary.
2. Write local news items suggested by events of the past week. Let each item contain words enough for ten or more printed lines.
   Answers will vary.
3. Write an item for a newspaper, on one of the following subjects:
   A. Need of a new school house
   B. Damage done by storm
   C. The baseball game

    D. The act of a brave boy

    E. Increase in shipments of fruit

    F. The automobile races

    G. The water supply inadequate

    H. Great fire in the business section

    I. Need of rain

    J. Frost in the south, the orange crop injured

    K. Suffering among the poor caused by the continued cold

    L. A distinguished visitor; his comments on local conditions

Refer students to Lesson 153 and review the newspaper article rubric, page 224. Students should write their article so that it is organized starting with the most important details to the least important details. Students should answer the 5 Ws: Who, What, Where, When, and Why.

Extended Activity

Have students create their own newspaper based on "The Story about George Washington," Lesson 196, and other Revolutionary War facts. Students can create want ads, advertisements, obituaries, cartoons, etc. "Page layout" computer programs such as Microsoft Publisher, Adobe InDesign, Quark Express, etc. can aid students in this project.

Lesson 210
Dictation

Note: *Ship* is the name of something that sails on the sea.

Note: *Sea* is the name of a great body of water.

  1. How many other names can you find in the paragraph?

    plow, train, freight, market, seamstress, industry

  2. Make a list of the nouns in the paragraph.

    ship, sea, plow, field, mine, treasure, ship, train, freight, market, smoke , furnace, loom, garret, seamstress, needle, industry

  3. Write the paragraph from dictation.

    Verify students' work with the passage on page 220. It may be beneficial to discuss the proper use of semi-colons so that students understand that the length of the passage is not a run-on.

Lesson 211
Nouns

    Answers will vary. The following are suggested answers:

  1. Write five nouns that are names of objects at your home.

couch, chair, table, lamp, bed, book

2. **Write five nouns that are names of object you saw on the way to school.**

    trees, road, cars, mountain, bridge, sign, stores

3. **Write five nouns that are names of articles of food.**

    carrots, pizza, hamburgers, milk, cereal, bread

4. **Write five nouns that are names of musical instruments.**

    trombone, piano, violin, guitar, trumpet

5. **Write three nouns that are names of materials used for clothing.**

    cotton, wool, nylon, elastic, buttons, thread

6. **Write three nouns that are names of parts of a wagon, motorcycle or automobile.**

    wheel, headlight, window, windshield wiper, motor

7. **Write five nouns that are names of parts of the human body.**

    arms, legs, ears, eyes, nose, mouth

8. **Write five nouns that are names of flowers.**

    tulip, rose, poppy, dandelion, gardenia

Lesson 212

Selection for Study—"The Music of Labor"

1. **Read the lines that refer to the work of the tailor, the shoemaker, the author, the farmer, the engineer, the weaver, the blacksmith, the carpenter.**

Occupation	Line numbers	Poetry Lines
Carpenter	1-7	The banging of the hammer/the whirling of the plane/The crashing of the busy saw/The creaking of the crane/The ringing of the anvil/The grating of the drill/The clattering of the turning lathe
Weaver	8-10	The whirling of the mill/The buzzing of the spindle/The rattling of the loom
Engineer	11-12	The puffing of the engine/The fan's continual boom
Tailor	13	The clipping of the tailor's shears.
Blacksmith/Shoemaker	14	The driving of the awl
Author	17-20	The clinking of the magic type/The earnest talk of men/The toiling of the giant press/The scratching of the pen
Farmer	23-26	The halloo from the tree top/As the ripened fruit comes down/The busy sound of thrashers/As they cleave the ripened grain

2. **Which industry referred to in this lesson do you know most about? Tell what you can about it.**

    Answers will vary.

Lesson 213
Michael Angelo

1. **Why did the block of marble mean more to Michael Angelo than it did to other people?**
   The marble meant more to Michael Angelo than it did to other people because he saw its potential.
2. **What sort of mental picture do you think he had as he gazed at the block?**
   As he gazed at the marble, he probably had a mental picture of the boy, David, more splendid than any other boy.
3. **Tell the story of the making of the statue.**
   This question is asking students to write a summary: In the city of Florence a great block of marble was ignored. Michael Angelo saw its potential as a great statue. For 18 months Michael Angelo worked chiseling away at the marble. Finally, Michael Angelo finished his statue of David the Shepherd Boy. People were amazed at Michael Angelo's work.
4. **Tell the story of "David the Shepherd Boy," as it is told in the Bible.**
   David was chosen by God to be King Saul's successor. David was the youngest son of Jesse. One day when young David brought his brothers food, he heard the giant Philistine, Goliath, challenge the Israelites. David insisted that he could defeat Goliath. So with a sling and a stone, David slew Goliath. After many trials and battles, Saul was killed, and David was made King of Israel.

Lesson 214
Pronouns

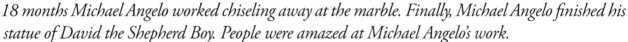

1. **In the first paragraph of Lesson 213 who is meant by *he*? To whom does the word *his* refer?**
   In the first paragraph of Lesson 213 he *and* his *refer to Michael Angelo.*
2. **In the second paragraph to whom does *it* refer? In the fourth paragraph *he* is used instead of what word? For what word is *they* used?**
   In the second paragraph it *refers to the block of marble. In the fourth paragraph* he *is used instead of Michael Angelo.* They *is used for the people of the city.*
3. **In the fifth paragraph *his* is used instead of what word?**
   In the fifth paragraph his *is used instead of the words Michael Angelo.*
4. **Copy the pronouns in Lesson 198.**
   The pronouns in Lesson 198 are they, them, them, we, and she.

Note: A word that is used in place of a noun is called a *pronoun*.

Note: The noun for which a pronoun stands is called its *antecedent*.
5. Write after each pronoun its antecedent.
    They—leaves, them—leaves, we—the narrator, she—autumn.

Lesson 215
Composition—Description of a Place

Travelers going to a strange city find of great service a guidebook containing the names and short descriptions of the principal places of interest.

1. Write a travelers' guide for the place in which you live.
2. If you live in the city, write of the buildings, stores, parks, etc., that would be of interest to visitors.
3. Give a short description of each of the more important.
4. If you live in a small town, write of the surroundings, the places of natural beauty, fine farms, or any local industry that would interest a visitor.

Students can use publishing software to help them design their guidebook. Use the guidebook rubric, page 223, in the Teacher Aids section of this book to evaluate the travel guide.

Lesson 216
Common and Proper Nouns

In Florence, near the gate of the city, there was a huge block of pure white marble.

1. Name the nouns in this sentence.
    The nouns are Florence, gate, city, block, and marble.
2. Does block refer to any particular object, or to one of a class of objects?
    Block refers to one class of objects.
3. Does Florence refer to a particular place, or to one of a class of places?
    Florence refers to a particular place.
Note: A noun that refers to a particular person, place, or object is called a *proper noun*. *Florence* is a proper noun.
Note: A noun that belongs to one of a class of persons, places, or objects is called a *common noun*. *Block* is a common noun.
4. With what kind of letter do all proper nouns begin?
    All proper nouns begin with a capital letter.
5. Write the names of five cities.
    Answers will vary.

6. **Write the names of five states.**
   Answers will vary.
7. **Write the names of five countries.**
   Answers will vary.
8. **Write the names of five rivers.**
   Answers will vary.
9. **Write the names of five great men.**
   Answers will vary.

Lesson 217
Selection for Study—"Down to Sleep"

1. **What is meant by the third line of the first stanza?**
   The third line of the first stanza reads, "Each noon burns up the morning chill." This means that as the sun comes out, it warms the air from the night chill.
2. **Why does the author use the word "reverent," in the sixth line?**
   The author uses the word reverent *because* reverent *means to be respectful. When the speaker is walking, he wants to respect the peacefulness of the woods.*
3. **What words describe "November woods"?**
   "Bare" and "still" describe the "November woods."
4. **What words describe "November days"?**
   "Clear" and "bright" describe the "November days."
5. **How does the forest "spread beds"?**
   The forest "spread(s) beds" when the leaves fall on the ground covering it up.
6. **Explain lines one and two of the third stanza.**
   "Each day I find new coverlids/ Tucked in, and more sweet eyes shut tight" means that more and more leaves are covering the ground and more and more flowers are shutting themselves up.
7. **Who is meant by the "viewless mother"?**
   The "viewless mother" is the earth.
8. **From what are the words "down to sleep" quoted?**
   The words "down to sleep" come from a children's prayer: "As I lay me down to sleep, I pray the Lord my soul to keep. If I should die before I wake, I pray the Lord my soul to take."
9. **Describe a picture that might illustrate this poem.**
   Answers will vary.
10. **Who wrote this poem?**
    Helen Hunt Jackson wrote this poem.
11. **Find in this book "October's Bright Blue Weather." Compare it with this poem. Which has prettier word pictures?**
    "October's Bright Blue Weather" is on page 133. The author is the same as "Down to Sleep" Students should contrast the description of October to the description of November. October is described as bright and colorful, whereas November is described as bare and still. The tone of

the poems are also different. The October poem has a more cheerful tone while the November poem is somber. For an extended activity, students could fold a paper in half and draw October on one side and November on the other. Instruct students to use the colors that are named in the poems.

12. **Read again the quotation from Henry Ward Beecher, Lesson 198. Compare it with this poem. Do you find similar ideas in the two?**

    Lesson 198 is on page 207. Beecher describes October as "calm" and "tranquil." He also describes the woods as becoming "thinner." These ideas are similar to the ideas in "Down to Sleep."

Lesson 218
Composition—A Lost Article

Lost, between the courthouse and the post office, a black silk umbrella; hand of gold, with initials E. G. C. Reward offered for its return to Edwin G. Curtis, 642 Linn St.

1. **Using this as a model, write a notice regarding a lost article.**

   Answers will vary. To guide students have them write about a cell phone, purse, or computer game that was lost at the grocery store.

Lesson 219
Possessives

   A. The morning's snow is gone by night.
   B. The stars are the night's candles.
   C. The sculptor's chisel cut the block of marble.
   D. Sculptors' chisels are sharp.
   E. The artists's greatest picture was not sold.
   F. Artists' materials are sold at this store.

1. **Copy from the sentences all the nouns in the possessive form. Which are in the possessive singular? Which are in the possessive plural?**
   Singular—morning's, night's, sculptor's, artist's; Plural—sculptors', Artists'
2. **Write the possessive singular of each of the following nouns.**

A. day *day's*	**E. forest** *forest's*	**I. river** *river's*
B. bed *bed's*	**F. oak** *oak's*	**J. robin** *robin's*
C. rose *rose's*	**G. town** *town's*	**K. maple** *maple's*
D. oriole *oriole's*	**H. village** *village's*	**L. winter** *winter's*

3. **Write the possessive plural of each of the nouns.**

A. day *days'*	**E. forest** *forests'*	**I. river** *rivers'*
B. bed *beds'*	**F. oak** *oaks'*	**J. robin** *robins'*
C. rose *roses'*	**G. town** *towns'*	**K. maple** *maples'*
D. oriole *orioles'*	**H. village** *village'*	**L. winter** *winters'*

4. **How is the possessive of nouns in the singular formed?**

   The possessive nouns in the singular are formed by adding apostrophe s.

5. **How is the possessive of nouns in the plural ending in *s* formed?**

   The possessive nouns in the plural are formed by adding s then the apostrophe.

6. **Write six nouns whose plural forms do not end in *s*.**

   Suggested answers: children, geese, teeth, men, women, oxen.

   Note: The possessive plural of such nouns is formed by adding the apostrophe and s to the plural form.

7. **Form the possessive plurals of the nouns you have written.**

   Suggested answers: children's, geese's, teeth's, men's, women's, oxen's

Lesson 220
Conversation—Coal

Students can access http://www.eia.doe.gov/fuelcoal.html to find out more information about coal.

1. **What sections of the United States produce much coal?**

   Kentucky, West Virginia, and Pennsylvania are large coal mining states.

2. **Tell what you can of the way in which coal is mined.**

   Coal is mined in two ways. Surface mining is done when coal is less than 200 feet below the ground's surface. The soil and rock are simply removed to expose the coal. Underground mining is when the coal is more than 200 feet below the ground's surface. Workers and machinery go into mine shafts to move the dirt and rock around to expose the coal. Sometimes these mines can go as deep as 1,000 feet below the surface.

3. **Tell uses of coal for transportation, manufacturing, heating, etc.**

   The main use for coal in the United States is to create electricity. Coal generates 50% of electricity in the U.S. Today, coal is rarely used for transportation, manufacturing or heating.

4. **What is the difference between soft coal, anthracite, and semi-anthracite? (Bring specimens.)**

   Anthracite coal is a type of coal that is compact, hard and has a high luster. Anthracite is often used for decorative purposes. Soft coal is the most common and abundant form of coal. It is used primarily to generate energy.

5. **Compare coal and wood as its value for fuel.**

   Coal is a more valuable resource for fuel. It lasts longer, burns hotter, and can be used in more ways than wood.

Lesson 221
Composition

Write a composition on coal. Include the points discussed in Lesson 220.

To be more specific, students are writing an expository essay. Have them write their paper in third person. Students may use the planning sheet to organize their ideas. Use the short story rubric, page 219, to evaluate this assignment.

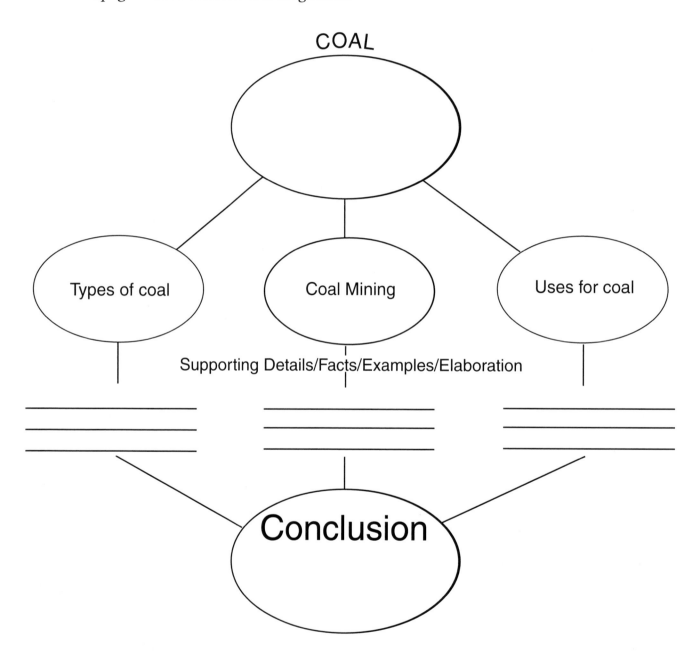

Lesson 222
Conversation—Electricity

1. **Tell what you can of the way in which houses are lighted by electricity.**

   Electricity that is in a home is first generated at a power plant. The electricity is then moved by wire to a transformer. From the transformer, the electricity is sent on a nationwide network of transmission lines, the big tower lines one sees when driving down the highway. Electricity then is carried over distribution lines that deliver electricity to your home.

2. **Compare electric lights with other means of lighting.**

   Electric lights cost money depending on the wattage that is used. Electricity is a safe, easy way to light one's home. Other means of lighting are battery-operated lights and fire. Neither of these methods is efficient for they give out a small amount of light. Battery-operated lighting can be expensive and fire can be dangerous.

3. **How does electricity enable us to talk long distances.**

   A telephone transfers sound into electricity, and electricity into sound. When a person speaks into a handset, the transmitter or microphone makes a diaphragm vibrate. This vibration varies the electrical current causing the receiver's diaphragm to vibrate thus duplicating the sound.

4. **What machines are run by electricity?**

   Answers will vary. Many machines are operated by electricity: can openers, microwaves, CD players, televisions, etc.

5. **How does electricity aid in transportation?**

   Electricity aids in transportation because many of our vehicles use electricity. All cars have batteries that are a mode of transmitting electricity. The batteries provide energy to start the vehicle, run the air conditioner, and radio. Subway cars are run on electricity as well. Many hybrid cars are operational by using a combination of electrical energy and gas.

6. **Find out what you can about one of the following, and be prepared to tell the rest of the class about it:**

   A. airplanes   D. motor boats
   B. motor cars   E. telephones
   C. motorcycles   F. radios

   Have students use the Internet or encyclopedia to research the topic of their choice.

Lesson 223
Picture Study and Letter

1. **Tell what you see in the picture.**
   The picture is of an old steam train.
2. **Describe the engine and coaches.**
   The engine appears to be burning coal because dark

smoke is coming out of the smoke stack. There is an engineer at the front of the train operating it. The cars look like old stagecoach wagons. The passengers are sitting on top of the cars. The second car has barrels and possibly the passengers' luggage.

3. **What is the power that moves the train?**

The power that moves the train is steam.

4. **How is that power generated? How is it controlled?**

Coal creates heats water, which produces steam, which produces pressure, which in turn moves the engine of the train. The pwer is controlled by increasing or decreasing the heat.

5. **Describe a modern engine and compare it with this one.**

A modern engine is operated by fuel. A modern train can go much faster than a train operated by coal. Today some trains can go hundreds of miles per hour. Modern trains are sleek compared to the bulkiness of the steam train. Have students use the Internet to research steam trains and modern trains. Students may want to complete a Venn Diagram, page 227, showing the similarities and differences.

6. **Imagine yourself one of the persons who went to see the first railway train, and write a letter to a cousin describing the wonderful event. Tell your impression when you first saw the engine when it began to move.**

Answers will vary. Use the letter writing rubric, page 221, to evaluate this assignment. Make sure that the letter includes: a description of the first train ride, the student's impression of the engine and his or her wonder when it began to move.

Lesson 224
Conversation—
Transportation

1. **Talk about the various means of transportation. When and where was the prairie schooner used?**

Prairie Schooners were a type of covered wagon that usually measured four feet wide and twelve feet long. Settlers to the West traveled in these wagons. Most families would live in them for months at a time. The wagons would carry a family's bedding and cooking supplies.

2. **Where are dogs and sleds used?**

Dogs and sleds are used in extremely cold regions of the world like Alaska and the North and South Poles. Dogs and sleds were often used to help haul heavy supplies, and the dogs would help guard camps.

3. **Where are camels used?**

Camels are used in desert regions of Asia and North Africa. Camels are popular means of transportation in these areas because they can travel at speeds up to 40 miles per hour and can go long periods of time without water.

4. **What advantages have camels over horses, for the kind of work they have to do?**

Camels are stronger than horses, being able to carry more weight, can also go much longer without food and water and have more endurance. They are thought to be gentler than horses. Have students complete a Venn Diagram, page 227, listing the similarities and differences between camels and horses.

5. **Tell what you can about sailboats.**

   Answers will vary. Sailboats are of all sizes and can be used for racing or cruising. Sailboats are partly or entirely propelled by sails. Students can use the encyclopedia to find out more information about specific sailboats.

6. **In what respects is the steamboat an improvement over a sailboat?**

   A steamboat is an improvement over the sail boat because a steamboat can move much faster. A steamboat does not rely on the wind; therefore, it is not inhibited as much by weather and can move directly into the wind.

7. **Tell what you can of the equipment of a modern passenger train.**

   A modern passenger train has cars for sleeping and dining. Passengers can have private rooms or they can sit in a public area.

8. **Bring pictures showing various means of transportation.**

   Answers will vary.

9. **Write a description of one of the following:**

A. a sailboat	D. a street car
B. an ocean steamer	E. an automobile
C. a passenger train	F. a motor cycle

   Answers will vary.

Lesson 225

Debate

Resolved, that the study of geography is of more value to the pupil than arithmetic.

1. **Debate this subject. For suggestions regarding a debate see Lesson 108.**

	Pros	Cons
Geography	_____	_____
	_____	_____
	_____	_____
	_____	_____
	_____	_____
Arithmetic	_____	_____
	_____	_____
	_____	_____
	_____	_____
	_____	_____
	_____	_____

Lesson 226
Dictation—Transportation

1. **Write the paragraph from dictation.**
   Compare students' work with the paragraph on page 236.
2. **Copy fifteen nouns from the paragraph; place the singular nouns in one list and the plural nouns in another.**
   Plural nouns: goods, railroads, ships, trucks, roads, boats, rivers, canals, freighters, tankers, articles.
   Singular nouns: market, railroad, boat, mode, transportation, airplane, ocean, truck.
3. **What pronoun do you find? State its antecedent each time that it is used.**
   The pronoun is it. It—trucks, it—airplane, it—transportation
4. **Use the following words in a sentence.**
   A. transported   D. canal
   B. comparatively E. especially
   C. bulky   F. distance
   Answers will vary. Make sure students understand the meaning of each word and its part of speech.

Lesson 227
Conversation—Good Roads

1. **Where are the best roads in your neighborhood?**
   Answers will vary.
2. **How were they made?**
   Answers will vary.
3. **What materials are best for country roads?**
   Materials that are best for country roads are asphalt or tar. Many country roads are dirt or gravel, but modern vehicles travel better on paved roads.
4. **How are town or city roads paved?**
   City or town roads are paved by tar or asphalt. First engineers plan where the road will be located. Equipment is used to clear away the route of the road. Most of the time gravel is laid in thick layers before the asphalt is poured. A roadroller is used to flatten and make the surface even.
5. **How should a road be graded?**
   Gravel roads need more maintenance than paved roads and should have crown in the middle to allow water to run off, rather than pool in the road. After rains or frequent use, a gravel or dirt road becomes uneven. A vehicle called a grader will be used to even out the road.
6. **Of what advantage to the farmer are good roads?**
   Farmers need good roads so that they can transport their goods to and from the market. They may also need to travel from one area of the farm to another.

Lesson 228
Railroads

1. **Tell the names of all the railroads you know.**
   Answers will vary. Students can access the Federal Railroad Administration to find information regarding the history of railroads, names of railroads, and their routes. The web site is http://www.fra.dot.gov

2. **What line, or lines, would you take to go from your home to one of the following places: New York, Chicago, Denver, San Francisco, Minneapolis, Kansas City, New Orleans, Cincinnati?**
   Answers will vary.

3. **Plan trips to one or more of the following places: Yellow Stone National Park; Washington, D.C.; Florida; Colorado; Yosemite Valley; Grand Canyon, AZ; Niagara Falls; California.**
   Students can use an atlas to help them plan their trip. Students can also contact local Chambers of Commerce to get more information about specific cities.

4. **Which of these places would you most like to visit?**
   Answers will vary.

5. **At what time of year would your trip be most pleasant?**
   Answers will vary.

6. **What places of interest would you like to visit on the way?**
   Answers will vary.

7. **Bring to class descriptions and pictures of interesting places you would like to visit, or find poems describing any of the places.**
   Answers will vary.

Extended Activities

1. Have students create a travel brochure for their favorite place.
2. Have students write a daily journal recording their trip and the exciting places they visited.
3. Students could also follow the letter format and write to a local Chamber of Commerce requesting information about the town.

Lesson 229
Picture Study—
The Breaking Wave

1. **Study this picture. What does it suggest to you?**
   This picture suggests a terrible storm, possibly a hurricane.

2. **What other name might the painter have given to the picture?**
   Answers will vary.

3. **Have you seen a storm on the ocean or on a large lake? Tell about it if you have.**
   Answers will vary.

4. **Why does the artist show so much of the sea and so little of the sky? Find another picture where the opposite is true.**

   The artist probably shows much of the sea since that is the focus of the picture—showing the unrest and violence of a sea during a storm.

5. **Compare this picture with *The Return of the Fishing Boats,* page 103. Which picture do you like better?**

   The Return of the Fishing Boats *shows a more tranquil sea. Sailboats seem to be safely moving across the waves which are smaller than the waves in* The Breaking Wave. *It is possible that there are no ships in* The Breaking Wave *because it would be too dangerous.*

6. **What colors do you think were used in painting this picture?**

   Dark colors such as grey, dark blue and green were probably used to paint this picture.

7. **Can you find any poem or description suggested by the picture?**

   Answers will vary. Several poems about the sea are "Aboard at Ship's Helm" by Walt Whitman, "Break, Break, Break" by Alfred Lord Tennyson, and "O Listen to the Sounding Sea" by George William Curtis. John Masefield is also well-known for his many seafaring-themed poems.

Lesson 230
Advertisement and Answer

Bookkeeper wanted, for real estate office; chance for promotion. State experience and salary desired. Best of references required. D 643, Times.

1. **Write a letter which might be sent in answer to this advertisement. The letter should be sent to D 643, Times Office.**

   Use the letter writing rubric, page 221, to evaluate this response. Be sure that the letter includes the criteria stated in the advertisement.

Lesson 231
Writing Advertisements

1. **Bring advertisements clipped from newspapers.**
2. **Study them and select ones you consider the best.**
3. **Write an advertisement of not more than thirty words for each of the following:**
   A. **To Rent—Furnished Room**
   B. **For Sale—House**
   C. **Wanted to Purchase—Pony**
   D. **Situation Wanted—Stenographer**
   E. **Lost—Dog**
   F. **Wanted to Rent—House**
   G. **Found—Pocketbook**

Answers will vary. Have students compare a written advertisement, one found in the classifieds, with a product advertisement. How are they different? Students could be made aware of common propaganda techniques. The most common are:

A. Bandwagon—This technique appeals to one's sense of belonging. You should join in (or buy a product) because everyone else is doing/buying it.

B. Testimonial—This technique states that because a famous person is doing it, you should too.

C. Glittering Generalities—This technique uses words or images that have different positive meaning for individual subjects, but are linked to highly valued concepts.

D. Name Calling—This technique is used when negative words or words with negative connotations are used when describing the other brand.

E. Plain Folk—This technique is used when the product tries to reflect the view of the common person; the product is good enough for the common folk.

Lesson 232
Selection for Study—"The Blue Jay"

1. **Explain: "azure," "dye," "bonniest."**
   Azure is a shade of blue, and dye is a liquid that stains items a color. Bonniest in the last line of the third stanza means pleasing to the eye.
2. **What is meant by the second and third lines of the second stanza?**
   The second and third lines of the second stanza reads: "When April began to paint the sky,/That was pale with the winter's stay?" It is saying that when spring arrives, the colors turn from pale to pretty pastels. The second line: "April began to paint" is an example of personification.
3. **State in your own words the thought of the author concerning the making of the Blue Jay.**
   The main thought of the author is that the Blue Jay was created as pretty as flowers and fields of spring.

Lesson 233
Conversation—Birds' Nests

1. **Find out about the nests of as many of the following birds as you can:**

A. robin	I. duck	Q. mockingbird
B. cowbird	J. crow	R. chimney swallow
C. wren	K. hawk	S. Baltimore oriole
D. heron	L. owl	T. barn swallow
E. sparrow	M. eagle	U. cliff swallow
F. blue jay	N. flicker	V. goldfinch
G. catbird	O. swan	
H. shrike	P. blackbird	

Students can use an encyclopedia to research information regarding the nests of the birds listed. Have students rearrange the names of the birds in alphabetical order to aid in looking up the encyclopedia entries.

2. **How many of these birds can you recognize when you see them?**
    Answers will vary.

Lesson 234
Dictation

1. **Find in this paragraph a compound word.**
    Compound words in this paragraph are: framework and horsehairs.
2. **Find a sentence containing a series of words.**
    The sentences containing a series of words reads: "The framework of the nest is made of twine or long horsehairs, through which the oriole weaves fine grass, hair, and bits of wood fiber.
3. **How is the sentence punctuated?**
    The sentence is punctuated by using commas between the items listed.
4. **Write the paragraph from dictation.**
    Compare students' work with the paragraph.

Lesson 235
Biography of an Oriole

Tell of—
A. **Its early home**
B. **Learning to fly**
C. **Learning to sing**
D. **How it spent the summer**
E. **Its flight south**
F. **The difference between north and south**
G. **The winter in the south**
H. **The return of the north**
I. **Try to include some adventure that might happen to a bird—perhaps it was almost caught by a hawk, a cat or a big snake.**
    Most of these answers will contain information that is imaginary. Here are some basic facts regarding the oriole: The oriole lives in northern regions with a moderate climate. They migrate to the South in the winter. Male orioles are typically yellow. The females lay three to

six eggs at a time. Orioles are shy, living in tree canopies. The song of the oriole is a beautiful fluting. Use the short story rubric, page 219, to evaluate this entry.

Lesson 236
Selection for Study— "Winter"

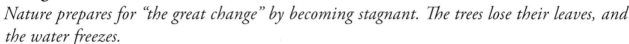

1. **Why is the wind compared to the "blast of a trumpet"?**

   The wind is compared to a trumpet, because in winter, the wind sounds are roaring.

2. **In what ways does Nature prepare "for the great change"?**

   Nature prepares for "the great change" by becoming stagnant. The trees lose their leaves, and the water freezes.

3. **Explain "Nature ceases from her labors".**

   "Nature ceases from her labors" by ceasing new growth.

4. **Describe the picture that this paragraph suggests.**

   The picture above the paragraph, A Winter Scene, is a good description of this paragraph. The words in the paragraph describe frozen pools and ditches, hanging bows, and a "shroud" of snow.

5. **What word describes "leaves"?**

   The word "dry" describes "leaves."

6. **What word describes "water"?**

   The word "stagnant" describes "water."

7. **What word describes "figures"?**

   The word "fantastic" describes "figures."

8. **Find other words in this paragraph that describe.**

   Other adjectives are: great, low-hanging, sharp, busy, melancholy, continual, tall, funeral, dying.
   Note: word that describes a noun or a pronoun is called an adjective

9. **Write the paragraph from dictation.**

   Verify students' writings with the paragraph.

Lesson 237
Conversation

1. **Discuss the following sentences in class; tell what you think each means and if possible illustrate with some short story.**

A. Wealth cannot buy health.

Wealth cannot buy health means that money cannot buy one's health. Rich and poor people alike have health issues. Diseases like cancer have no prejudices. A rich person may be able to provide better health care, but money cannot prevent one from becoming sick.

B. Evil news rides fast.

Evil news rides fast means that most people like to speak ill of others. It is human nature to spread bad news more than good news. Ask students if they think this is right or wrong. Why? Ask students what they think about the saying "If you cannot say anything good about someone, don't say anything at all."

C. Every cloud has a silver lining.

In every situation, a person can find some good; thus, every cloud (a bad thing, person, or situation) has a silver lining (a benefit, a goodness, or a positive attribute).

D. A good name is rather to be chosen than great riches.

A good name is rather to be chosen than great riches means that one's name stays with him or her always. One's reputation is worth more than any material possession one may own.

E. A soft answer turneth away wrath.

Another saying may be "You can get more with honey than with vinegar." If you want people to treat you well, you need to treat others well.

Lesson 238
Dictation—"The Bells"

1. **In this poem the author tried to reproduce in verse the music made by sleigh bells.**
2. **Memorize the poem.**
3. **Write the poem from either memory or from dictation.**
   Use the memorization rubric, page 218, to evaluate this lesson. For dictation, compare the student's work with the poem.

Lesson 239
Composition

1. **If you had been given a large sum of money to spend for improvements in your neighborhood, tell what you would do.**
   (See below.)
2. **If roads or bridges need repairing, tell how you would have the work done; if public buildings need tearing down, tell which ones, and how you would replace them.**
   The prompts given are problem—solution. When students write their essay they need to identify the problem. Many students make the mistake of assuming that their readers are aware of the

problem. Next students should clearly describe the solution to the stated problem, supported by strong reasons. A problem—solution essay is in many ways a persuasive type of writing since the writer is attempting to gain the audience's support of his or her opinion. Hint: It often helps to have students connect the problem to a personal experience. Students should plan their ideas before they begin to write. It might be helpful to conduct a brainstorming session to generate ideas before students attempt to formally plan.

Use the essay rubric, page 220, to evaluate this assignment.

Lesson 240
Choice of Adjectives

1. **Copy the following nouns, placing a suitable adjective before each.**

A. wind	G. snow	M. mountains	S. fruit
B. forest	H. trees	N. valleys	T. night
C. leaves	I. flowers	O. plains	U. engine
D. water	J. bells	P. river	V. picture
E. clouds	K. waves	Q. ocean	W. story
F. air	L. rocks	R. moon	X. song

Answers will vary for each noun given. Below are some descriptive words that might help students expand their adjective vocabulary:

Touch: cool, icy, lukewarm, tepid, rubbery, elastic, crisp, fragile, tender, prickly, fleshy, hairy, oily, satiny, gritty, sharp, smooth, dull

Taste: tangy, rotten, oily, buttery, salty, spoiled, burnt, raw, mellow, fruity, flat, ripe

Smell: sweet, minty, fragrant, tempting, rancid, earthy, moldy, fresh, stagnant

Sounds: melodious, pattering, humming, snapping, hissing, crackling, deafening, clashing, screeching, roaring, jangling, barking, clapping, inaudible

Colors: sandy, almond, tawny, snowing, milky, ivory, ashen, beige, buff, apricot, citron, mauve, lilac, fuchsia, crimson, coral, vermillon, licorice, jet, persimmon, topaz, turquoise, aqua, sapphire, violet, mint, lime, apple

Lesson 241
Selection for Study

1. **Find the meanings of these words:**
   A. revelation *(noun) the act of making something known*
   B. existence *(noun) state of being*

   C. unforeseen *(adjective) not expected*

   D. larvae *(noun) the young of any invertebrate*

   E. community *(noun) a social group whose members live in a specific locality*

   F. compressed *(adjective) pressed together*

2. **Use the words in sentences.**

   Answers will vary. Make sure students use the word as its correct part of speech.

3. **What is meant by "insect-angels"?**

   "Insect-angels" means that flying bugs will hover around the open flowers like angels.

4. **To what does "their golden disks" refer?**

   "Their golden disks" refers to the blooming, open flowers.

5. **How do you explain the expression, "poisoned by sunshine"?**

   The expression "poisoned by sunshine" means that the insects who live under the rock like the darkness. The sunshine is like poison to them.

6. **Did you ever have an experience similar to the one the author describes?**

   Answers will vary.

7. **From this selection copy—**

   A. Ten nouns in the singular

   stone, grass, hedge, stick, foot, housewife, revelation, surprise, community, existence, dismay, maturity, light, day, region, sunshine, bird, beetle, dandelion, buttercup

   B. Ten nouns in the plural

   fields, edges, fingers, members, blades, creatures, crickets, filaments, whips, stagecoaches, creatures, larvae, legs, retreats, fans, insect-angels, disks

   C. Five pronouns and write after each its antecedent

   you/reader, it/stone, she/housewife, herself/housewife, its/community, they/blades, them/ community

   D. Ten adjectives and write after each the word that it modifies

   large/stone, flat/stone, little/hedge, odd/revelation, unforeseen/surprise, unpleasant/surprise, small/community, sudden/ dismay, old/stone, colorless/grass, hideous/creatures, crawling/creatures, black/crickets, glossy/crickets, long/filaments, four-horse/stagecoaches, motionless/creatures, slug-like/creatures

Lesson 242
Composition

1. **Write a composition on one of the following subjects:**

   A. My first ride on horseback

   B. My first ride on a bicycle

   C. My first ride in a rowboat

   D. My first ride in an automobile

   E. My first ride in a motor boat

   a. When it was

b. Where you went
c. With whom you went
d. Some interesting experience connected with the ride

Use the essay rubric, page 220, to evaluate this composition. Have students use the visual diagram to help them with their planning. Remind students that a narrative is best organized chronologically.

<table>
<tr><td></td><td>My first—
_____</td><td></td></tr>
<tr><td>When?</td><td></td><td>People involved:</td></tr>
<tr><td>Where?</td><td></td><td>Experience:</td></tr>
</table>

Descriptive phrases:

About your place:

Lesson 243
Debate

More pleasure can be obtained from a horse and carriage than from an automobile.

1. **Debate this subject. Read suggestions regarding a debate, Lesson 108.**
   Students may not have ever ridden in a horse and carriage. It may be helpful to change the debate to: More pleasure can be obtained from riding in a (boat, airplane, train) than from riding in an automobile.

Lesson 244
Picture Study—
The Horse Fair

1. **Look carefully at the picture; notice the different positions of the horses. Think how many sketches the artist needed.**

   The artist needed many sketches of horses. Some of the horses in the picture are facing forward, some sideways and some backwards. Some are bucking and some are running.

2. **Which horse is the principal one in the picture? Which did you notice first? Is it in the center of the picture? Does an artist ever place the principal subject exactly in the center?**

   The principal horse in the picture is the big white one to the right of the center. One's eye is drawn to this because of its light coloring compared to the rest of the picture. An artist does not always place the principal subject in the center of a picture.

3. **Can you name another artist who painted pictures of animals? In what country did he live?**

   Some artists who painted animals are: Edward Hicks (American, 1780-1849), John James Audubon (American, 1785-1851, painted birds), Abraham Cooper (British, 1787-1868, painted horses), Sir Edwin Henry Landseer (British, 1802-1873).

Lesson 245
Selection for Study—"The Horse's Prayer"

1. **Mention some ways in which a horse should be cared for.**

   A horse should be cared for by providing it with "shelter, a clean, dry bed and a stall wide enough for [the horse] to lie down in comfort." A horse needs companionship and careful examination of its hooves and teeth. It should be well fed and when its usefulness is done a horse would prefer for its owner to "take [its] life in the kindest way."

2. **Mention some ways in which a horse should not be treated.**

   A horse should not be mistreated. One should not "jerk the reins," "strike or beat" it. Nor should the horse be overloaded. Its head should not be tied in an "unnatural position."

3. **In this selection find words in a series.**

   Words in a series are: "provide me with shelter, a clean, dry bed and a stall", "Never strike, beat or kick", and "give me clean, cool water."

4. **Give the rule for punctuation of words in a series.**

   The rule for punctuating a series is to put a comma between the words.

5. **Find the nouns; write the nouns in the singular in one list, those in the plural in another.**

Singular	Plural
master	*reins*
prayer	*blinders*

work	*eyes*
shelter	*teeth*
bed	*flies*
stall	*signs*
comfort	*hands*
voice	*glanders*
hill	
harness	
feet	
head	
water	
teeth	
position	
defense	
tail	
power	
disease	
condition	
shelter	
sun	
blanket	
cold	
bit	
mouth	
strength	
owner	
life	
way	
God	

6. **In the first line the word petition might have been used instead of prayer.**

   Two words that have the same meaning are called synonyms. Petition and prayer are synonyms.

7. **Find words that might have been used instead of the following: offer, provide, examine, condition, shelter, reward.**

   Some synonyms are: offer—present, submit, tender
   provide—endow with, impart, give
   examine—inspect, observe, check
   condition—situation, circumstance, state
   shelter—haven, sanctuary, refuge
   reward—repay, compensate, pay

8. **In the first line why is there a comma before *my* and one after *Master*?**

   "My Master" is an appositive. An appositive is a phrase that renames the subject.

9. **Write the first and second paragraphs from dictation.**

   Verify students' work with the passage.

Lesson 246
Composition

1. Read again "The Horse's Prayer," Lesson 245, then write a dog's prayer. Let your composition tell of ways in which dogs are sometimes neglected or abused.
    Use the essay rubric, page 220, to evaluate this composition.

Extended Activity

Have students visit an animal shelter. What do they observe? If possible, have students volunteer time helping to care for animals in a shelter.

Lesson 247
Adjectives and Nouns

1. Copy the following adjectives, and write after each a suitable noun:

A. transparent	I. porous	Q. smooth
B. downy	J. sticky	R. fleecy
C. slippery	K. brittle	S. acid
D. bitter	L. fragrant	T. grand
E. crisp	M. juicy	U. delicious
F. spacious	N. delicate	V. hug
G. extensive	O. slender	W. indelible
H. nutritious	P. industrious	X. stiff

Answers will vary. Make sure students know the meaning of the adjectives so that their nouns are suitable. It would be beneficial to divide students into groups and have them write their answers on large paper then display around the room. Discuss the students' answers.

Lesson 248
Summary—Continued from Lesson 195

Extended Activity

A. For each sentence, identify the subject and the predicate.
    1. During the game, Thomas scored a goal.
    Subject—Thomas, Predicate—scored
    2. James blocked the ball from the side of the goal.
    Subject—James, Predicate—blocked
    3. The coach congratulated the team on its good effort.

Subject—coach, Predicate—congratulated

    4. **The other team shook hands after the game.**

Subject—team, Predicate—shook

    5. **All the players ate pizza together to celebrate.**

Subject—players, Predicate—ate

B. **Which sentence has a compound subject?**

    1. **During the game, Thomas kicked the ball to James.**

    2. **During the game, Thomas and James passed the ball.**

Sentence 2 has a compound subject: Thomas and James.

C. **Write your own sentence using the subjects: Thomas and James.**

Answers will vary.

D. **Which sentence has a compound predicate?**

    1. **During the game, Thomas kicked the ball and scored a goal.**

    2. **During the game, Thomas kicked the ball too far to the right of the goal.**

Sentence 1 has a compound predicate: kicked and scored.

E. **Write your own sentence using the predicates: run and jump.**

Answers will vary.

F. **In the following passage identify the nouns:**

    The fall weather was beginning to ascend upon the little valley town. The soccer players were excited for the season to come to an end. While the players, especially Megan and Madison, enjoyed the exciting game, they were looking forward to riding on their snow sleds. Madison's sled had never been used, while Megan's sled was old. The girls' dad made sure each sled was in perfect condition.

G. **Which nouns above are common nouns and which are proper nouns?**

Common nouns: weather, town, players, season, end, game, sleds, sled, dad, condition

Proper nouns: Megan, Madison

H. **In the passage above, identify the adjectives and the noun it describes.**

Adjectives/noun—fall/weather, little/town, valley/town, soccer/players, exciting/game, snow/sleds, new/sled, old/sled

I. **In the passage above, identify a plural noun that is possessive.**

A plural noun that is possessive is girls'.

J. **In the passage above, identify singular nouns that are possessive.**

Singular nouns that are possessive are: Megan's and Madison's.

Lesson 249
Selection for Study—"Landing of the Pilgrim Fathers"

1. **Describe the picture given in the first six lines of the poem.**

The picture given in the first six lines describes a scary, bleak, undiscovered land. The "breaking waves" and the "rock bound coast" indicate possible danger.

2. **What do you understand by "rock bound coast"?**

   "Rock bound coast" describes a rocky shore line rather than a sandy beach.

3. **What other words might have been used in place of bark?**

   Another word that could have been used instead of "bark" is ship. Bark indicates that the Pilgrim's means of transportation was a wooden ship.

4. **Would any other words give the same idea?**

   Answers will vary.

5. **What does the fifth stanza tell of the character of the people who had come to the new world?**

   In the fifth stanza the speaker says that the Pilgrims "sang" an "anthem of the free." This indicates that the Pilgrims were hopeful and possibly joyful about their new freedom in a new land.

6. **What welcome did they receive?**

   Their welcome involved an "eagle" who soared, and the forest that "roared."

7. **Read the lines that describe the different persons in this band of exiles.**

   Lines that describe the different persons in this band of exiles can be found in the seventh and eighth stanzas.

8. **Why had they come to America?**

   They came to America to find "freedom to worship God."

9. **Use in sentences:**

      A. breaking waves   **D. giant branches**

      B. wild New England shore   **E. stormy sky**

      C. hoary hair   **F. dim woods**

   Answers will vary.

Lesson 250
Selection for Study

Note: The word *shine* expresses the action of the sun. *Says* also expresses an action. A word that expresses action is called a *verb*

1. **Copy twelve nouns.**

   sun, light, moon, night, brook, breeze, rain, trees, daisies, star, birds, child

2. **Find in the selection divided quotations. How are they punctuated?**

   The divided quotations are: "We sing," chant the birds, "How happy we all are!" Notice the comma at the end of the first quotation "sing," and a comma after "birds." The end mark comes at the end of the second quotation.

3. **Copy ten verbs from the selection.**

   shine, says, glimmer, adds, ripple, whisper, sighs, patter, laughs, dance, nod, twinkle, shine, sing, chant, smile, cries.

4. **Write the selection from dictation.**

   Verify students' work with the original poem.

Lesson 251
Verbs

1. Write a sentence containing—
   A. Five verbs that tell what a horse can do.
   B. Three verbs that tell what a dog can do.
   C. One verb that tells what the sun does.
   D. One verb that tells what the wind does.
   E. One verb that tells what the fire does.
   F. Three verbs that tell what the bird can do.
   G. Five verbs that tell what the farmer does.
   H. Five verbs that tell what you can do.
   Answers will vary. Have students underline the verb in each of their sentence. Verify its agreement with the subject.
2. Copy five verbs from Lesson 236
   Verbs from Lesson 236: sweeps, whirl, covers, ceases, prepares, weaves

Lesson 252
Verbs—Continued

   A. In every seed there is a plant.
   B. November woods are bare and still.

Note: Some verbs do not express action.
In the first sentence we assert no action, but express being.
In the second sentence we express a condition or state of being.
A word that expresses action, being, or state of being is called a *verb*.
Sometimes a verb consists of more than one word: *as, was running, had been running, might have been running,* etc.

1. Copy five verbs from Lesson 198.
   Verbs from Lesson 198: shake, drop, begin, swing, touch.
2. Copy five verbs from Lesson 204.
   Verbs from Lesson 204: tells, makes, murmurs, pulls, lean.
3. Copy ten nouns from Lesson 204.
   Nouns from Lesson 204: cardinal, dragonfly, breeze, nest, trees, lullaby, July, cobweb, cap, lilies, wall, butterfly.
4. Copy nouns, pronouns, adjectives, and verbs from Lesson 208.
   Nouns: years, book, hand, printing, pictures, pen, brush, labor, time, book, person, bookstores, schools, monasteries, men, copyists, business, copies, illuminators, initials, headings, pages,

borders, colors, ink, plan, copy, page, wood, carvings, substance, paper, sheet, block, leaves.
Pronouns: they, it, one, we, he.
Adjectives: Seven hundred, every, great, costly, rich, few, great, large, written, such, beautiful, chapter, different, some, several, new, same, wood, thin, inky, carved, one, handsome, fifty, one.
Verbs: was written, was, were, were drawn, painted, required, was finished, could afford, was, ornamented, encircled, had, carved, are made, was wet, was laid, was printed, was treated, could be printed, were stitched, made, been engraved, could make.

Lesson 253
Letter Writing

1. Write one of the following:
   A. You have moved, and wish to have the address of a paper or magazine to which you have subscribed changed. Write the letter, giving both the old address and the new.
   B. The pupils in your room wish to use a vacant lot for baseball games. Write a letter to the owner asking permission.
   C. Write a note to your teacher asking if you may be excused from school for part of the day. State why you wish to be absent.
   Answers will vary. Use the letter writing rubric, page 221, to evaluate this response.

Lesson 254
Conversation

1. **Tell what you can of the duties of a judge.**
   The duties of a judge are to read and listen to the arguments of the defense and the prosecution, and order the sentence of those who are guilty.
2. **Suppose a man is accused of stealing a sum of money, tell what you can of the manner of conducting a trial.**
   The prosecution will gather evidence against the person who is accused of stealing a sum of money. This evidence may include witnesses to the crime as well as other material evidence. The prosecution has a duty to share this information with the defense so that the defendant's attorneys can put together arguments against the evidence. The attorneys then pick a jury. The two sides then go to court where they present their arguments before the judge and jury. The judge will issue directions to the jury, then the jury will vote as to whether there was sufficient evidence to find the defendant guilty. The case will either be dismissed or the defendant will be found guilty in which the judge will then pronounce a sentence. The sentence could be a fine, jail time, or some other appropriate punishment.
3. **How is the jury chosen? Of how many people is it composed?**

A jury is chosen randomly. The court selects people by calling them to appear through their voter identification card or their driver's license. The attorneys ask questions and select those they want to serve. Depending on the type of case being tried, a jury can consist of as few as six people to as many as twelve.

4. **Who decides whether the accused is guilty?**

   The jury or the judge decides whether the accused is guilty.

5. **Who pronounces the sentence?**

   The judge pronounces the sentence.

6. **Explain the terms attorney for the defense, acquittal.**

   Attorney for the defense is the lawyer who defends the accused. Acquittal means that the accused has not been found guilty and is let go.

Lesson 255
Selection for Study— "The Burial of Sir John Moore"

1. **Why was there no sound of drum or funeral note as the hero was buried?**

   There was no sound of drum or funeral note as the hero was buried because they were burying him on the battlefield. The poem insinuates that the enemy is near. To make noise would arouse their whereabouts.

2. **Read the lines that tell the time of the burial.**

   The first line of the second stanza tells that the time of the burial was midnight: "We buried him darkly at dead of night."

3. **What lines tell of the feeling of the soldiers toward Sir John Moore?**

   The first line of the last stanza tells how the soldiers felt towards Sir John Moore: "Slowly and sadly we laid him down."

4. **Explain the meaning of these words: "rampart," "bayonets," "shroud," "martial," "random."**

   A "rampart" is a mound of dirt used for fortification. A "bayonet" is a blade fastened to the end of a rifle. It is used in close combat. A "shroud" is a cloth laid over a dead body. "Martial" means suitable for war. "Random" means without plan or order.

Lesson 256
Correct Use of Words

   A. I shall see you soon,
   B. This lesson is difficult, but I will learn it.

   C. My cousin will see you soon.

   D. My cousin shall go to school, even if he does prefer not to go.

1. **Which of the sentences express determination?**

   The sentences that express determination are sentences B and D.

2. **What verb is used with I? What verb is used with my cousin?**

   Will is used with I and shall is used with my cousin.

3. **Which of the sentences state that something will occur in the future? What verb is used with I? What verb is used with my cousin?**

   Sentences A and C state that something will occur in the future. The verb used with I is shall and the verb used with my cousin is will.

Note: To express simple future use *shall* with I and we, use *will* with all other words. To express determination use *will* with I and we, use *shall* with all other words.

4. **Use shall and will in sentences expressing simple, future, showing that—**

   A. You expect to go away this summer.

   B. Your mother expects to go with you.

   C. You both expect to see many strange sights.

   D. Your father expects to be with you part of the time.

   E. You expect to send post cards to many of your friends.

   F. You expect to return before school begins in the fall.

   Answers will vary. Example sentences:

   A. I shall go on vacation this summer.

   B. My mother will go with me.

   C. We shall see many strange sights.

   D. My father will be with me part of the time.

   E. I shall send post cards to many of my friends.

   F. I shall return before school begins in the fall.

5. **Fill each of the following blanks with shall or will, so that the sentences shall express determination.**

   A. I *will* finish this work.

   B. My dog *shall* learn this trick.

   C. You *shall* not hurt this boy.

   D. I *will* tell the truth.

   E. You *shall* give me my book.

   F. We *will* go even if it does rain.

Lesson 257
Composition

Write a description of the prettiest spot near your home. It may be some place on a river or stream, it may be a part of a park, or a shady nook in the woods. Describe the place, tell how to reach it, and state what there is that makes it especially beautiful.

Use the essay rubric, page 220, to evaluate this descriptive essay. Students may use the visual organizer to plan their essay. Lines under circles are for specific supporting details. Refer to Lesson 240, Teacher's Guide to offer students suggestions of adjectives.

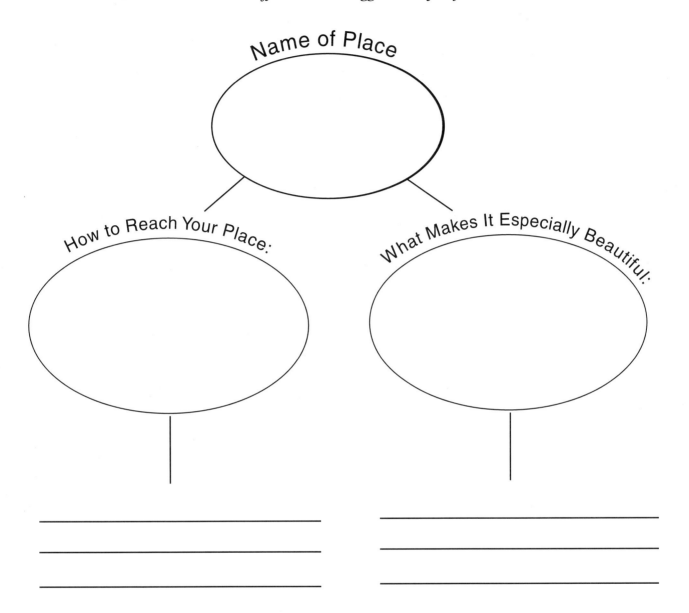

Lesson 258

Selection for Study—"The Seasons"

1. **How can you tell that Mr. Holmes loved nature? Where do you think he spent much of his time?**
   One can tell that Mr. Holmes loved nature because this passage has many specific details of animals and plants. He probably spent much of his time outside.

2. **Do parts of the selection make you think of any poems you have studied?**
   Yes, this selection is reminiscent of many of the poems that have been studied. Some are:

"The Robin" page 13, "The Red-headed Woodpecker" page 18, "The Apple Tree" page 33, "October's Bright Blue Weather" page 133, "July" page 213.

3. **Explain the first part of the sixth paragraph.**

   The first sentence of the sixth paragraph reads: "June comes in with roses in her hand, but very often with a thick shawl on her shoulders, and a bad cold in her head." This means that while June is pretty and flowers are blooming, often times it still remains cold in the morning and/or in the evening.

4. **Describe pictures that might be used to illustrate each paragraph.**

   Have students read each paragraph and draw a picture stating the main idea for each paragraph. Each paragraph should feature: 1—birds, 2—geese or toads, 3—flowers, 4—baby birds, nests and bees, 5—fruit trees, 6—roses or fireflies, 7—meadows, 8—yellowing leaves, 9—colored trees, 10—barren trees and snow.

5. **Mr. Holmes lived in New England, where the coming of spring is often late. Are conditions he mentions different in your state?**

   Answers will vary.

6. **What trees, flowers, or birds he refers to do you not have? What kinds do you have that he does not mention?**

   Answers will vary.

7. **Copy from this selection, in separate lists, the names of birds, insects, flowers, trees.**

   Birds: bluebirds, robins, sparrows, blackbirds, phoebe birds, wild pigeons, geese, wrens, brown thrushes, swallows, martins, orioles, catbirds, golden robins, bobolinks, whippoorwills, cuckoos, yellow birds, humming birds.

   Insects: flies, grasshoppers, bees, fireflies, katydids, crickets.

   Flowers: dandelion, violet, lilac, roses, azalea, honeysuckle, marigold, dahlia, zinnia, hollyhock, aster, goldenrod, cowslip, chickweed, strawberry, bellroot, dogtooth violet.

   Trees: laurel, oak, apple, peach, cherry, beech.

8. **Give the meaning of "linger," "clamor," "heralds," "tapestry," "desolate," "minstrels," "ignominiously."**

   The meanings of the following words are: "linger"—(verb) to stay awhile, "clamor"—(noun) discordant noise, "heralds"—(verb) to proclaim, "tapestry"—(noun) a decorative fabric with many colors, "desolate"—(adjective) barren, by oneself, "minstrels"—(noun) a singer or poet, "ignominiously"—(adverb) humiliatingly.

Lesson 259
Review

1. **Copy from Lesson 258: six pronouns, fifteen adjectives, fifteen verbs.**

   Pronouns: them, us, themselves, his, it.

   Adjectives: ground, cold, wild, few, wild, strange, rarer, bright, green, dark, brown, new, mellow, breezy, busy, great, ever-spreading, pink, white.

Verbs: peep, shown, make, linger, drop, wedging, are, piping, straggle, seen, heard, opening, found, springing, growing, pouring.

2. **Write after each pronoun its antecedent.**

Pronouns/Antecedents: them/Robins, us/the speaker and the reader; themselves/toads, tree toads, martins, and swallows; his/bumblebee; it/warmth.

Lesson 260
Sentences Like Model

1. **Copy the first sentence in Lesson 258. Using it as a model, complete the following sentences:**
   A. As late as the last of October _____.
   B. As early in the summer as _____.
   C. As early as the first of November _____.
   D. As late as the middle of April _____.
   Let the sentences be about insects, flowers, birds, fruits or the coming snow.

   As early as the first of March ground squirrels peep out of their holes, and bluebirds have also shown themselves.

   Answers will vary for sentences A-D.

2. **Write sentences containing the following expressions: "heralds of spring," "flowering meadows," "saddest days of the year," "gorgeous tapestry."**

   Answers will vary. Example sentences:

   Robins flying into our yard are the heralds of spring.

   My friends and I run through the flowering meadows.

   When the sun sets early, the saddest days of the year have arrived.

   When the leaves on the trees turn to red and gold, they create a gorgeous tapestry of autumn.

Lesson 261
Quotations

People often keep notebooks in which they write beautiful quotations.

1. **Select quotations of poetry or prose that especially please you. Read them and tell why you like them. Copy them in your notebook and add to them the best quotations that other members of the class read. Select quotations that are not given in this book.**

   Answers will vary for this assignment. Students might enjoy binding their notebook somehow and illustrating the quotations they include.

Lesson 262

Selection to be Memorized— "The Year's at the Spring"

1. **What time of the year is described?**
   The time of year described is spring.
2. **What time of day?**
   The time of day is "the morn."
3. **What shows that Pippa was contented?**
   The line "All's right with the world" shows Pippa was contented.
4. **What contractions do you find in the poem?**
   Contractions in the poem are: year's, day's, morning's, hillside's, lark's, snail's, God's.
5. **Memorize the stanza.**
   Compare students' answers with the poem.
6. **Write the stanza from memory.**
   Compare the students' writing with the poem.

Lesson 263

Adverbs

A. The ground squirrels peep timidly out of their holes.
B. The flowers will blossom soon.
C. Beautiful trees grow here.

For Lessons 263-265, example sentences can be given to students for the purpose of additional practice in identifying adverbs.

1. **What is the verb in the first sentence? What word modifies the meaning of the verb by telling how?**
   The verb in the first sentence is peep. The word that tells how is timidly.
2. **What is the verb in the second sentence? What work modifies the meaning of the verb by telling when?**
   The verb in the second sentence is will blossom and the word that tells when is soon.
3. **What is the verb in the third sentence? What word modifies the meaning of the verb by telling where?**
   Note: A word that modifies a verb is an adverb.
   The verb in the third sentence is grow and the word that tells where is here.
4. **Add to each of the following sentences adverbs that tell how.**
   A. The bluebirds are singing.
   The bluebirds are singing melodiously.

B. The brook murmurs.

The brook murmurs softly.

C. The child plays.

The child plays heartily.

D. The fire burns.

The fire burns brightly.

E. The dog barks.

The dog barks loudly.

F. The children did their work.

The children did their work diligently.

G. The lion roared.

The lion roared ferociously.

5. **Use these adverbs in sentences: quietly, patiently, kindly, quickly, carefully, fiercely, roughly, loudly, carelessly.**

Example sentences:

Quietly the girl slept.

The teacher listened patiently.

The man smiled kindly on the servant.

The boy ran quickly.

Carefully the woman took the cake out of the oven.

The horse ran fiercely to the finish line.

The sea roughly hit the shore.

The children sang loudly.

It is unwise to do your homework carelessly.

6. **Use these adverbs in sentences: often, seldom, daily, yearly, early, late, always, soon, never.**

Example sentences:

Often I visit my grandmother.

Seldom do I see her sleep.

I pick the daisies daily.

I have to give a report yearly.

I do not like to rise early.

The tree will bloom late in the summer.

I always do what I am told.

I hope to go on vacation soon.

I hope I never wreck my car.

7. **Use these adverbs in sentences: there, here, down, up, backward, forward.**

Example sentences:

I hope to visit there.

Here is where I laid my books.

I put the pencil down.

I looked up into the sky.

I could turn the chair backward.

I drove the car forward.

8. **Which adverbs tell how?**
    The adverbs in question five tell how.
9. **Which adverbs tell when?**
    The adverbs in question six tell when.
10. **Which adverbs tell where?**
    The adverbs in question seven tell where.

Lesson 264
Adverbs—Continued

   A. **We crossed a high mountain**
   B. **We crossed a very high mountain.**

1. **What adjective do you find in the first sentence?**
    The adjective in the first sentence is high.
2. **In the second sentence what word modifies the adjective?**
    The word that modifies the word high is very.

Note: A word that modifies an adjective is an adverb.

3. **Copy the following adverbs and place an adjective after each: too, so, quite, very, more, most, less, least.**
    Examples: too shy, so quiet, quite sad, very tired, more fearful, most happy, less excited, least able.
4. **Use in sentences the expressions you have formed.**
    Example sentences:
    The girl was too shy to give a speech.
    The children were so quiet.
    I was quite sad when I learned we had to leave.
    At the end of the day I was very tired.
    I was more fearful this time than last.
    I was most happy when my package arrived.
    I was less excited than I thought I would be.
    Tom was the least able to carry the heavy logs.

Lesson 265
Adverbs—Continued

   A. **You must listen carefully.**
   B. **You must listen more carefully.**

1. **What adverb do you find in the first sentence?**
   The adverb in the first sentence is carefully.
2. **In sentence B what word modifies the adverb?**
   Note: A word that modifies another adverb is an adverb.
   In sentence B the word that modifies the adverb is more.
3. **Copy the following words and place a suitable adverb after each: very, more, least, quite, too.**
   Examples: very carefully, more often, least likely, quite loudly, too early.
4. **Use in sentences the expressions formed.**
   Example sentence:
   I did my homework very carefully.
   I will visit you more often.
   Tom was least likely to start a fight.
   The child spoke quite loudly in the restaurant.
   It was too early to go to sleep.
5. **Complete the following definition: An adverb is a word that modifies a** <u>*verb*</u>**, an** <u>*adjective*</u>**, or another** <u>*adverb*</u>**.**

Lesson 266
Composition

1. **Bring to school business circulars, or advertisements clipped from papers.**
2. **What special points must be observed in writing such articles?**
3. **Write an article suitable for a circular advertising the business of one of the following: grocer, plumber, florist, dry goods merchant, jeweler.**

Responses will vary.

Lesson 267
Selection for Study, A Biography—"Samuel Morse"

1. **Tell what you can of the way in which messages are transmitted.**
   Messages are transmitted electronically through a wire.
2. **Of what value is the telegraph?**
   The value of the telegraph was that people could communicate over long distances. The telegraph was much faster than sending a letter through the mail.
3. **Why did Mr. Morse want a patent on his invention? What kinds of things are patented?**
   Mr. Morse wanted his invention patented so that it was protected and the credit for the invention would go to Mr. Morse. Many kinds of inventions are patented such as a printer, a game (such

as Game Cube or Nintendo), a mechanical pencil, etc.

4. **What protection does the government give the author of a book?**

   The government offers copyright to authors. Copyright protects the work of an author from being copied and sold by someone other than those granted permission to do so.

5. **Find in this book the mark of the copyright.**

   The copyright for this book (the textbook) is 1996.

6. **Tell the story of the invention of the telegraph.**

   Samuel Morse, an inventor, was returning from a trip to Europe when he met a man who told Morse about some experiments the French were performing. These experiments involved transmitting messages electronically. Morse went to work trying to create an apparatus that would be used as a communication device. It took him about three years to invent one that worked. After that, his invention was patented and a company was formed to put telegraph lines throughout the country.

Lesson 268
Telegrams

1. **Tell what you can about telegrams.**

   A telegraph is the machine that sends a message and a telegram is the message itself. The message is sent in code—The Morse Code.

2. **Why are telegrams sent instead of letters?**

   Telegrams were sent instead of letters because it arrived much faster than a letter. Today, telegrams are no longer used. Today many people use facsimile (fax) machines or e-mails to communicate.

3. **If you wish to send a telegram, where would you take it?**

   If one wished to send a telegram, he could go to a number of businesses like Western Union (often located in grocery stores and post offices).

4. **Write telegrams for the following so that each will contain not more than ten words besides the address and signature:**

   A. To a relative who lives in another city—your mother and yourself will arrive on the six o'clock train, Saturday morning; ask the relative to meet you at the train; mention the name of the railroad.

   B. To a dealer in bicycles in another city—order a boy's or girl's bicycle; state the make wanted; ask that it be shipped at once by freight or express.

   C. To someone in the country, or a small town, asking him to ship fruit to a store in the city: state the price that will be paid, and the quantity wanted.

   Answers will vary. Examples:

   A. Mother and I arriving on Transatlantic, Saturday AM, please meet.

   B. Request girl's Schwinn bike. Ship immediately by express.

   C. Ship two cases of oranges at $3.00 a case.

Lesson 269
Prepositions

1. **Read again the first paragraph of Lesson 267. What word shows the relation of Charlestown to the other part of the sentence? What word shows the relation of New York to the other part of the sentence? What word shows the relation of his native town to the other part of the sentence?**

   The word at *shows the relation of Charlestown to the other part of the sentence. The word* in *shows the relation of New York to the other part of the sentence and the word* of *shows the relation of his native town to the other part of the sentence.*

   Note: A word that shows the relation of a noun or something used as a noun to the rest of the sentence is called a preposition.

2. **Copy five prepositions from Lesson 267.**

   Five prepositions are: from, after, for, at, in.

3. **Use the following prepositions in a sentence:**

A. about	G. before	M. except	S. behind
B. for	H. till	N. above	T. below
C. from	I. To	O. across	U. beneath
D. in	J. into	P. toward	V. after
E. beside	K. against	Q. of	W. on
F. under	L. between	R. with	X. over

   Answers will vary. Example sentences:
   A. I will go about my business.
   B. I can look for my shoes under the bed.
   C. I walked from the school to the field.
   D. In the yard grew a tall tree.
   E. The bee flew beside the flower.
   F. The bird hid under the branch.
   G. We ate lunch before the program.
   I. I went to the ball game.
   J. The boy went into the dug out.
   K. I will sit against the tree.
   L. The boy was tagged between first and second base.
   M. Everyone hollered except me.
   N. The eagle will soar above the mountain.
   O. The man will swim across the lake.
   P. The farmer will drive the tractor toward town.
   Q. He drove right off the road.
   R. Tom and Sally went with the farmer to the market.
   S. The animals followed behind the cowboy.
   T. The flower withered below the snow.
   U. I dug beneath the snow to see if the seed was still there.

V. After winter the flowers will bloom again.
W. I rode on the big stallion.
X. I hope to fly over my house someday.

Lesson 270
Composition—A Biography

1. **Make an outline from Lesson 267.**
   Note: The written history of a person's life is called a biography.
   I. Life
   > *A. Born April 27, 1791—Charlestown, Mass. Died April 2, 1872—New York, NY*
   > *B. Graduated from Yale*
   > *C. Became an artist*
   > > *1. Studied Royal Academy, London*
   > > *2. Became portrait artist—Boston and Charleston*

   II. Telegraph
   > *A. Met Mr. Jackson who told of the experiments of the French*
   > *B. Morse designed an apparatus and devised an alphabet*
   > *C. After three years first model completed*
   > *D. 1837—received patent and built trial line from Washington to Baltimore*
   > *E. Companies formed to erect telegraph lines in all U.S.*
   > *F. Morse received many honors at home and abroad*

2. **How does a biography differ from an autobiography?**
   A biography is a written account of someone's life. An autobiography is a written account of someone's life written by that person.

3. **Write a short biography of one of the following: George Washington, Abraham Lincoln, the President of the United States, an author, an artist, a prominent man in your neighborhood.**
   Use the essay rubric, page 220, to evaluate this assignment. Before students write, have them plan their writing. Have students include some of the following information: When and where the person was born and educated, some descriptions of the person's personality, and some contributions the person has made to his or her community.

Lesson 271
Correct Use of Words

1. **Write questions beginning with the following: of whom, with whom, for whom, by whom, to whom, from whom.**
   Of whom will you secure the deposit? With whom are you going to the dance? For whom is the gift?

By whom are you sitting? To whom does the book belong? From whom was the package?
Note: The word *who* is never used after a preposition.

2. **Write five questions beginning with who.**

    Examples: Who is the person in the red shirt? Who is going to bring the snacks? Who is talking so loud? Who is sitting on the bench? Who is writing the article?

3. **Write questions which the following statements might answer; begin each question with *Whom*.**

    As, A. Samuel Morse met a friend on the ship. *B. Whom did Samuel Morse meet on the ship?*

Teacher Note

This usage is not commonly practiced or encouraged today. Typically, whom is preceded by a preposition, as in: ***With whom*** did Samuel Morse meet on the ship? Today this would more comonly be expressed as: ***Who*** did Samuel Morse meet on the ship? The answers below reflect modern usage. This lesson is a good place to start a discussion with pupils about how language changes. State abbreviations have been contracted from three to two letters. How else has the way we write and speak changed?

C. The people praised Michael Angelo.

Who did the people praise? or By whom was Michael Angelo praised?

D. Millet loved the poor people.

Who did Millet love? or By whom were the poor people loved?

E. The Pilgrims feared the Indians.

Who did the Pilgrims fear? or Of whom were the pilgrims afraid?

F. Echo laughed at Juno.

Who laughed at Juno? or At whom did Echo laugh?

G. The teacher praised industrious pupils.

Who praised the industrious people? or By whom were the industrious people praised?

H. I saw many friends at the park.

Who did I see at the park?

I. I took my brother for a ride.

Who did I take for a ride?

Lesson 272
Selection for Study—"The Coming of Spring"

1. **What month does this poem suggest?**

    This poem suggests either April or May because it refers to the "scent of summer things" and "The coming of the spring."

2. **Use in sentences: "morning sky," "changing tint," "frozen sleep," "wintry sky."**

    Answers will vary.

3. **Copy from the poem four contractions, and write each with its equivalent.**

    There's—there is, that's—that is, there's—there is, that's—that is, there's—there is, winter's—winter has

4. **Memorize the part of the poem that you like best.**

    Use the memorization rubric, page 218, to evaluate the memorization of the poem.

Lesson 273
Selection for Study

1. **Copy in separate lists, from the selection:**
   A. nouns
   bird, home, place, summer, family, winter, pleasure, eating, traveler, kind, food, season, place, home, food, mouthful, cold, birds, place, world, lovers, place, year, year, tree, next, families, land, pleasure, bodies, home, South, house, scrap, spot, food, food, season, meal, family, minutes, minutes.
   B. verbs
   is, is seen, brings, travels, may be, is, calls, could induce, love, prove, nest, repair, were, would think, appear, to do, choose, living, are, to be found, imagine, getting having, to go, to work, to build, would have, to search, carry, imagine, having, to hunt, trying, to get, think, having, get, wonder, would be.
   C. pronouns
   he, he, where, his, he, he, you, his, he, his, them, they, other, they, themselves, anywhere, some, they, they, they, they, they, yourself, you, yourself, every, you, yourself, ones, I,
   you, all, they.
   D. adverbs
   up, too, ever, better, so, just, never, once, so, perfectly, really, immediately, for, away, later, every, often, every.
   E. adjectives
   real, winter, severe, whole, home, same, same, same, old, contented, far, free, industrious, little, every, same, hungry, little, five, ten, two, cheerful.
   F. prepositions
   in, in, for, of, for, of, at, in, of, for, in, to, after, in, in, in, for, from, of, in, for, of.
2. **Copy the first paragraph, so changed that each of the nouns and pronouns will mean more than one.**
   Birds' real homes are the places where they are seen in summer and where they bring up their families. They travel in winter for pleasure—the pleasure of eating; for if they are winter travelers, you may be sure that their kinds of food are not to be found at that season in the places which they call their homes.
3. **What verbs was it necessary to change? What verbs add s when the subject means only one?**
   The verbs that were necessary to change were: is—are, is—are, brings—bring, travel—travels, is—are, calls—call.
4. **What is the central thought in each paragraph?**
   The central thought in each paragraph is:
   Paragraph 1—birds travel for food;
   Paragraph 2—birds stay in the place they love;
   Paragraph 3—birds return home;
   Paragraph 4—birds are industrious;

Paragraph 5—birds have to hunt for food and work hard to build their shelter;
Paragraph 6—feeding little ones.

5. **Make an outline of this selection.**

    An outline will follow the main ideas given in #4. Be sure to check that students have used Roman numerals for main ideas.

6. **Close the book, and using the outline you have made, reproduce as much as you can of the thought of the author.**

    Follow the outline as students recall what they read.

7. **Find a sentence in the transposed order.**

    Never once would they think of going to housekeeping or bringing up families in that land so far away.

8. **Name a subject of each sentence in the third paragraph.**

    Subjects: They, Some, they.

Lesson 274
Selection to be Memorized—"The Flag Goes By"

1. **Why the command "Hats off"?**

    "Hats off" is a call for people to show respect by removing their hats when the flag passes.

2. **Explain "blare of bugles."**

    "Blare of bugles" describes the sound of the parade as it approaches.

3. **What do you understand by "steel-tipped lines"?**

    The "steel-tipped, ordered lines" describes how the flag flies over the members of the band.

4. **Explain the last line of the second stanza.**

    The last line of the second stanza reads, "Live in the colors to stand or fall." This means that we need to take pride in our country—the colors of the flag symbolize our great county. Good citizens support our country in good times and bad.

5. **What are mentioned in the third, fourth, and fifth stanzas, as living in the colors of the flag?**

    Many things are mentioned as living in the colors of the flag: "Sea fights and land fights," "Weary marches and sinking ships," " cheers of victory," "Equal justice," and "Pride and glory and honor."

6. **Memorize the poem.**

    Use the memorization rubric, page 218, to evaluate students' recitation of the poem.

7. **Write the first and second stanzas from memory.**

    Compare students' writings with the poem.

Lesson 275
Dictation

1. **Write the paragraph from dictation.**
   Compare students' writing with the original.
2. **Write a list of the nouns in the paragraph.**
   Nouns: mind, flag, flag, nation, symbols, insignia, flag, government, principles, truths, history, nation.
3. **Write a list of verbs.**
   3. Verbs: sees, sees, may be, reads, belong, sets

Lesson 276
Conversation—The Soldier

1. **Tell what you can of the life of a soldier.**
   Answers will vary.
2. **What kind of uniform does he wear?**
   An American soldier in the army wears either Army Green (olive green shirt and necktie) or Army White (white shirt and tie). Have students use the encyclopedia or Internet to see the different army uniforms.
3. **What are his duties in time of peace?**
   A soldier's duty during times of peace is to train so as to be ready should there be war.
4. **Name some of the titles of officers in the United States Army. Who is highest in command? How is the rank of an officer indicated by his uniform?**
   The highest ranking officer in the army is a Five Star General or General of the Army. The ranks below him in descending order are: Brigadier, Colonel, Major, Captain, Lieutenant, Warrant Officer, Sergeant, Corporal, and Private. The officer's rank is indicated by stars or stripes on the shirt of his uniform.
5. **Explain the following terms:**

A. artillery	E. cavalry	I. infantry
B. commissary	F. department	J. barracks
C. rations	G. fortifications	K. flag of truce
D. captain	H. corporal	L. lieutenant

   A. artillery—(noun) large weapons such as a cannon or missle.
   B. commissary—(noun)a store that sells food and goods to military personnel
   C. rations—(noun) portions of food or other items
   D. captain—(noun) a military leader
   E. cavalry—(noun) the part of a military that serves on horseback
   F. department—(noun) a section or division of a business or army
   G. fortifications— (noun) a military works made to protect or strengthen

H. corporal—(noun) a noncommissioned officer ranking about private first class

I. infantry—(noun) a division of soldiers who fight on foot

J. barracks—(noun) the sleeping quarters for military personnel

K. flag of truce—(noun) a flag flown to show the opposition that one side wishes the fighting to cease

L. lieutenant—(noun) an officer in the army who is ranked below captain.

6. **When is a city said to be besieged?**

    A city is besieged when the enemy surrounds it and does not allow food, arms, ammunition, or people to enter or leave.

7. **When is an army said to be intrenched?**

    An army is said to be intrenched when they are positioned in a location and cannot get out.

8. **How are the wounded cared for?**

    The wounded are cared for at military hospitals. On the field injured soldiers are sent to M.A.S.H. camps (Mobile Army Surgical Hospital).

9. **Of what use is the bayonet?**

    The bayonet is a sharp sword at the end of a rifle. It is used when fighting hand to hand.

10. **What are the duties of a scout?**

    The duties of a scout are to assist in reconnaissance and security.

11. **Why is it necessary to keep a standing army in time of peace?**

    It is necessary to keep a standing army in time of peace so that the army can train and be prepared for times when we are not at peace. Some army units help cities and states in times of disaster or civil unrest.

12. **Where is the national military school located?**

    The national military school is located in West Point, New York.

Lesson 277
Selection for Study—"A Man without a Country"

1. **Read this several times. Tell the incident, and repeat as much as you can of the paragraph quoted.**

    Answers will vary.

2. **If possible read the book, *A Man without a Country*.**

    Answers will vary.

Lesson 278
Conjunctions

1. **In Lesson 277 what words does *or* connect?**

    The word or *connects two nouns: "paper or magazine."*

2. **In the second paragraph what does *but* connect?**
The word but *connects two sentences: "At first the punishment seemed light but as the years passed, his desire to hear of his country grew almost greater than he could bear."*

3. **In the fourth paragraph what does *and* connect?**
In the fourth paragraph the word and *connects two prepositional phrases: "For your country, boy, and for that flag."*
Note: A word that connects words, sentences, or parts of sentences is called a conjunction.

4. **Write a sentence in which *and* connects two or more words.**
Answers will vary.

5. **Write a sentence in which *and* connects parts of sentences or whole sentences.**
Answers will vary.

6. **Write a sentence in which *but* connects two sentences.**
Answers will vary.

7. **Write a sentence in which *or* connects words.**
Answers will vary.

8. **Write a sentence in which *or* connects sentences or parts of sentences.**
Answers will vary.

Lesson 279
Composition—The Flag

1. **Find out something concerning the history of our flag; tell by whom the first flag was made.**
The first flag was made by Betsy Ross, a Philadelphia seamstress. George Washington, our first president, is thought to have helped to create its design. On June 14, 1777, the Continental Congress passed the first Flag Act which designated the design to be the official flag of the United States of America.

2. **Describe the flag. How many stripes has it? What is the historical significance of the stripes?**
The flag has a blue section (called the Union) with 50 stars. There are 13 red and white alternating stripes representing the original 13 colonies.

3. **How many stars are there now in the blue field? How has this number been changed?**
There are now 50 stars in the blue field representing the 50 states. This number has changed as states were added to the Union.

4. **For what does the flag stand? What feelings should the sight of it rouse in every citizen of the United States?**
The flag stands for the citizens and government of the United States of America. The sight of the flag should arouse pride in our country.

5. **Write a short composition on "The Flag of the United States."**
Answers will vary. Have students use the Internet or encyclopedia to get more information on how the flag has changed over time. Information on folding the flag, flying the flag at half-mast, and how to display the flag can also be researched.

Lesson 280
Conversation

1. **Who is governor of your state?**
   Answers will vary.
2. **To what political party does he belong?**
   Answers will vary.
3. **Mention some of his duties.**
   A governor's duties include communicating with the legislature those issues of concern regarding the state and country. He can appoint notaries public and other officials provided by law. The governor makes sure that the laws are executed.
4. **For how long a term is he elected?**
   A governor's term is four years.
5. **When does his present term expire?**
   Answers will vary. gubernatorial elections are held two years after a presidential election.
6. **By whom are the laws of your state made?**
   The laws of the state are made by the state legislature.
7. **Tell something about the legislature.**
   The legislature consists of a Senate and House of Representatives.
8. **How are the expenses of the state government paid?**
   The expenses of the state government are paid through state taxes. Some of these taxes are income taxes, sales taxes, gas tax, etc. The types of taxes vary from state to state.

Lesson 281
Interjections

A. Soldiers, awake!
B. Hark! I hear the bugles and drums.
C. Hurrah! The soldiers are coming.

1. **What words in the sentences above are used to address, to attract attention, or to express feeling?**
   Soldiers *is used to address,* hark *is used to attract attention and* Hurrah *is used to express feeling.*

Note: A word used by itself to address, to attract attention, or to express feeling is called an interjection. It is not to be regarded as a part of a sentence, but as an independent word. The interjection is usually followed by an exclamation point.

2. **Write sentences containing the following words used as interjections:**

   A. what   C. behold   E. alas   G. good
   B. oh   D. hark   F. pshaw   H. hurrah

Answers will vary.

Note: The interjection *O* should always be written with a capital. It is used with a noun denoting the person or thing spoken to. It is not followed by any special mark of punctuation. As,

O Mother; O God

Oh, is an interjection of surprise, joy or grief. It is usually followed by a comma. As,

Oh, I am so sorry!

Lesson 282
Selection for Study—"Columbus"

1. **Find in the dictionary the meaning of "mutinous," "ghastly," "swarthy," "blanched," "naught."**
   Definitions: "mutinous"—(adjective) involving revolt against authority, "ghastly"—(adjective) shocking or frightful, "swarthy"—(adjective) dark skin color, "blanched"—(adjective) to turn white or pale, "naught"—(noun) nothing

2. **Who is the Admiral?**
   The Admiral is Columbus.

3. **Where are the Azores?**
   The Azores is a group of islands in the eastern North Atlantic belonging to Portugal.

4. **What reasons did the mate give for wishing to turn back?**
   The mate wished to turn back because his "men grow mutinous...wan and weak." Also the mate thinks they are so far gone that "not even God would know should [he] and his men fall dead."

5. **What is meant by "shoreless seas"?**
   "Shoreless seas" describes the fact that the men are so far from home that no shore can be seen.

6. **Who speaks the words in the last line of the first stanza?**
   Columbus speaks the last line of the first stanza.

7. **Explain lines one and two of the second stanza.**
   The first two lines of the second stanza relate how the men are wanting to revolt and turn back and that they have grown weak and tired.

8. **Read the words of Columbus, in the second stanza.**
   Columbus says in the second stanza: "Why, you shall say at break of day 'Sail on! Sail on! Sail on! And on!'"

9. **Why did they sail "as winds might blow"?**
   They sailed as the "winds might blow" because they sailed in the direction the wind blew at were at its mercy.

10. **What is the meaning of lines two, three, and four in the fourth stanza?**
    The description of a raging sea is given in lines two, three and four of the fourth stanza.

11. **Why was the fear of the sailors so great?**

The fear of the sailors was so great because they didn't know where they were going.

12. **Give in your own words the thought in the fifth stanza.**

The thought in the fifth stanza is that Columbus persevered even though the odds were against him. He gained a world (the Americas) by continuing on his journey.

13. **Try to imagine the scene on the ship when a light on shore was discovered.**

Have students write a description and illustrate it.

14. **Read what Columbus said in the first stanza. Find the quotation within the quotation.**

"Why, say, 'Sail on! Sail on! And on!'"

Note: Notice that it is enclosed in single marks ('). Find in the second stanza a quotation within a quotation.

15. **Memorize the stanza that you like the best.**

Compare students' recitation with the poem.

Lesson 283
Picture Study—*Columbus*

1. **Before the discovery of America what did most people believe about the shape of the earth? What did Columbus believe?**

Before the discovery of America most people believed the shape of the earth was flat. Columbus must have believed it to be different since he was willing to travel beyond the then-known world.

2. **What did Columbus wish to find?**

Columbus was looking for a new way to get to the Indies. He did not want to sail around Africa.

3. **Why did he have difficulty in securing aid?**

Columbus had difficulty securing money for the trip because people thought he was foolish.

4. **Who helped him finally?**

King Ferdinand and Queen Isabella of Spain finally helped him. They wanted Columbus to find gold and a new way to get to the Indies.

5. **How many ships was he given?**

Three ships were given to Columbus: the Nina, *the* Pinta, *and the* Santa Maria.

6. **Tell something of the voyage.**

The ships did not see any land for a month and endured false land sightings. Columbus's men even threatened mutiny.

7. **Why were the men afraid?**

The men must have been afraid because they did not see land for so long.

8. **What were the first signs of land?**

The first sign of land was a tropical environment. Columbus landed first in San Salvador. He thought they were in India.

9. **What were some of the things that Columbus and his men found in the new world?**
   Columbus and his men found gold.
10. **Describe the picture showing his return to the court of Spain.**
    Students can use the picture on page 297 to help with their description.
11. **What are some of the things that you can imagine Columbus had told the king.**
    Columbus told the king of the beauty of the new land. He also told him that he claimed the new land for Spain.
12. **What effect did his words have upon the king and the people who heard?**
    The people were amazed and excited to find that there was undiscovered, rich land.
13. **What did Columbus carry back with him from the new world?**
    Columbus carried back things such as gold, spices, and cotton.

Lesson 284
Selection for Study

1. **This paragraph describes the close of the day. Using this as a model, write a description of the break of day.**
   A. Begin in this way: The sun rises suddenly from behind the great castle-crested mountains _____ .

   B. Tell how the dewdrops glisten, how the river grows brighter and brighter, and how the birds sing their morning songs. Tell how the cattle go out to the hills, and the men start to work in the fields.

   Use the essay rubric, page 220, to evaluate this exercise.

Lesson 285
Words Derived from Proper Nouns

A. Japanese lanterns are made of paper.
B. French toys are expensive.

1. **From what proper noun is the word Japanese derived?**
   The word Japanese is derived from Japan.
2. **From what proper noun is the word French derived?**
   The word French is derived from the word France (or Frank).
3. **With what kind of letter do words derived from proper nouns begin?**
   Proper nouns begin with a capital letter.
4. **Name the proper nouns from which the following words derived.**

A. Russian	E. German	I. English
B. British	F. Portuguese	J. Irish
C. Scotch	G. Italian	K. Spanish
D. Mexican	H. Norwegian	

A. Russia	E. Germany	I. England
B. Britain	F. Portugal	J. Ireland
C. Scotland	G. Italy	K. Spain
D. Mexico	H. Norway	

5. **Use the words in sentences.**

Answers will vary.

Lesson 286
Invitations

1. **Study these forms.**
2. **Write a formal invitation to a party.**
3. **Write the acceptance which a friend might send.**
4. **Write a note regretting your inability to accept the invitation which a friend has sent you.**
5. **Write a formal invitation from the school for Patron's Day.**

Have students research the variety of invitations available. For an extra activity, have students use a software program to create an invitation. Many craft stores also have creative ways to write invitations.

Lesson 287
Letter Writing

T. L. Barnes, grocer, 1820 Main Street, St. Paul, MN, writes to George L. Owens, asking him to settle his account which is overdue.

1. **Write the letter in a courteous way.**

Use the letter writing rubric, page 221, to evaluate this assignment.

For formal business letters, students should use the business styles shown below:

Semi-Block Form

Sender's Name
Address
City, State Zip Code

Date

Receiver's name
Address
City, State Zip Code

Dear _____,

Body of the letter.

Salutation,
Signature

Block Form

Sender's Name
Address
City, State Zip Code

Date

Receiver's name
Address
City, State Zip Code

Dear _____,

Body of the letter.

Salutation,
Signature

Lesson 288
Selection for Study—"May"

1. **Use in sentences:**
   A. **secret sign**
   B. **enchanting notes**
   C. **magic touch**
   D. **amid the grass**
   E. **transformed**
   F. **confessed**
   G. **miracle**
   H. **burnished**

   Answers will vary. Make sure students understand the meaning of the words.

2. **Write three questions about the first stanza.**

   Possible questions:

   A. Identify a sentence that is written in inverse order. ("And merrily sang he.")

   B. To what is the brook compared? ("a silver string")

   C. What did echo repeat? ("Enchanting notes in every nook")

3. **Write two questions about the second stanza.**

   Possible questions:

   A. Identify the possessive nouns ("morning's", "day's")

   B. What does "o'er" mean? (over)

4. **Write two questions about the third stanza.**

   Possible questions:

   A. What time of year is the poem? (May)

   B. What is a banner? (a flag or sign of allegience)

Lesson 289
Conversation

1. **Who is the President of the United States?**

   Answers will depend on the time in which this question is being asked.

2. **To what political party does he belong?**

   Answers will depend on who is the sitting President.

3. **For how long a term was he elected?**

   Presidents are elected every four years.

4. **When does his present term expire?**

   Presidential elections will take place in 2008, 2011, 2015, 2019. Presidents take office in January.

5. **What are some of his duties?**

   A president's duties are to be Commander in Chief of the Armed Forces, enforce international and national policy, develop a budget, and sign bills into law, among other things.

6. **Who is Vice President of the United States?**

   Answers will depend on the time in which this question is being asked.

7. **Who makes the laws of the United States?**

   The Congress makes the laws of the United States.

8. **Of what two parts is Congress composed?**

   Congress is composed of the House of Representatives and the Senate.

9. **What are some of the duties of Congress?**

   Congress designs laws.

10. **How are the expenses of the Government paid?**

    The expenses of the government are paid though the taxes its citizens pay.

Lesson 290
Quotations

Bring quotations and stories to illustrate the following subjects:
   A. **obedience**
   B. **cleanliness**
   C. **promptness**
   D. **honesty**
Students can find a variety of stories by searching the Internet. The Elson Readers also have stories focusing on these traits.

Lesson 291
Selection for Study—"Daffodils"

1. **Give the meaning of**
   A. **jocund** *(adjective) cheerful*
   B. **continuous** *(adjective) uninterrupted in time*
   C. **sprightly** *(adjective) animated or lively*
   D. **margin** *(noun) a border or edge*
   E. **solitude** *(noun) the state of being alone*
   F. **vales** *(noun) valleys*
2. **Give synonyms for glee, wealth, bliss.**
   glee—delight, happiness, joyfulness; wealth—affluence, prosperity; bliss—pleasure, enjoyment
3. **Explain the first and second lines of the first stanza.**
   "I wonder'd lonely as a cloud/That floats on high o'er vales and hills" means that the speaker was leisurely walking observing the surroundings.
4. **What is the "Milky Way"?**
   The Milky Way is a spiral galaxy that contains our solar system.
5. **In the second paragraph find an example of transposed order.**
   An example of transposed order is: "Ten thousand saw I at a glance."
6. **What do you understand by the last line of the third stanza?**
   The last line of the third stanza compares the fluttering of the speaker's heart to the "dancing of the daffodils."
7. **What meaning do you find in the last stanza?**
   The last stanza tells that when the speaker is inside on his "couch" his mind wonders to the fields with the daffodils. This puts him at ease.
8. **Describe the picture which the poem presents.**
   The picture presents beautiful fields of daffodils swaying in the wind.

Lesson 292
Selection for Study—"Summer Rain"

1. In the first paragraph what is compared to the coinage of money?
    Rain is compared to the coinage of money.
2. To what are the roots compared?
    The roots are compared to machinery.
3. In the second paragraph to what are the clouds compared?
    The clouds are compared to a bank. While a bank holds money, clouds hold rain.
4. In the last paragraph why does He begin with a capital?
    He begins with a capital because the word is referring to God.
5. Write the first paragraph from dictation.
    Compare students' writings with the original paragraph.
6. Use in sentences:
    A. when the heavens send clouds
    B. the mountains of California
    C. a rain of riches
    D. every drop is silver
    E. the soft mines of heaven
    F. summer rain
    G. hidden gold
    Answers will vary.

Lesson 293
Description— Plan of a House

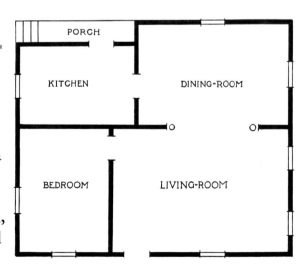

1. Here is a plan for a house of four rooms. Draw a plan for a larger house.
2. Write a description of your plan.
3. In your description, give the size of each room, the number of windows, and the color of wall paper to be used.
4. State how each room is to be furnished.

Answers for this lesson will vary greatly. For an extra activity, have students make a floor plan of their house. See if students can draw it to scale.

Lesson 294
Selection to be Memorized—
"Home, Sweet Home"

1. **Explain the second line of the first stanza. What does the third line mean?**
    The second line of the first stanza reads: "Be it ever so humble, there's no place like home." In other words, it doesn't matter how lowly one's home is, it is always good to be there. The third line, "A charm from the skies seems to hallow us there" means that something from the heavens make us revere our home.
2. **Explain the first line of the second stanza.**
    "An exile from home, splendor dazzles in vain" means that regardless of what seems to be attractive, that which sparkles does so without significance if we have no home.
3. **Have you ever been anywhere and longed for a home?**
    Answers will vary.
4. **What is meant by "peace of mind"?**
    "Peace of mind" means being content or happy in one's situation or location.

Lesson 295
Letter Writing

Frank Darby has applied for a position in a wholesale furniture store. The manager, C. S. Ferguson, writes to Prof. Charles Barnes, principal of the _____ School, telling him that Frank has applied for a position, and asking if Professor Barnes can recommend his former pupil.

1. Write the letter.
2. Write the reply of Professor Barnes, telling of Frank's good habits, his promptness, his honesty, and other good points which an employer might wish to know. Begin the body of your letter in this way: Your letter of the ____ was received today. Frank Darby was a pupil in my school for six years _____.
3. Write another reply to the first letter saying that Professor Barnes regrets he cannot recommend Frank Darby for the position in the furniture store, state why.

Use the letter writing rubric, page 221, to evaluate these responses. Have students research different ways one can write letters of recommendation. This research can help with the wording of the letter. Explain to students that letters of recommendation are very important. Some day they will need to ask a teacher, former teacher, principal, friend, or employer for a recommendation. Many colleges require letters of recommendation for admittance. It is important for students to work hard and develop good relationships with others.

Lesson 296
Conversation

1. **Study these proverbs; what does each one teach? If possible, give stories or incidents to illustrate them.**

    A. Necessity is the mother of invention. Suggestion for story: A boy who wishes to have a wagon but has no money to buy one.

    It is from necessity that we find ways to solve problems.

    B. Vinegar catches no flies. Suggestion for story: A merchant who is cross and discourteous to all who enter his store.

    Vinegar is sour and will not attract a fly; therefore, to attract good things, one must be good.

    C. A word to the wise is sufficient.

    An intelligent person can take a simple hint. He does not need long explanations.

    D. God helps them that help themselves.

    If one makes an effort, God will assist. If we don't try, God will not come to our aid.

    E. Experience is a good teacher.

    Sometimes we learn from our mistakes and experiences.

    F. A bird in the hand is worth two in the bush.

    Things we currently have can be more valuable than those we hope to get.

    G. A stitch in time saves nine.

    If one pays attention to and cares for things now, it will save time having to fix them later.

    H. All work and no play make Jack a dull boy.

    One needs to work hard, but also take time to enjoy life.

    I. All is not gold that glitters.

    Things that may appear to be valuable may not be.

    J. A rolling stone gathers no moss.

    If one is constantly on the move, then he develops no roots or a place to be grounded.

    K. It is never too late to mend.

    There is always time to heal—a broken friendship, etc.

    L. An ounce of prevention is worth a pound of cure.

    Taking time to prevent something is worth more than having to fix it later.

2. **Write one of the stories.**

    Have students plan their story and then use the short story rubric, page 219, to evaluate the story. For examples of stories with morals, have students read some of Aesop's Fables.

Lesson 297
Selection for Study—"The Day is Done"

1. **In the first stanza to what is the falling of darkness compared?**

    The falling of darkness is compared to "a feather is wafted downward from an eagle in its flight."

Note: Such a comparison is called a simile. A simile usually is introduced by the words *as* or *like*.

2. **Find a simile in the third stanza. What are compared?**

   The feeling of sadness and longing is compared to the mist as it resembles the rain (fourth line of third stanza).

3. **Explain the third stanza. What is the meaning of "akin"?**

   The third stanza states that a feeling of sadness and longing are not related to pain. Akin means related.

4. **Find a simile in the seventh paragraph. What are compared?**

   The way that songs "gush" from a writer's heart is like rain ("showers") that falls from the sky or tears from an eyelid.

5. **Read the fourth stanza. If such a request were made of you, what would you select to read? Mention one of the poets referred to in the sixth stanza.**

   Answers will vary.

6. **Which stanza pleases you most?**

   Answers will vary. Have students explain the reason for their selection.

7. **Define and use in sentences these words:**

A. wafted	D. resist	G. resembles
B. banish	E. bards	H. corridors
C. martial	F. devoid	I . endeavor

   Definitions:
   A. *wafted—(verb) to go gently through the air*
   B. *banish—(verb) to drive away or put one in exile*
   C. *martial—(noun) having to do with war*
   D. *resist –(verb) to stand against something*
   E. *bards—(noun) a person who recited poems*
   F. *devoid —(adjective) empty*
   G. *resembles—(verb) to look like someone or something else*
   H. *corridors—(noun) hallways*
   I. *endeavor—(noun) a strenuous effort*
   Sentences will vary.

8. **Who wrote the poem?**

   The author of the poem is Henry Wadsworth Longfellow.

9. **Mention some other poems that Longfellow wrote.**

   Poems in this book can be found in Lesson 65, "The Village Blacksmith" and Lesson 88,"Daybreak."

10. **Memorize this poem.**

    Compare student's recitation with the poem.

11. **Copy sentences containing similes, from Lessons 169, 236, and 241.**

    Lesson 169—"Her cheeks were as rosy as the skies at dawn, her eyes were as tender and bright as the starlight."
    Lesson 236—"The wind sweeps through the forest with a sound like the blast of a trumpet."
    Lesson 241—"...and turned it over as a housewife turns a cake".

Extended Activity

This poem was written by Henry Wadsworth Longfellow (Lesson 65), who along with William Cullen Bryant (Lesson 30), John Greenleaf Whittier (Lesson 35), Oliver Wendell Holmes (Lesson 178), and James Russell Lowell (Lesson 189) were generally regarded as the first great American poets known as "The Fireside Poets." They were also referred to as the "Schoolroom" or "Household Poets" since their poems were easy to memorize and were read and recited in schools and at home around the family fireside. They lived and wrote in the nineteenth century. These men shared many common interests and activities. From your research of these poets, complete the following chart and then identify their similarities and differences.

	Date of Birth	Place of Birth	Father's Occupation	Age When First Published	Career	Other Interests/ Expertise	Date of Death
BRYANT	November 3, 1794	Cummington, MA	Doctor	Thirteen	Lawyer Journalist Editor	Antislavery Movement	June 12, 1878
WHITTIER	December 17, 1807	Haverhill, MA	Farmer	Nineteen	Editor	Antislavery Movement	September 7, 1892
LONGFELLOW	February 27, 1807	Portland, ME	Lawyer Congressman	Thirteen	Educator Linguist	Wrote books and taught French, Italian, and Spanish at Harvard	March 24, 1882
HOLMES	August 29, 1809	Cambridge, MA	Clergyman and author of *Annals of America*	Twenty-one	Doctor	Good Friend of Helen Keller	October 7, 1894
LOWELL	February 22, 1819	Cambridge, MA	Clergyman	Twenty-two	Writer	Diplomacy and Studied Law	August 12, 1891

Teacher Note

Students may find additional points of interest that they may wish to include in their chart. If so, feel free to adapt the chart to their research.

William Cullen Bryant (Lesson 30)
John Greenleaf Whittier (Lesson 35)
Henry Wadsworth Longfellow (Lesson 65, Lesson 88, Lesson 297)
Oliver Wendell Holmes (Lesson 178)
James Russell Lowell (Lesson 189)

Lesson 298
Selections for Study

1. Discuss the following selections in class; write the first one from dictation.

    A. This selection discusses the importance of working or playing with gusto and pride. If something is not done well, it is not worth doing.

    B. This selection discusses the importance of doing good things and being happy in life. It encourages one to enjoy those things which one is given each day.

Lesson 299
Suggestions for Descriptions

1. Write a description of a pleasant bedroom. Tell about the wall paper, windows and curtains, the furniture, and the good order in which it is kept. Make your description so clear that others will see the picture as you do.
2. Write a description of an untidy dining room. Tell about the things that make it unattractive.
3. Describe some building in your neighborhood without telling where or what it is.
4. Suppose that you have a large yard in which you wish to plant trees, ornamental shrubs, and flowers. Draw a diagram of the lot, showing location of house, flower beds, etc. Would you leave a space for a kitchen garden? What would you plant in it? Write a description of it as you would have it appear.
5. Write a description of some character in a book that you have read recently.

    Answers will vary.

Lesson 300
Selection for Study

1. What is this poem intended to teach?

    This poem is intended to teach one to keep the city clean.
2. Write five rules for keeping streets, sidewalks, and yards in good condition.

    Answers will vary.

Extended Activity

Have students write a poem which is intended to teach a lesson.

Lesson 301

Summary, Continued from Lesson 248— To Remember

A. **Identify whether the statements below are true or false. If the statement is false, explain why.**

1. Subjects of sentences are nouns and pronouns.

True

2. Verbs only show action.

False; verbs can show state of being.

3. The verb of a sentence can come after the subject.

True

4. Conjunctions are used to address or call attention or express feeling.

False; a conjunction connects words, phrases, and sentences—interjections are used to address or call attention or express feeling.

5. A word derived from a proper noun begins with a capital letter.

True

B. **For each sentence identify the adverb and what it modifies.**

6. Camels can travel quickly through the desert.

quickly—travel

7. Some people dislike the very bumpy ride of a camel.

very—bumpy

8. Camels can wander aimlessly through the desert.

aimlessly—wander

C. **For each sentence identify the preposition.**

9. Out of the dark roared the thunder of a cannon.

out, of, of

10. After four years of conflict came a time of reconstruction.

after, of, of

11. A Civil War museum is in Atlanta, Georgia.

in

D. **Write two sentences using an interjection.**

E. **Choose the best word for each sentence.**

12. I (*shall*, will) visit you soon.

13. I cannot talk on the phone now, but I (shall, *will*) call back later.

14. My teacher (shall, *will*) read to the class in a little while.

15. My teacher (*shall*, will) go to the workshop.

Teacher Aids

Rubrics for Student Evaluation Worksheets

Copy these aids as needed.

Memorization Rubric

Criteria	Rating Scale Not Very				Very
	1	2	3	4	5
Fluency *Reader speaks with appropriate pauses and speed.*					
Pronunciation *All words are pronounced correctly and clearly.*					
Emphasis *Appropriate emotion is used when reciting piece.*					
Memorization *Selection is memorized, and the student does not need prompting*					
TOTAL					

Short Story Rubric

Criteria	Rating Scale — Not Very (1) to Very (5)				
	1	2	3	4	5
Focus and Directions *Student has included words and/or story line specified in the directions. Conflict and resolution is obvious.*					
Organization *Story has a beginning, middle, and end.*					
Use of Language *Spelling* *Varies sentence structure and makes good word choices.* *Grammar and punctuation*					
Legibility					
TOTAL					

Essay Rubric
Criteria

	Rating Scale Not Very				Very
	1	2	3	4	5
Audience and Purpose *Contains an engaging introduction; main idea clearly stated.*					
Organization *Well organized, with transitions helping to link words and ideas (First, second, most important, finally, etc.).*					
Elaboration *The essay is effectively developed with specific details.*					
Use of Language *Spelling* *Varies sentence structure and makes good word choices.* *Grammar and punctuation*					
Legibility					
TOTAL					

Letter Writing Rubric

Criteria	Rating Scale Not Very / Very				
	1	2	3	4	5
Audience and Purpose *Addresses the intended audience appropriately.*					
Organization *Follows standard letter writing (greeting and salutation); uses uniform spacing; organizes information.*					
Elaboration *Clearly states and supports reasons for writing.*					
Use of Language *Uses appropriate formal language; few errors in spelling, punctuation, and grammar.*					
TOTAL					

Scrapbook Rubric

Criteria	Rating Scale Not Very				Very
	1	2	3	4	5
Completed On Time					
Evidence of Time and Effort					
Materials Used Creatively					
Appealing and Neat					
Correct Spelling and Punctuation					
TOTAL					

Guidebook Rubric

Criteria	Rating Scale				
	Not Very				Very
	1	2	3	4	5
Points of Interest *Points of interest are described.*					
Pictures					
Presentation *Articles and descriptions are neat and orderly.* *Writing is legible.*					
Use of Language *Spelling* *Varies sentence structure and makes good word choices.* *Grammar and punctuation*					
Legibility					
TOTAL					

Newspaper Article Rubric

Criteria	Rating Scale Not Very				Very
	1	2	3	4	5
Audience and Purpose *Contains an engaging introduction stating clearly the 5 Ws: WHO, WHAT, WHY, WHEN, WHERE.*					
Organization *Article is arranged from most important to least important*					
Elaboration *The article is effectively developed with specific details, making sufficient use of concrete nouns.*					
Use of Language *Spelling* *Mature word choice* *Grammar and punctuation*					
Legibility					
TOTAL					

Story Map

There are six parts to a plot.

STORY:

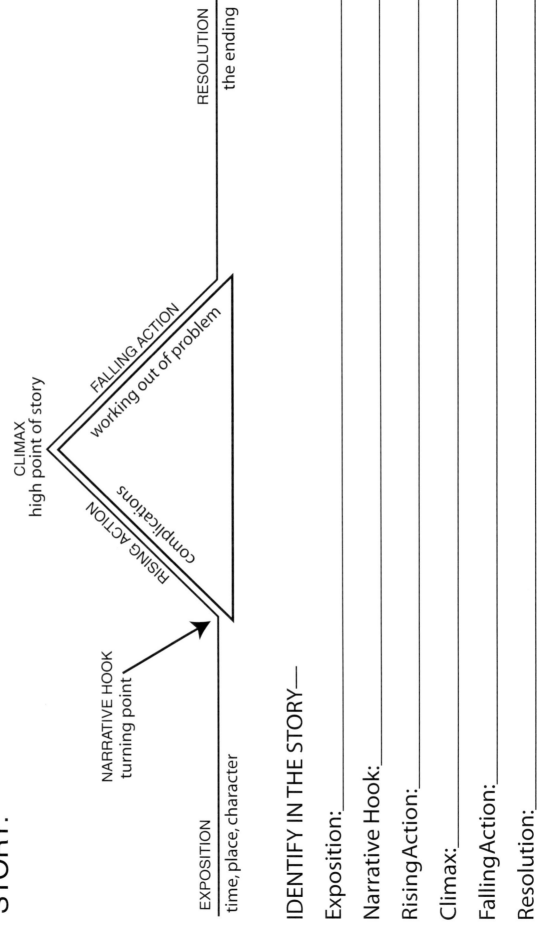

RESOLUTION
the ending

FALLING ACTION
working out of problem

CLIMAX
high point of story

RISING ACTION
complications

NARRATIVE HOOK
turning point

EXPOSITION
time, place, character

IDENTIFY IN THE STORY—

Exposition: _____

Narrative Hook: _____

Rising Action: _____

Climax: _____

Falling Action: _____

Resolution: _____

Envelopes

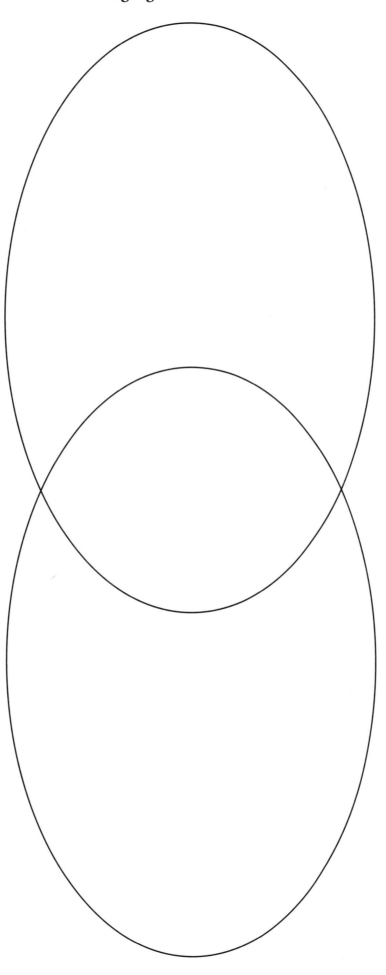

Venn Diagram

Writing and Dictation Worksheets

Books Available from
Lost Classics Book Company

American History
Stories of Great Americans for Little Americans................................ Edward Eggleston
A First Book in American History ....Edward Eggleston
A History of the United States and Its People....................................Edward Eggleston

Biography
The Life of Kit Carson... Edward Ellis

English Grammar
Primary Language Lessons .... Emma Serl
Intermediate Language Lessons ....Emma Serl
(*Teacher's Guides Available for Each Reader in This Series*)

Elson Readers Series
Complete Set .... William Elson, Lura Runkel, Christine Keck
The Elson Readers: Primer.. William Elson, Lura Runkel
The Elson Readers: Book One .... William Elson, Lura Runkel
The Elson Readers: Book Two .... William Elson, Lura Runkel
The Elson Readers: Book Three..William Elson
The Elson Readers: Book Four ....William Elson
The Elson Readers: Book Five .... William Elson, Christine Keck
The Elson Readers: Book Six .... William Elson, Christine Keck
The Elson Readers: Book Seven.. William Elson, Christine Keck
The Elson Readers: Book Eight... William Elson, Christine Keck
(*Teacher's Guides Available for Each Reader in This Series*)

Historical Fiction
With Lee in Virginia .... G. A. Henty
A Tale of the Western Plains .... G. A. Henty
The Young Carthaginian.. G. A. Henty
In the Heart of the Rockies .... G. A. Henty
For the Temple .... G. A. Henty
A Knight of the White Cross .... G. A. Henty
The Minute Boys of Lexington... Edward Stratemeyer
The Minute Boys of Bunker Hill... Edward Stratemeyer
Hope and Have .... Oliver Optic
Taken by the Enemy, First in *The Blue and the Gray Series*............................ Oliver Optic
Within the Enemy's Lines, Second in *The Blue and the Gray Series*.....................Oliver Optic
On the Blockade, Third in *The Blue and the Gray Series*................................Oliver Optic
Stand by the Union, Fourth in *The Blue and the Gray Series* ....Oliver Optic
Fighting for the Right, Fifth in *The Blue and the Gray Series*...............................Oliver Optic
A Victorious Union, Sixth and Final in *The Blue and the Gray Series* ....Oliver Optic
Mary of Plymouth...James Otis

For more information visit us at: http://www.lostclassicsbooks.com